*Crime Victims*

R.I. MAWBY · M.L. GILL

# Crime Victims
## Needs, Services, and the Voluntary Sector

Tavistock Publications
London and New York

First published in 1987 by
Tavistock Publications Ltd
11 New Fetter Lane, London EC4P 4EE

Published in the USA by
Tavistock Publications
in association with Methuen, Inc.
29 West 35th Street, New York NY 10001

© 1987 R.I. Mawby and M.L. Gill

Printed and bound in Great Britain by Biddles Ltd
Guildford and Kings Lynn

All rights reserved. No part of this book may be reprinted or reproduced or utilized in any form or by any electronic, mechanical or other means, now known or hereafter invented, including photocopying and recording, or in any information storage or retrieval system, without permission in writing from the publishers.

*British Library Cataloguing in Publication Data*
Mawby, R.I.
　Crime victims: needs, services and the voluntary sector.
　1. Victims of crimes—Great Britain
　I. Title II. Gill, M.L.
　362.8'8'0941　　　HV6250.3.G7

ISBN 0-422-61450-5

*Library of Congress Cataloging in Publication Data*
Mawby, R. I.
　Crime victims.
　Bibliography: p.
　Includes index.
　1. Victims of crimes—Great Britain. 2. Victims of crimes—Services for—Great Britain. 3. Volunteer workers in criminal justice administration—Great Britain. I. Gill, M. L. II. Title.
　HV6250.3.G7M39　1987　　362.8'8'0941　　87-10025
ISBN 0-422-61450-5 (alk. paper)

# Contents

*Acknowledgements* vi
*Introduction* vii

## PART I *CRIME VICTIMS*
1 Crime and its victims 3
2 The impact of crime 18

## PART II *STATE RESPONSES TO CRIME VICTIMS*
3 State responses to the needs of victims and the introduction of criminal injuries compensation 35
4 State responses to the needs of victims: compensation orders and reparation 51

## PART III *THE RESPONSE OF THE VOLUNTARY SECTOR*
5 The community and the voluntary sector 67
6 Victims support schemes in Britain, 1971–87 87
7 Victims services in the United States 115

## PART IV *VICTIMS SUPPORT SCHEMES IN THE SOUTH WEST*
8 Victims services in a rural area 137
9 Victims support schemes and the police 154
10 Victims support schemes and the probation service 179
11 Volunteers and victims support schemes 200

## PART V *DISCUSSION*
12 Discussion 221

*Notes* 235
*References* 241
*Author index* 255
*Subject index* 259

# Acknowledgements

We would like to take this opportunity to thank our colleagues and fellow travellers whose time we have misused, good offices we have exploited, and ideas we have misinterpreted. We are particularly indebted to Plymouth Polytechnic and the Department of Social and Political Studies for financial backing for the research and a number of educational visits. Within the Department, special thanks are due to our research aides, notably Vicki Firkins, Bridie Johnstone and Lindsay Harris, and to the secretarial team who translated our imperfect scratchings into real, typed words.

We are also grateful to the various agencies – victims support, police and probation – which allowed us access to their records and considerable assistance in developing our research and ideas. Most especially, we appreciate the co-operation of volunteers, police officers and probation staff who responded to our questions, and the help of Kay Coventry and latterly John Pointing, from the NAVSS, and the irrepressible regional chairperson, Pauline Letheridge. In a rather different context, we are indebted to Mike Hough and the Home Office Research and Planning Unit for allowing us to carry out analyses of the 1984 British Crime Survey, and to Mike Maguire from whom some of the BCS questions originated.

Our appreciation of international victimological issues has been aided through the kind offices of a number of people, only a few of whom are cited in the notes to the text. Among these, Sarah Sopkin was especially helpful in arranging a programme for one of us to visit a number of schemes in Florida in 1986.

Finally, we would like to take this opportunity to thank each other. Research as a joint enterprise is fraught with difficulties. It is, additionally, a special kind of learning experience. That we have emerged unscathed comes as both a surprise and a relief to us.

*Rob Mawby and Martin Gill*
*January, 1987*

# Introduction

This book represents the product of three separate elements of our interest in victimology, the study of victims. The original interest came from the involvement of one of us (R.I. Mawby) in one of the earlier local victim surveys in Britain, in Sheffield, reflecting concern over the 'dark figure' of unreported crime. The British Crime Survey (BCS), first carried out in 1982 and repeated in 1984, allowed this interest to develop, especially since the Home Office Research and Planning Unit has encouraged outside academics to become involved in subsequent analysis. This enabled us to consider not only the extent of crime against the public, and variations between different social groups, but also to focus in more detail on the impact of crime and relate this to the availability of services.

In this latter respect we were already aware that services for crime victims were minimal. With the exception of free medical services through the National Health Service, and a rather separate concern with child victims of violence, few policies were directed at crime victims. This was reflected in a dearth of research, with the result that courses on applied social studies, social policy and administration, and social work included little of practical relevance. Thus, for example, a trained probation officer or social worker might have been expected to cover a wealth of detail of needs and problems in society, and the response of different welfare agencies (statutory or otherwise) to meeting those needs, but little of this would be directly related to crime victims.

Yet the 1970s saw the development of a number of voluntary agencies concerned with victims of one crime or another. In Britain, for example, Refuges for Battered Women emerged, first in Chiswick and then across the country. Similarly, Rape Crisis Centres were set up in many urban areas, in this case particularly influenced by developments in the United States. Somewhat separately, victims support schemes emerged to help victims of crimes in general.

These initiatives raised for us the question of how far such voluntary-sector developments could be viewed in the same light as voluntarism in welfare services in general. It is, for example, often acknowledged that the lack of state response to the problems of urbanizing, industrializing nineteenth-century Britain led to growth in the voluntary sector. Could recent developments *vis-à-vis* crime victims be seen equally as filling the gap ignored by state provisions? If so, could a similar set of strengths and weaknesses be identified?

This in turn led to a further question. Could one make generalizations about the nature of the voluntary sector, or were there marked differences depending on the context of involvement and the social meaning ascribed to that context by its actors? Most especially, were those involved in the voluntary movement to help crime victims inspired by similar principles to those who volunteered for other work, or could one identify different ideologies of volunteering? To consider this further, one of us (R.I. Mawby) received a three-year research grant from Plymouth Polytechnic to finance a research assistant (M.L. Gill) to compare voluntarism in three rather different contexts of the criminal justice system – victims support schemes, the probation service and the police. From this emerged our local research on victims support schemes in the South West of England.

The structure of this book reflects these different influences on our interests in crime victims and social policy. In Part I we have concentrated on crime victims. In Chapter 1 we provide a general introduction, by considering the extent of crime, those most at risk, and the rather separate problem of fear of crime. Then, in Chapter 2 we focus on the impact of crime on its victims, using original data from the 1984 BCS. We then assess the problems caused by crime in the context of responses by the state and other service providers.

Part II contains a critical review of state involvement in helping crime victims. In Chapter 3 we provide a historical overview, culminating in an analysis of the creation and operation of criminal injuries compensation schemes. In Chapter 4 we then look at the later development of compensation orders in Britain, and more recent initiatives, in North America and lately in Britain, in the field of reparation and mediation. Here again we are fortunate in being able to include BCS data. In providing this review of state services we have two prime concerns. First, we shall suggest that policies only partly reflect a commitment to meet the needs of victims, much less acknowledge victims' rights. Second, as is readily appreciated, such initiatives apply to only a minority of victims.

Clearly, most services for crime victims are provided by the voluntary sector, and Part III concentrates on a critical overview of the role of voluntary organizations in this respect. In Chapter 5 we provide an introduction to voluntary organizations and the use of volunteers, and take the examples of Refuges and Rape Crisis Centres to illustrate diversity within the voluntary sector. Chapter 6 concentrates on victims support schemes in Britain as a very different manifestation. Developments in the United States are compared with British victims services in Chapter 7.

Part IV then focuses on our local research in the South West. In these four chapters we review the growth of victims support schemes in a relatively rural area and consider two crucial issues for the voluntary sector, namely the relationship between voluntary and statutory services (Chs 9 and 10) and the use of volunteers (Ch. 11).

Finally, in Part V we draw together our analysis of developments in Britain, experiences from abroad, and our more detailed study in the South West to suggest how services may best be developed in the future. In so doing we shall attempt to address those involved in policy initiatives *vis-à-vis* crime victims, and those who have to implement those policies through providing help for individual victims.

# PART I
## *Crime victims*

# 1 Crime and its victims

**Introduction: criminology and the victim**

Despite the pioneering work of Von Hentig (1948), the discipline of victimology is of relatively recent origin. Statements that the victim is the forgotten actor in the crime scenario and that criminal justice and welfare policies have tended to overlook victims are so common as to be almost clichés. Yet the lack of focus on the victim of crime is rather more widespread than this – it is also a black hole among theorists. Traditionally, criminology has ignored the victim; more recently, deviancy theory has compounded matters.

Recent texts on criminology and deviance, like those by Taylor, Walton, and Young (1973) and Downes and Rock (1982), illustrate the extent to which criminology's origins were offender-focused. Even postwar theories encompassing notions of anomie or subculture virtually ignored the victim, the exception being Sykes and Matza (1957), where techniques of neutralization, developed to explain how delinquents justify law violations, incorporate notions of victim-denial.

However, the influence of labelling theorists and symbolic interactionists in the 1960s amounted to a near disavowal of consideration of crime victims. Attacking conventional criminology for its conservative-reformist emphasis and its dependence upon official statistics, proponents of the new sociology of deviance redirected attention into issues of law-making and law enforcement. At the same time, and of particular relevance here, they concentrated attention on a number of victimless offences and challenged academics to consider 'Whose side are we on?' (Becker 1967) and appreciate the perspective of the 'deviant' rather than the system.

Moreover, scepticism over the use of official statistics led to a strange situation where some authors shifted from a doubt in the validity of police data, through a doubt in the possibility of *any* valid crime data, to an assumption that crime (or at least primary deviance) was equally distributed among the population. This led, on the one hand, to criticisms of studies which distinguished the social characteristics of offenders; on the other hand, it led to a denial of the reality of problem areas, whether as places where offenders lived *or* as areas vulnerable to offending. Thus, when one of us

(Mawby 1979a) argued that valid area variations in crime were evident, this was met with a certain degree of scepticism and incredulity.

Not so now. Researchers, many of them radical, are now almost universally willing to acknowledge the special concentration of crime, and to see crime as a significant feature of many inner-city areas. An interest in the victims of crime is evident in academic circles as well as among policy-makers

Amongst researchers there are at least three reasons for this. First, lack of evidence that different sentences had differing impact on offenders led policy-makers to consider the possibility that crime might be reduced, or at least constrained, through situational measures. This in turn led to an emphasis on the immediate circumstances surrounding the offence, of necessity incorporating the role of the victim, best illustrated in a number of studies carried out by the Home Office (Clarke and Mayhew 1980). Second, and in complete contrast, the developing impact of feminism in sociology, and latterly criminology, has encouraged a greater emphasis on women as victims, notably of rape and domestic violence, and has more widely stimulated an interest in the fear of crime. Finally, and perhaps most significantly, criticism of official statistics has resulted in a spawn of victim surveys, where sample surveys of individuals or households have enabled considerable data to be collated on the extent of crime and the characteristics of victims, irrespective of whether or not crimes become known to the police.

**Victim surveys**

Victim surveys were introduced primarily as a means of measuring the extent of crime (at least against individuals) and changes over time. The first major surveys were carried out in the United States in 1966 as part of the President's Commission on Law Enforcement and the Administration of Justice (Biderman *et al.* 1967; Ennis 1967), and these developed into periodic national surveys.

Since 1972 a nationwide victimization survey has been carried out twice yearly, using a panel of 60,000 households replaced at three-yearly intervals. At the same time, victim surveys were introduced in a number of other countries, including Australia, Canada, Israel, the Netherlands, Sweden (Block 1983), and Japan (Ishii 1982).

In Britain a certain amount of data was available from the General

Household Survey (GHS), which first included questions on domestic burglary in 1972. This was followed by a number of localized surveys in three London boroughs (Sparks, Genn, and Dodd 1977), in Sheffield (Bottoms, Mawby, and Xanthos 1981; Bottoms, Mawby, and Walker 1987; Mawby 1982a), and in Birmingham (Smith 1982).

Although these surveys provided local detail, the Home Office Research and Planning Unit was keen to produce a national picture. There was some government resistance to the idea – interestingly due to concern that the results would magnify the crime problem – but eventually the first British Crime Survey (BCS) was conducted in England, Scotland and Wales in 1982. A second survey in England and Wales followed in 1984, and a third is scheduled for 1988. In the mean time, local victim surveys in Liverpool (Kinsey 1984) and Islington (Jones and Young 1986; Jones, MacLean, and Young 1986) provided up-to-date information on crime in specific urban areas.

What, then, do such surveys tell us about crime? First, and not surprisingly, they demonstrate considerably higher levels of crime than is shown in official statistics. The extent of the disparity varies, according to the construction of the questionnaire, the offence descriptions used in it, the length of time covered by the questions, and so on, such that it is difficult to make valid comparisons between one survey and another. However, it is clear that for crimes against individuals – rather than against corporate victims like shops, offices or banks – only a small minority of crimes are reported to the police and not all of these are subsequently recorded.

At the same time there is some evidence that the increase in crime may not be as great as the increase in recorded crime. That is, for example, victims may be more willing to report crimes than in the past and the police may record more of the crimes reported to them. Thus, in a review of BCS and GHS data on domestic burglary, Hough and Mayhew (1985) argue that these crimes have probably increased at a far slower rate than have the numbers recorded in police statistics.

Moreover, it seems that in comparison with some other countries – notably the United States – crime in Britain is *not* particularly high. This is clear from comparisons of figures for homicides (United States Department of Justice 1982), where official data may be fairly valid, and also from victim survey data (Block 1983). In summarizing the findings of the 1982 survey, Hough and Mayhew (1983) point out that at 1981 levels the 'statistically average' adult in Britain could expect to be robbed once every five centuries, to be the victim of an assault resulting in an injury every century, to have the family car stolen every sixty years, and to be burgled every forty years. Thus:

> 'if the same total of offences were shared out equally between all the police in England and Wales, each officer would only have to deal with one offence every four days. . . . The "average" person can, for example, expect to be the victim of a burglary or car theft once or twice in their adult life. The chances of being injured in an assault are very much smaller, and the risks of robbery are smaller still.'

(Hough and Mayhew 1983: 15)

On the face of it such a statement is reassuring. However, it begs three important questions. First, while 'the statistically average person' may be relatively safe, are there groups in the population whose level of risk is significantly higher? Second, is the question of how safe people *feel* distinct from that of how safe they *actually are*? Finally, what is the impact of crime on those who are victimized? These three questions form the basis of this first part of this book. In this chapter we shall review research on the social characteristics of crime victims and fear of crime. In Chapter 2 we shall then consider the needs and problems experienced by victims.

## Victims of crime

Although victim surveys were initially seen as important in allowing more valid measurement of crime, they necessarily included considerable detail of the population surveyed. This was significant because earlier studies based on police statistics provided few details of victim characteristics, in part due to the lack of detail collated in police records, in part to the problems inherent in official statistics. That is, it could be argued, if official crime data are largely dependent upon the decisions of *victims* to report crime to the police (Bottomley and Coleman 1981; Mawby 1979a; Reiss 1971), such records may provide a clearer indication of 'willingness to report' than of actual victimization. Thus research which has been dependent on official statistics and which has included victim details (e.g. Amir 1971; McClintock 1963; Maguire 1982; Radzinowicz 1957) must be used with caution. Equally, studies which focus on the area distribution of crime and suggest that those living in certain areas (inner city or public housing) are more at risk of crime than others (Baldwin and Bottoms 1976) have been criticized for their reliance on police records.

There are, of course, some exceptions to this. Notably, crimes which are almost always reported to and recorded by the police – such as homicide and car theft – are better sources of valid data on victimization. With regard to the former, for example, British and American crime statistics regularly include details of homicide victims showing that homicide is anything but randomly distributed. Thus in 1984 in England and Wales, among victims aged 16 or more, male victims outnumbered females by 35 per cent, and rates decreased with age.[1] Additionally, 77 per cent of offenders were acquainted with their victims, whilst only 14 per cent were not (the remainder being unknown), and of the overall total of 563 victims, 23 per cent were killed by spouse/former spouse/lover, and so on, and 19 per cent by another family member (Home Office 1985a).

The United States Department of Justice (1982) similarly provides statistics to demonstrate variations in risk, for example contrasting area, gender, and race. These reveal both the higher risks in the United States and enormous variations among different populations. Thus in the early 1980s the lifetime chance of being a homicide victim was 1 in 606 for white females, 1 in 186 for white males, 1 in 124 for non-white females and a frightening 1 in 29 for non-white males (Karmen 1984).

Homicide statistics on victims are however exceptional. In most respects, victim surveys provided the first opportunity for researchers to consider the distribution of crime *vis-à-vis* the population at risk. From the first, details were included in surveys of the gender, age, social class, race, marital status, family composition, area of residence, and so on, of respondents. Rates of victimization could then be compared for different variables.

Before considering the findings it is perhaps worth pointing out that the ways in which the data are collated vary between surveys. As already noted, for example, the offences included in the survey, the descriptions of those offences, or the time period covered may vary. In addition, though, two other distinctions may be made. First, rates may be based on all crimes covered in the survey, specific offence types, or broader distinctions. In this respect, much analysis of the BCS (Gottfredson 1984; Hough and Mayhew 1983, 1985) draws a distinction between *personal* crime and *household* (including vehicle) crime. Second, rates may incorporate each offence against the individual or household into an *incidence rate* or may count only one incident per individual or household, providing a *prevalence rate* (Bottoms, Mawby, and Walker 1987).

Given these alternatives, what then are the findings? First, it is perhaps worth noting that *by and large* victim surveys have failed to show *consistent* variations in risk according to either social class or race (Hindelang 1976, Hough and Mayhew 1983; Smith 1982; Sparks, Genn, and Dodd 1977). Where differences do emerge, it appears that some categories are more at risk of certain crimes, other categories of different crimes. With regard to race, this is particularly interesting because others have argued that racial harassment is a significant factor behind much crime against minority groups, especially Asians in Britain, and it is arguable that large-scale crime surveys 'miss' such incidents, either due to under-sampling or the reluctance of racial minorities to list such incidents. If so, local specialist surveys like that in Islington may provide a more valid reflection of minority vulnerability (Jones, MacLean, and Young 1986).

Leaving this aside, considerable variations in risk have been found in many surveys on at least three other variables [2] – area of residence, gender, and age. With regard to the former, national surveys have demonstrated marked differences between urban and rural areas, with large conurbations particularly crime prone, even though, in some surveys at least, such a clear pattern is not evident for offences of violence (Hindelang 1976; Hough and Mayhew 1983). Nevertheless, using the ACORN classification of neighbourhood groups, Hough and Mayhew (1985) show clear differences between different neighbourhood types, with for example agricultural areas, better-off retirement areas and affluent suburban housing having lower rates for robbery/theft from the person than do multi-racial areas and the 'poorest council estates'. Similarly, local surveys show equally marked variations. Thus Sparks, Genn, and Dodd (1977) found differences between the three London boroughs they surveyed, Mawby (1982a) and Bottoms, Mawby, and Walker (1987) showed high rates in certain areas of privately rented and council accommodation in Sheffield, and more recently Kinsey, noting considerable area variations in Liverpool, concluded:

> 'There can be no doubt that both in terms of the quality and the impact of the crimes examined the poor suffer more than the wealthy. The problems appear critical for the 20 per cent of the Merseyside population living in the poorest council housing.'
>
> (Kinsey 1984: 16)

Comparisons by gender also reveal differences, with males more at risk than females (Gottfredson 1984; Hindelang 1976), with only the Islington survey producing any conflicting information (Jones and Young 1986; Jones, MacLean, and Young 1986). Given the very different public image of the vulnerability of females, we shall return to this issue later. It is, however, important to note that personal offences against females are more likely to be missed by a victim survey than are those against males – rapes or attempted rapes are unlikely to be mentioned (Hough and Mayhew 1985), and women may also be reluctant to give details of domestic violence, especially where they are still living with the offender (a problem apparently overcome in the Islington survey). Nevertheless, Clarke *et al.* (1985) show from BCS data that risk of 'street crime' alone is also markedly greater for males than females, at least nationally.

Just as it is surprising to find that males are more at risk of crime than females, so variations by age are contrary to public images. Thus it appears that the young are more at risk of crime than are the elderly. Moreover, while – with notable exceptions (Riger *et al.* 1978) – research on gender variations has been minimal, there is a wealth of data on victimization by age. Broadly, this shows that whether one uses police records or survey data, the elderly are least at risk. While there are variations by offence type, very few researchers have shown the elderly to be more at risk of any offence, and for most offence categories the young are at particular risk (Mawby 1982b). Similarly, surveys of juveniles reveal very high risks of victimization among school populations (Feyerherm and Hindelang 1974; Mawby 1979b).

These age variations are well illustrated in findings from the 1984 BCS.[3] In *Table 1.1* we have included rates for different age groups

Table 1.1 *Victimization rates per 100 units by age (BCS 1984)*

| age of respondents | household rates |  | personal rates |  |
|---|---|---|---|---|
|  | incidence | prevalence | incidence | prevalence |
| under 20 | 58 | 34 | 37 | 22 |
| 20–29 | 64 | 37 | 21 | 14 |
| 30–39 | 54 | 32 | 13 | 8 |
| 40–59 | 44 | 24 | 7 | 5 |
| 60 or over | 18 | 12 | 2 | 2 |
| total | 41 | 24 | 11 | 7 |

for household and personal offences separately, in each case distinguishing between incidence and prevalence rates. For the under-20 age group the pattern is unclear, given that for crimes against the household these rates may reflect the age group of head of household for those living with parents. In all other respects, though, age is seen to be negatively correlated with risk. Those aged 60 or above have the lowest rate on all four indices.

In *Table 1.2* we have focused on personal offences and compared males and females in each age group. As is evident, the rates for males are some 50 per cent higher than those for females, and marked for each age group except the eldest, where there is no significant gender difference. At the other extreme, the largest gender difference emerges for those aged under 20, where male rates are almost twice those of females. Thus while some 7 per cent of the population in 1983 were the victims of personal crime, this rate increased by no less than 300 per cent for males aged under 20. While 24 per cent of respondents lived in households which had been victimized, the rate was some 50 per cent higher among respondents aged between 20 and 29. Clearly, then, objectively, crime is more of a problem for some groups within the population than it is for others. Moreover, in respect of area of residence and age at least, victims appear to share certain characteristics with offenders, a finding substantiated by other studies which suggest particularly high rates of victimization among offenders, both adult (Gottfredson 1984) and juvenile (Mawby 1979b).

This immediately raises the question of *why* such variations exist. In this respect, some have attempted solutions by looking at the strategies deployed by offenders, especially burglars (Carter and Hill

Table 1.2 *Personal victimization rates per 100 units by age and gender (BCS 1984)*

| age of respondents | incidence |  |  | prevalence |  |  |
|---|---|---|---|---|---|---|
|  | male | female | total | male | female | total |
| under 20 | 49 | 24 | 37 | 28 | 15 | 22 |
| 20–29 | 22 | 19 | 21 | 16 | 11 | 14 |
| 30–39 | 16 | 10 | 13 | 9 | 7 | 8 |
| 40–59 | 9 | 5 | 7 | 6 | 4 | 5 |
| 60 or over | 2 | 2 | 2 | 2 | 2 | 2 |
| total | 14 | 9 | 11 | 9 | 6 | 7 |

1979; Maguire 1982; Repetto 1974), suggesting that certain environments may be particularly vulnerable. This has been expressed most forcefully, if somewhat simplistically, in the notion of 'defensible space' (Newman 1972).

However, while it may be true that for certain types of crime high-rise buildings may be easy targets and, say, terraced houses, relatively well protected, explanations which rely on offenders' strategies are somewhat weak. For example, we might then expect those least able to protect themselves (the elderly) and those with the most which could be stolen (higher incomed; higher social classes) to be most at risk, which is clearly not always the case.

Instead, it is more productive to look at the victims themselves, to see how far their status or behaviour may have 'encouraged' the crime to take place. Early victimologists referred to this as victim precipitation (Amir 1971; Von Hentig 1948; Wolfgang 1958; see also Wolfgang 1985) and, in arguing that the actions of the victim in many ways precipitated the crime, seemed – to a greater or lesser extent – to suggest that victims were at least partly to blame for their crimes.

Since, as we shall note later, in policy initiatives the issue of desert is frequently intertwined with the concept of need, it is important to clarify this point.[4] There is a distinction between saying that the status or behaviour of an individual increased his or her chance of being the victim of a crime and saying that, because of this, victims are partially to blame. To confuse the two issues is as illogical as it is to argue that if a particular stretch of road is an accident black spot, all those involved in road accidents there are at fault!

Alternatively, let us take the more contentious case of the female hitch-hiker who is raped. On the one hand, clearly those who hitch lifts may be more at risk than those who do not, partly because they become easier targets, partly because males may be more likely to perceive them as sexually willing or available. On the other hand, clearly alternatives to hitching may be less available to some females than others – inability to afford a taxi or the unavailability of public transport. Finally, the victim could justifiably argue that she has the right to expect to be safe in our society, and a society where behaviour such as hitching a lift is 'off limits' for females is itself open to criticism.

While we would accept that victimization rates can be explained in terms of the victim's status and behaviour, we therefore do not accept that this necessarily implies that victims share some of the responsibility for the crime. However, as the above example illustrates, the precise nature of the behaviour which is held to increase risk varies. Early victimologists tended to focus on behaviour by the victim which either provoked the offender or encouraged him to see the victim as a willing participant or easy target. Certainly, some crimes may be explained in this way, but it is scarcely a sufficient explanation for the variations in risk we have described. More important, perhaps, is the concept of location – where victims live or spend their time. Thus we know that within urban areas, residential areas with high offender rates tend also to have high offence rates. In this context, then, those who are trapped into accepting accommodation in such areas immediately place themselves at more risk of crime.

Further, though, we also know that much crime is located in city centres, and in the evenings, that multi-storey car parks are particularly vulnerable, and that burglars prefer empty houses to occupied ones. All other things being equal, then, we might expect those who spend most time outside the home, especially in the evening, to increase their risk. The elderly, who in contrast spend more time at home, reduce their risk of burglary and avoid the possibility of street crime. The young, who spend most time out of the home and frequent city centres in the evenings, increase their risk (Garofalo 1986).

Life-style is not a *sufficient* explanation for victimization. As Clarke et al. (1985) show, the elderly have low victimization rates even when one controls for time spent outside the home. Nevertheless, analysing the 1982 BCS, Gottfredson concludes:

> 'Going out in the evening (particularly at the weekend) and heavy drinking are apparently risk-enhancing activities, accounting for some of the risks associated with age, sex and urbanisation. Daytime activities – especially working out of the home, going to school, and travelling on public transport – affect the chances of both personal and household victimization. Some of the factors associated with household and motor vehicle victimization also suggest that individual behaviour patterns serve to enhance or to decrease the opportunity for these crimes.'
>
> (Gottfredson 1984: 31)

The life-styles of the elderly and women may thus explain their low risk of crime. However, one controversial issue remains, which will be covered in the next section. That is, is life-style independent of risk of victimization, or does the threat of crime affect life-style? Do the elderly and women spend more time in the home because they fear to go out? If so, those who are not 'actually' crime victims may, to some extent, be considered victims of crime, or at least of the fear of crime – what Conklin (1971) calls 'indirect victimization'. With this in mind, it is important to consider fear of crime as a separate issue.

## Fear of crime

As well as measuring *experiences* of crime, early victim surveys introduced questions aimed at tapping respondents' *anxiety* over crime. In the United States, for example, respondents to the National Crime Survey were asked: 'How safe do you feel or would you feel being out alone in your neighbourhood at night?' (Garofalo 1979). Additionally, respondents were asked about their feelings of safety in different areas, whether they felt people limited their activities because of fear of crime, and about national crime trends (Gaquin 1978). In the first victim survey in Britain (in London), Sparks, Genn, and Dodd (1977) used a similar question on feelings of security *within the home*. The BCS, in both 1982 and 1984, incorporated the question: 'How safe do you feel walking alone in this area after dark?' Additionally, respondents were asked whether or not they worried about being the victim of crime, and about which specific crimes concerned them most.

It is important to emphasize the types of question asked to elicit 'fear of crime' both because it is unclear what responses to such questions signify *and* because different questions elicit markedly different answers. For example, respondents answering that they felt unsafe about being out alone at night may do so because:

1. They feel vaguely worried about the extent of crime generally.
2. They consider their chances of being attacked to be great.
3. They have heard of others being victimized in the area.
4. They feel that should they be attacked they would be seriously harmed.

Alternatively, others may deny feeling unsafe because:

1. They do not see crime as a salient social problem.
2. They think it unlikely that they will be attacked.
3. They do not think such crimes are common.
4. They feel able to handle an attack, should it occur.

5. Or perhaps most tellingly, they feel too embarrassed to admit to being afraid.

The problem is compounded by the finding that different questions produce responses which appear contradictory. Thus, while many people admit to a fear of crime, considerably more perceive crime rates to be high and/or rising and see the crime problem as a serious social problem (Mawby 1982a). On the other hand, asked specifically about crime in their area (compared with elsewhere), respondents tend to *understate* the problem. Thus both Herbert (1976) and Mawby (1982b) found that even in residential areas with high crime rates the majority of residents did not see the local crime rate as above average.

This is well illustrated if we consider the responses of residents of Sheffield's 'red light district', an area characterized by high offence and offender rates according to both police statistics and victim survey data. Yet only 46 per cent of those interviewed felt the local offender rate was above average for Sheffield, and half this number felt it had risen within the last few years. In terms of offences committed in the area, only a quarter felt the area rate to be above average (Bottoms, Mawby, and Xanthos 1981). Similar evidence emerged from studies in the United States, as McPherson summarizes:

'Most information about fear and concern for crime comes from national-level data which do not make distinctions between the fear of being personally victimized and a more generalized concern about crime as a national problem. Results of the Law Enforcement Assistance Administration's survey (of the public's attitudes towards crime) indicate, however, that there is a real and significant difference between individuals' perception of crime nationally versus their perception of crime in the neighbourhood where they live. Specifically, more people perceive rising crime as a national, rather than a neighbourhood, problem; and people tend to believe that the fear of crime affects other people more than it affects them.'

(McPherson 1978: 319–20)

Returning to questions specifically about fear of crime, there are, however, further ambiguities, centring on the relationship between fear and risk.

On a general level, for instance, people may worry about certain problems more than about others which are, objectively, more likely to occur. For example, approximately 15 per cent of respondents to the 1982 BCS were very worried about assaults, more than were worried about road accidents (9 per cent), domestic fires (10 per cent) or accidents in the home (8 per cent) (Maxfield 1984). Yet in 1984 in Great Britain, approximately 127,000 crimes of violence against the person were recorded by the police (Central Statistical Office 1986), of which a minority involved injury and less than 1 per cent death, whilst in the same year, over 78,000 people were killed or seriously injured on the road, and from 14,259 accidental deaths 5,789 occurred in road accidents and 5,759 in the home (Central Statistical Office 1986). Similarly, the 1982 BCS found that within the last year 3 per cent, 4 per cent and 6 per cent of respondents, respectively, answered that they or other members of their household had required medical treatment following a motor vehicle accident, household fire or other accident in the home, in each case as many or more than had been injured as a result of a crime.

Clearly, then, the public may be more at risk from vehicle-related or other accidents, but fear of crime is greater. A further difficulty over measures of fear of crime, however, arises where comparisons are drawn between those who fear crime and those who are most at risk of crime.

Reports from early victim surveys noted that those respondents who appeared most in fear of crime were not necessarily those who were most at risk. Indeed, in some cases quite the reverse. Thus, whilst males and young people were most likely to be the victims of crime, females and the elderly were most worried about crime. Garofalo (1979), for example, used 1975 National Crime Survey data from eight cities to compare personal victimization rates with responses to the question on feelings of safety out alone in the neighbourhood at night. Whilst victimization rates fell from 12.5 per cent for the 16 to 19 age group to 3.4 per cent for the 65-plus age group, the corresponding proportions who said they felt somewhat or very unsafe rose from 37 per cent to 63 per cent. At the same time, 9.0 per cent of males and 5.4 per cent of females were the victims of personal crimes, but 26 per cent of males and 60 per cent of females expressed fear of crime, by this definition. These contrasting patterns led Garofalo to consider the extent to which fear is based on not merely risk and experience of crime but also role socialization, media presentations of crime, and the extent to which respondents felt reassured by police performance.

Others have concentrated on the paradox as it relates to specific subgroups. Riger *et al.* (1978), for example, argue that higher levels of fear among women are partly the result of women's lesser ability to defend themselves, partly the impact of fear of rape, a point taken up in both the Islington crime survey (Jones, MacLean, and Young 1986) and the 1984 BCS (Hough and Mayhew 1985).

However, most attention has been focused on the position of the elderly. High levels of fear among the elderly have been explained on a number of levels. For example, they may reflect concern over the *effects of crime should it occur* rather than risk of crime *per se*. Alternatively, some have argued that fear of crime itself produces low crime rates, in that it affects life-style (Balkin 1979). That is, because they fear crime the elderly are reluctant to leave their homes – especially on foot or alone at night – thereby reducing their risk of crime. Such an image of the elderly as virtually imprisoned in their homes because of the fear of crime is particularly potent: freedom from crime may be bought 'at the expense of richness of life-style, such as the freedom to visit friends and relatives, to sit in outdoor locations, to participate in the free activities of the city, or to traverse the neighbourhood' (Lawton *et al.* 1976: 28).

Moreover, it signifies a shift in emphasis in studies of fear. Whereas a few years ago fear of crime was considered somewhat irrational, numerous authors now appear to take crime, and fear of crime, very seriously indeed. At least three elements are involved here.

First, more recent studies suggest that fear is indeed greater in high-risk neighbourhoods. Put another way, within the inner city, residents may see crime as one of the most serious social problems. Thus Kinsey (1984) in Liverpool and Jones and Young (1986) in Islington have aroused controversy in arguing that local crime problems are indeed 'real' problems. Similarly, Hough and Mayhew (1985), in summarizing the 1984 BCS, shift away from their earlier emphasis and suggest that fear of crime is indeed greater in areas of urban deprivation.

Second, and allied to this, is the argument that fear of crime is associated in people's minds with a number of other aspects of one's area of residence. In a sense, fear of crime becomes a shorthand way of expressing a concern for community, an experience of the quality of life. Fear of crime may thus include anxiety about strangers, concern over moral standards, worries about the respectability of the neighbourhood, fear of the incivility of local children, and so on

(Garofalo and Laub 1978; Wilson and Kelling 1982), which is compounded by the powerlessness of the elderly, women (Eve and Eve 1984) and inner city residents to change the conditions of their environment (Smith 1986).

Third, as we have noted, and as a result of this, fear of crime is taken seriously where it is seen to affect life-style. Thus, if one cannot alter the environment within which one lives, a rational response may be to limit excursions into the more dangerous areas of that environment, resulting in indirect victimization through a restriction of life-style for women (Riger *et al.* 1978) and the elderly (Balkin 1979; Berg and Johnson 1979; Lawton *et al.* 1976).

Evidence on the extent to which fear of crime does actually affect behaviour is conflicting with some studies seeing the association as minimal (Hindelang 1976; Skogan 1986; Yin 1982). However, in analysing the 1982 BCS, Maxfield produces evidence:

> 'That behaviours associated with risk management are common, and that they frequently reflect fear for personal safety and worry about crime. Those whose anxieties centre on street crime distance themselves from these threats by staying off the streets and by avoiding night-time activities they perceive as risky. Such actions are more common among vulnerable groups and those living in inner-city areas, places where street crime is more common.'
>
> (Maxfield 1984: 36)

There are, however, problems arising from this type of perspective. For example, if, as has been suggested, fear of crime is a shorthand expression of a number of undesirable features of neighbourhood, it may equally be used as a global justification for behaviour. It becomes, for some, a convenient reason to give to the interviewer when asked to account for lack of leisure activities. Moreover, while it may be true that those in high-risk areas show higher levels of fear than do other citizens, a sizeable minority of the latter apparently express levels of fear above what one might expect. It is difficult to argue that the 11 per cent of respondents to the 1984 BCS who lived in agricultural areas and were 'very worried' about mugging, or the 14 per cent of those who lived in affluent suburban housing who answered similarly (Hough and Mayhew 1985: 73), were expressing rational fears.

Nevertheless, as we have already noted, fear of crime depends not just on risk but also on perceived effects should a crime occur. It is therefore pertinent to consider the impact of crime upon its victims.

# 2 The impact of crime

**Needs and problems of crime victims**

Interestingly, while discussions on fear of crime are almost endless, the amount of attention paid to the needs of crime victims is negligible. The exception to this is research on rape, a point not lost on Burt and Katz in a comparison of the effects of crime on the elderly and rape victims:

> 'Research on the elderly and crime has focused on fear to the virtual exclusion of responses on recovery patterns following actual victimization. No one seems to care what happens to the elderly after they are victimized, except to see whether they are more fearful. This is a very different research picture from that for rape.'
>
> (Burt and Katz 1984: 1)

Indeed, as the authors note, in an excellent review of the literature, the effects of rape are well documented. The physical act of rape, compounded by the social meanings ascribed to the rape and the victim by legal and medical agencies, relatives and friends, and ultimately the victim herself, results in financial costs, physical ill-health, behavioural maladjustments, and 'emotional, psychological and relationship outcomes'. Burgess and Holstrom (1974) described the effects in terms of a 'rape trauma syndrome', and Sutherland and Scherl (1970) posit a three-stage model. This includes a period of initial crisis, during which there is a disruption of all aspects of life functioning, a period of pseudo-adjustment, and finally a phase of long-term adjustment. However, little research has considered the effects of rape over a year after the event, and as Burt and Katz (1984) point out, there is some evidence that problems may persist for considerably longer periods (Ellis, Atkeson, and Calhoun 1981).

While much of this research took place in the United States (Becker, Abel, and Skinner 1979; Burgess and Holstrom 1974; Katz and Mazur 1979; McCahill, Meyer, and Fischman 1979; McCombie 1976; Williams and Holmes 1981), British research (Chambers and Millar 1983) and evidence from those involved in the helping process (London Rape Crisis Centre 1984) provide a similar picture, and it is undoubtedly the case that the effects of crime are most devastating and long-term for the victims of rape.

Research on other victims of serious crimes is less common. However, in one exception, Harris Lord (1986) notes the dramatic impact on next-of-kin in drink-driving cases. Nevertheless, despite political emphasis on the serious impact of crime, especially in the United States (President's Task Force 1982; Young and Stein 1983), much of the research which uncovers extreme effects is based on dramatic events, including holocaust, fires, experiences in prisoner of war camps, hijacking, hostage-taking and hurricanes (Bard and Sangrey 1979; Galvin 1986a; Salasin 1981; Symonds 1982), which in many cases do not involve crimes. In contrast, as Maguire (1984) has pointed out, the effects of mundane crime (i.e. that which is most likely to be experienced) are less well researched.

Of course, police records and victim survey data provide information on the most common types of crime, including details of financial losses and the extent of physical injuries. However, further information is less readily available and is frequently limited to small-scale studies. In one of the earliest of these, based on 826 victims in Milwaukee interviewed during the court proceedings, Doerner *et al.* (1976) found that seven different problems were mentioned by more than 20 per cent of the sample, the most common being 'mental or emotional suffering' cited by 57 per cent.

In Britain details of the impact of specific offence types comes from Maguire's (1980, 1982) study of household burglary and Shapland's (1984) research on the victims of violent crime (see also Shapland, Willmore, and Duff 1985). Maguire found that only 32 per cent of his sample focused on loss, damage, or disarrangement of property as the worst problem, while 41 per cent cited intrusion on privacy and 19 per cent emotional upset. Moreover, while only a minority felt that the effects were considerable, they were sometimes persistent:

> 'At least one-quarter of victims experienced some very unpleasant moments after discovering that they had been burgled. It is perhaps a matter for more concern that 65 per cent of victims interviewed 4 to 10 weeks after the event said it was still having some effect upon their lives. The most common persisting effects were a general feeling of unease or unsecurity and a tendency to keep thinking about the burglary.'
>
> (Maguire 1980: 264)

Shapland (1984: 142) also noted 'the persistence and consistency of the prevalence of physical, social and psychological effects over time', although in the case of violent crime financial needs were less marked and less persistent.

Shapland's longitudinal study illustrates perhaps the most appropriate means of assessing changes in impact over time. However, different research techniques may also result in different conclusions. To illustrate this, Maguire and Corbett (1986) compared data from the 1984 BCS with the results of their own, in-depth interviews with selected groups of reported burglary victims. Noting that only 36 per cent of the former who were victims of reported burglary, but between 60 and 80 per cent of the latter, were 'very much' affected by the crime, the authors suggest that, allowing for the selective sampling, survey-based attempts to measure the effects of crime produce estimates almost one-third lower than do in-depth interviews.

This is not, of course, to say that the latter are a more valid measurement. One could, indeed, make a case that in-depth interviews encourage victims to magnify the effects of the crime. Nevertheless, it is an important methodological qualification, most pertinently because we wish here to dwell on the 1984 BCS in some detail.

## The impact of crime: data from the BCS

In the 1984 survey, victims were asked how much they had been affected by the crime, and how much it was still affecting them at the time of the interview.[1] They were also asked what problems the crime had caused them and what the worst problem had been.

Including the replies from all victims – whether or not the crime had been reported to the police – it is clear, from *Table 2.1*, that only a minority said they were affected 'very much' or 'quite a lot' at the time, and very few were still affected at the date of interview. In all, 41 per cent of victims cited practical problems resulting from the crime and 33 per cent mentioned emotional or personal problems. Of these, 13 per cent had experienced worry, fear, loss of confidence, or wariness as a result of the crime, and 9 per cent admitted to feelings of anger, frustration, or annoyance.

Clearly, the proportions citing problems might be expected to vary according to offence type and whether or not the crime is reported (see also Maguire and Corbett 1986). Dividing victims of personal

Table 2.1 *Percentage of victims who felt that the incident had affected them or their household (BCS 1984)*

|             | in the first few days | at time of interview |
|-------------|-----------------------|----------------------|
| very much   | 11                    | 2                    |
| quite a lot | 17                    | 5                    |
| a little    | 31                    | 12                   |
| not at all  | 39                    | 80                   |
| total       | 98                    | 99                   |

and household crime, for example, 37 per cent of the former but only 25 per cent of the latter said the crime had affected them 'very much' or 'quite a lot' at the time, with the proportions falling to 9 per cent and 6 per cent respectively, at the time of interview. By the same token, 51 per cent of victims of personal crimes known to the police and 42 per cent of victims of reported household crimes said they were significantly affected at the time, and 14 per cent and 12 per cent, respectively, were still affected when interviewed.

But, if certain subgroups of the population are more at risk of crime, it is equally important to ask whether the effects of crime are greater for some victim categories than others. For example, Gay, Holton, and Thomas (1975) found the elderly, women, and those living alone to be most affected by the crime; Maguire (1980) found that among burglary victims the separated, divorced, and widowed were additionally adversely affected; Jones, MacLean, and Young (1986) found greater effects among the elderly, low-incomed, and blacks.

Using the 1984 BCS, we considered the impact of crime according to three sets of variables. First, we tested whether the effects varied according to *victim* characteristics; then we considered variations according to *offender* characteristics; finally we considered the influence of victim–offender relationships. In each case we distinguished between personal and household crimes.

The results are summarized in *Tables 2.2* to *2.4*, which illustrate marked variations. In line with earlier research, we found that female, older, and separated/divorced or widowed victims, and those living in single-adult households reported themselves to be particularly affected by the crime, and that these variations persisted over time. In contrast, single people, males, those aged under 20, and those with other adults in their households, were least likely to say that crime had affected them. Similar patterns emerged where we

## 22  Crime Victims

Table 2.2 *Percentage of victims who were 'very much' or 'quite a lot' affected by the incident, according to victim characteristics (BCS 1984)*

|  | during first few days |  | when interviewed |  |
|---|---|---|---|---|
|  | personal | household | personal | household |
| *marital status* |  |  |  |  |
| single | 26 | 24 | 6 | 5 |
| married | 39 | 24 | 9 | 5 |
| divorced/separated | 64 | 31 | 17 | 10 |
| widowed | 57 | 41 | 32 | 14 |
| *family structure* |  |  |  |  |
| single-person household | 51 | 34 | 16 | 12 |
| one-parent household | 74 | 42 | 18 | 17 |
| adults only | 29 | 24 | 9 | 5 |
| adults and child(ren) | 37 | 22 | 7 | 4 |
| *gender* |  |  |  |  |
| male | 24 | 22 | 6 | 4 |
| female | 59 | 29 | 15 | 8 |
| *age* |  |  |  |  |
| under 20 | 23 | 17 | 6 | 3 |
| 60 or more | 51 | 33 | 29 | 11 |
| *tenure* |  |  |  |  |
| owner-occupiers | 32 | 21 | 6 | 4 |
| council tenants | 46 | 36 | 14 | 10 |
| *income* |  |  |  |  |
| under £5,000 | 62 | 36 | 22 | 10 |
| £15,000 or more | 32 | 18 | 11 | 4 |
| *socio-economic grouping* |  |  |  |  |
| professional | 31 | 23 | 5 | 6 |
| semi/unskilled manual | 45 | 36 | 14 | 9 |
| *school-leaving age* |  |  |  |  |
| minimum | 41 | 28 | 11 | 8 |
| above minimum | 32 | 22 | 8 | 4 |

considered the proportions who said they suffered practical or emotional difficulties as a result of the crime. For example, at the extreme 85 per cent of respondents from one-parent households said they suffered emotional or personal problems as a result of personal crimes, and 58 per cent admitted to practical problems resulting from household crimes.

Additionally, there is some indication of variations by socio-economic status, with lower-status victims most affected. For example, council tenants more often said they were affected than did owner occupiers, and twice as many of those with incomes under £5,000 said they were affected compared with the high-income brackets. This was, moreover, more than a matter of relative financial loss, since the differences by socio-economic status were greater for emotional or personal problems than for practical ones.

Victims were also asked if they had any idea who committed the crime, and specifically about the number of offenders, and gender, age, and race of offenders. We therefore considered whether the effects varied according to offender characteristics. The main findings are included in *Table 2.3*, and it is clear from this that variations are neither as great nor as consistent as by victim characteristics. Taking the victims of personal offences, it seems that at the time older offenders caused victims most distress. However, the long-term impact did not differ by offender's age but was greater where four or more offenders were involved and, intriguingly, for the small number of cases involving female offenders. Turning to household crimes, victims were most likely to say they were affected at the time where four or more offenders were involved, where the offenders were at least 16, and in the small number of cases involving

Table 2.3 *Percentage of victims who were 'very much' or 'quite a lot' affected by the incident, according, where known, to offender characteristics (BCS 1984)*

|  | during first few days | | when interviewed | |
| --- | --- | --- | --- | --- |
|  | personal | household | personal | household |
| number of offenders | | | | |
| one | 38 | 29 | 8 | 9 |
| four or more | 34 | 44 | 13 | 16 |
| gender | | | | |
| male | 36 | 36 | 8 | 13 |
| female | 39 | 35 | 17 | 3 |
| age | | | | |
| school-age | 30 | 32 | 10 | 13 |
| 16–25 | 31 | 42 | 10 | 16 |
| older | 47 | 40 | 10 | 12 |
| race | | | | |
| white | 35 | 34 | 11 | 11 |
| West Indian/African | 37 | 55 | 8 | 16 |

black offenders. However, while number of offenders and race were also related to feelings at the time of the interview, age was less significant, and offences by males were considered to have had more impact than those by females. As a result, there is no consistency on any one variable, the nearest exception being that victims were in most circumstances affected more frequently where four or more offenders were involved. However, even this tendency is undermined by the finding that victims of one offender were *more* likely to mention either practical or emotional/personal problems than were victims of four or more offenders.

The BCS also allows us, however, to consider the relationship between victim and offender (Mawby and Firkins 1986). Those victims who said they knew who was responsible were subsequently asked if their offenders were strangers or known personally; if the latter, if they were known casually/by sight or well known; and if well known, what the precise relationship was. We are therefore able to distinguish four levels of victim–offender relationship: those where the victim has no idea who committed the crime (*offender unidentified*); those where the offender is known to be a *stranger*; those where the offender is no more than a *casual acquaintance*; and those where the offender is *well known*.

For household crimes it is clear from *Table 2.4* that victims were least affected by crimes where the offender was unidentified. For personal crimes, where only a small number of 'offender unidentified' situations arose, this pattern was not evident vis-à-vis victims' feelings at the time. Rather, crimes by strangers were *least* upsetting to victims, crimes by offenders well known to the victim most likely to have an effect. Thus 53 per cent of those victims who said the offender was well known to them said they were 'very much' or 'quite a lot' affected by the incident at the time, and this rose to 62 per cent for crimes by neighbours and 81 per cent when only 'spouse'-related crimes were considered.[2] The pattern is illustrated in a rather different way in *Figure 2.1*, where we have compared the victim–offender relationship for those who said they were 'very much affected', with those who were 'not at all' affected at the time of the offence, and in *Figure 2.2* where we have repeated the exercise according to whether or not victims cited emotional problems. The clear message from *Table 2.4* and *Figures 2.1* and *2.2* is that, at the time of the offence, it is not personal crimes by strangers but offences by those well known to the victim, especially personal crimes by spouses, which most affect victims. A similar conclusion can be

Table 2.4 *Percentage of victims who were 'very much' or 'quite a lot' affected by the incident, according to victim–offender relationship (BCS 1984)*

|  | during first few days |  | when interviewed |  |
|---|---|---|---|---|
|  | personal | household | personal | household |
| offender unidentified | 41 | 22 | 4 | 4 |
| stranger | 29 | 33 | 9 | 12 |
| casual acquaintance | 40 | 37 | 9 | 13 |
| well known | 53 | 36 | 11 | 9 |

drawn from *Table 2.4*, concerning feelings at the time of interview, although at this juncture offences by neighbours appear most upsetting. In any event, quite clearly the impact of the crime varies both for different subgroups of victims and according to the nature of the victim–offender relationship.

Whilst only a small percentage of crime victims in general suffer physical harm, practical/financial and emotional/personal problems are cited by a large number of victims. Only a small proportion of these are long-term. Nevertheless, the evidence suggests that for some victims problems arise which may require outside help, and that some types of victim – women, the divorced or separated, one-parent families, those living alone, the elderly, the poor, and victims of personal crimes who know their offenders well – may be most vulnerable. In the final section of this chapter we therefore move on to consider the development of policies in the context of the needs and rights of such people.

## Needs, rights, and policies

In the last sections we have suggested that while fear of crime may in itself be a problem, and the crime problem perceived as a major social issue, crime is not as prevalent as is often thought, and our risks from crime may be lower than from other sources, like traffic accidents, which arouse far less concern. Nevertheless, some subgroups within the population are more at risk than others. Equally, if we consider the effects of crime, it is clear that in only a small minority of cases are victims affected a great deal, or for a long time. This is not to say that, for the rest, crime is insignificant or unimportant. Rather, it may be for many a nuisance, an inconvenience, an irritant, or an imposition rather than a crisis, and where

26  *Crime Victims*

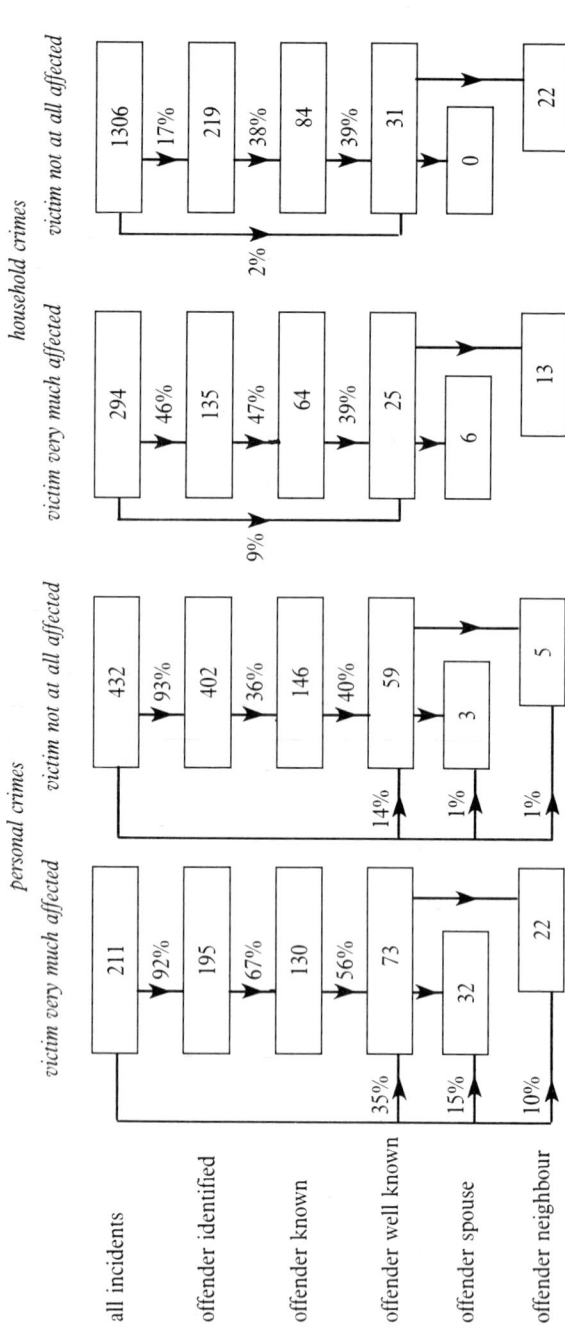

*Figure 2.1* Victim–offender relationship, comparing those 'very much' and those 'not at all' affected at the time of offence, controlling for offence type (BCS 1984)

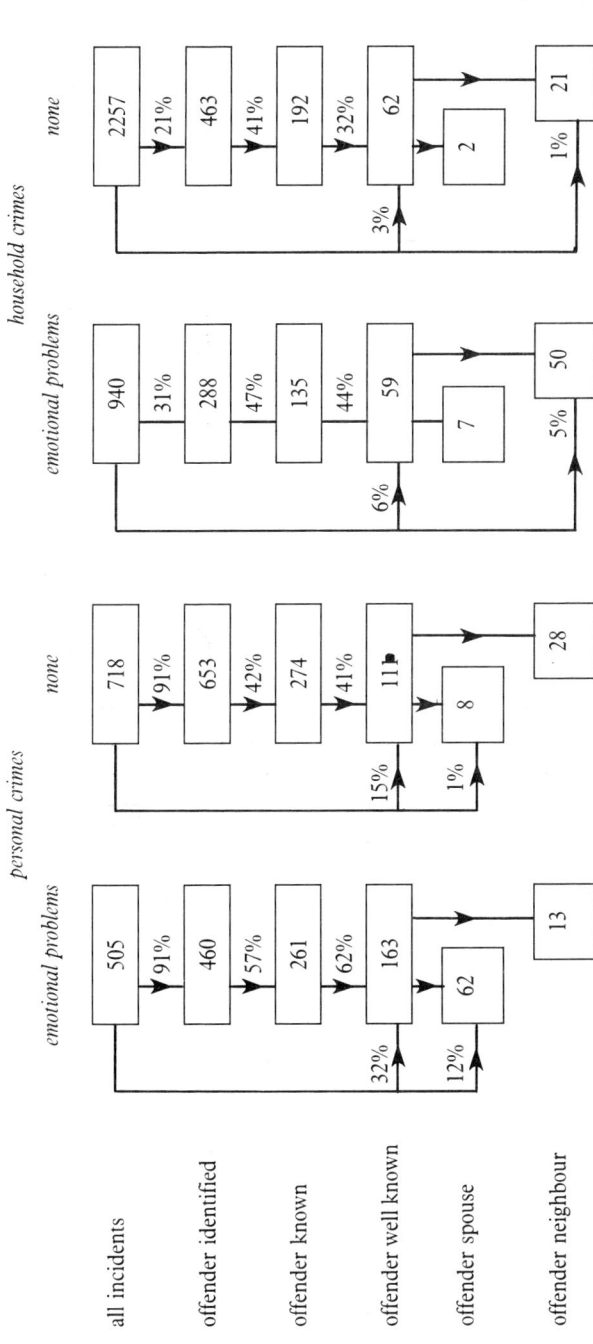

*Figure 2.2* Victim–offender relationship, comparing those who cited emotional/personal problems with those who cited no emotional/personal problems, controlling for offence type (BCS 1984)

minor incidents occur regularly, the cumulative impact may be considerable. Moreover, some victims are badly affected by 'their' crimes.

It is, however, rather more difficult to estimate just which victims from a given population will be among those most affected. For example, while it seems that the elderly and women are particularly affected, they are also less at risk than other groups. Thus the number of young male victims of personal crimes who say they are experiencing problems may be greater than the number of older female victims!

On a wider level, the path between crime effects and policies is fraught with difficulties, arising from the inadequacy of using 'needs' as a basis for service provision. There are at least two elements of importance here, related to the definition of need and the delineation of responses.

Considering first the question of defining need, we are confronted with a range of difficulties identified by social administrators and leading one to talk, somewhat mischievously, of the discipline of 'needology' (Williams 1974). As we have noted, some crime victims say they are 'affected' to some degree by the crime; they describe a range of emotional/personal and practical/financial problems. Just when these effects can be described as 'needs' is, however, problematic. As Plant, Lessor, and Taylor-Gooby note:

'If needs can be fixed in some straightforward, neutral, objective way, then the goals of the social services could equally be fixed objectively, thus by-passing contestable appeals to social and political values. Questions about the social services would no longer be questions about moral or political values but of matching needs, which might be thought a technical rather than an ideological problem.'

(Plant, Lessor, and Taylor-Gooby 1980: 21)

But the problem *is* an ideological one, as the controversy which surrounded Townsend's (1979) study of poverty well illustrates. Whether or not needs can be said to exist depends on both the type of definition employed and the definer.

Difficulties were less (but not absent) where researchers advocated survival standards (Rowntree 1901). However, in the context of crime, to argue that the dead (or dying) victim is in need is scarcely helpful! We may, therefore, turn to the expert, the scientist, to define standards for an adequate existence. But while there are some psychological approaches to defining the needs of crime victims (see, for example, Salasin 1981), definitions on some basic level of functioning for healthy existence are neither objective nor adequate.

Instead, we may, in desperation, turn to the studies described above and define need in terms of victims' own definitions. Unfortunately, as Runciman's (1972) classic study of poverty illustrates, we may unearth those who according to other definitions are clearly in need but who do not perceive themselves as such. Moreover, as Shapland (1984) observes, victims may base their responses on socially developed expectations of 'what one ought to need'. Thus, if victims have low expectations of help, they may understate their needs.

Clearly, though, if policies are to be initiated, they must be based on some definition, appropriately quantified, of what needs must be met. Problems concerning the delineation of responses are, however, even wider than this. To start with, we may accept that a level of need exists without considering that any outside help is appropriate, if the victim is considered undeserving. This is a common theme in the context of crime victims. We have already referred to the issue of precipitation and, as we shall detail in Chapter 3, policies have in general been restricted to those considered innocent or blameless victims.

Even where victims are considered deserving, there is no guarantee that the state will accept some responsibility for meeting needs. As is currently government policy vis-à-vis unemployment in Britain, the problem is accepted, but doctrine absolves the state from direct responsibility – it is an affair for private market forces to resolve. More commonly, with regard to welfare services, the state may accept the role of benevolent provider of help for extreme cases – what Titmuss (1974) calls 'the residual model of welfare' – but expects the voluntary sector to act as the primary provider. This stance may be justified on ideological and/or financial grounds.

Many of these difficulties are lessened if services are considered as rights rather than needs-based. In Britain the welfare state, as it has developed incrementally, incorporates both. For example, health services (with some high-cost exceptions) are available as of right to all citizens; education for those between the ages of 5 and 16 is similarly a right. In contrast, services in the sphere of housing, employment, income maintenance, and personal social services are more selective and tend to be defined as welfare provision for those in need rather than rights for everybody.

| sector | relevant agency mechanism | problems cited | help given |
|---|---|---|---|
| state | NHS | physical/psychological injury | medical services |
| state | CICB | physical/psychological injury (possibly leading to loss of income) | financial compensation |
| state | compensation orders | physical injury or financial loss | financial compensation |
| private | insurance | financial | financial compensation |
| voluntary | women's refuges | physical/psychological injury leading to financial hardship | advice, support, shelter |
| voluntary | Rape Crisis Centres | physical/psychological injury | advice, support, counselling |
| voluntary | victims support schemes | practical and emotional | advice, support, counselling |

*Figure 2.3* Role of relevant agencies in Britain *vis-à-vis* problems cited by crime victims

## The impact of crime

Given that services for crime victims have, as we shall see, developed only recently in Britain, they are almost entirely needs-based; victims' *rights* are either ignored or explicitly denied. Allied to this, the role of the state is minimal and the role of the voluntary sector is marked.

We shall return to the 'needs versus rights' issue in the final chapter. Here, however, we can conclude by identifying the various services provided for victims. As can be seen from *Figure 2.3*, excluding the crime prevention role of the police, the role of the state is almost exclusively confined to meeting the physical health and financial needs of (some) victims. There are principally two avenues for dealing with injuries caused to victims – first, the National Health Service and, second, the Criminal Injuries Compensation Board, which deals with *financial* compensation for physical injury and psychological harm. Compensation orders also relate to compensation for injury but most especially financial loss. In Chapter 3 we shall focus on the development of victims services and particularly criminal injuries compensation. Then, in Chapter 4 we shall concentrate on the later implementation of compensation orders and the recent widening of the principle of compensation to include mediation and reparation.

Financial help is also provided for victims, where eligible, by the private sector through insurance. However, although other help may be given informally by family or friends, the bulk of services are provided by the voluntary sector. Most victims are dependent upon the voluntary sector for information about their financial entitlements, and for providing for any other needs. The remainder of the book therefore focuses on the role of the voluntary sector. In Part III we provide a critical overview of voluntary services in Britain and compare these with services in the United States. Then, in Part IV we concentrate on our current research on victims services in south-west England.

# PART II
## *State responses to crime victims*

# 3 State responses to the needs of victims and the introduction of criminal injuries compensation

Victim studies have, as we noted in Chapter 1, been a comparatively recent development. Parallelling it, and to some extent feeding off it, there have emerged in the last two to three decades a variety of socio-political movements advocating incorporation of the victim's interests in policy. For convenience, we have labelled this conglomeration the victims' movement, but in reality it is a complex mixture of ideologies and issues which fits uneasily under one banner. Some have advocated victims' interests in the pursuance of 'law and order', championing for example bail restrictions and capital punishment (Carrington 1975); some have allied this to the search for a more effective criminal justice system where victim or bystander co-operation might be improved (Ziegenhagen 1976); others have seen the advantages of offender reparation for deterrent sentencing (Meiners 1978). In contrast, many have advocated restitution as in the offenders' interests (Harding 1982; Schafer 1960), especially as the treatment model has been superseded by a justice perspective, and this is at the core of many mediation initiatives. Others still have focused quite specifically on the victim and avoided wider sentencing issues, a deliberate policy of the NAVSS in Britain (NAVSS 1981), avoiding some of the embarrassment of the feminist movement, where focusing on women's rights (in the context of rape and domestic violence) has sometimes become associated with a more punitive approach towards offenders.[1]

Equally varied are the alternative structures which have emerged whereby victims' interests can be met. On the one hand, statutory services have developed in many countries, mainly within the criminal justice system but sometimes as part of welfare services. Alternatively, the voluntary sector has expanded to cater for many victim needs which are unmet by the state.

This chapter and the following chapter focus on the development and current status of services provided by the state, and in subsequent chapters we shall concentrate in more detail on the voluntary sector. As will become evident, state services focus predominantly on the *financial* solutions to the problems experienced by victims. We shall therefore consider these, in the context of both their development, the needs which they meet, fundamental and procedural problems which have been identified, and ultimately, the gaps in state provision.

**Criminal justice and the victim: a historical introduction**

It is now commonplace for writers on victim services, especially compensation, to note the decline, in urbanizing and industrializing societies, of the victim's role in the criminal justice system (Harding 1982; Meiners 1978; Schafer 1960). The place of compensation was – we are told – firmly located in Babylonian law, where the *lex talionis* is detailed, as well as in Greek, Jewish and Roman law (Fry 1951: 28–30; Schafer 1960: 3–4), although, as Burnham (1984) observes, all relied ultimately on bloody force and the power of kin to force or 'negotiate' compensation. Reparation is also evident in early English law, from about the seventh century, and among Germanic tribes (Fry 1951: 29–33). In Saxon England the *wer* (payment for homicide) and the *bot* (compensation for injury) were allied to the *wite* (the fine paid to the overlord). However, the development of a centralized state in the Middle Ages coincided with a diminution of the victim's right to compensation and the imposition of fines collected by the state. Nevertheless, as Burnham notes: 'it is clear that reparative solutions to problems were extensive until the introduction of the New Police and the extension of summary justice in the middle of the 19th Century', and restitution was applied under developing colonial law in seventeenth-century America (Meiners 1978: 8; Schafer 1960: 5).

However, the development of criminal law, and the distinction of criminal from civil law, saw the virtual exclusion of the victim from the criminal justice process – 'The victim became the Cinderella of the criminal law' (Schafer 1960: 8).

But, for those familiar with fairy tales, Cinderella did ultimately become star of the ball, and the fairy godmother eventually arrived! She appeared, briefly, with the classical school of criminology, where Jeremy Bentham argued that a utilitarian system of justice would provide for the victim, either from the offender's estate or, if impractical, from the state. Then, in the late nineteenth and early twentieth centuries, restitution was identified as an issue at a series of International Penal Congresses, where William Tallack from Britain,

Sir George Arney from New Zealand, and the Italian criminologist Raffaelo Garofalo were among those pressing for changes in criminal law. However, the penal lobby's influence was restricted to a series of rather weak resolutions, and Cinderella apparently went back to the ashes (Meiners 1978; Schafer 1960).

The word 'apparently' is inserted because, despite the lack of pressure for change – in Britain between William Tallack and Margery Fry (1951, 1957) – the rights of the victim to compensation were established in a variety of laws which allowed the courts to require reparation from the offender as a condition of sentence. Thus, reparation was introduced as an optional requirement of a probation order from its inception in America (Schafer 1960) and has continued to operate (Goldstein 1982), and a similar requirement was included in the 1907 Probation Act and 1948 Criminal Justice Act in Britain. Moreover, provisions for the offender to pay compensation to the victim were included in the 1870 Forfeiture Act and the 1914 Criminal Justice Administration Act, among others.

Of course, evidence of legal provision should not be equated with use, and with one exception (see below) there is little evidence on this count. Research on the introduction and use of these provisions appears non-existent. Without further evidence, we must assume that Cinderella did in fact languish among the ashes until the postwar period, when she was summoned forth to the ball by a rather appropriate fairy godmother in the guise of Margery Fry. Before considering developments in the 1950s, however, it is perhaps useful to reflect on the place of the victim in *welfare* systems, in the context of the British welfare state.

## Crime victims and the welfare state

Although Britain was by no means unique in the development of a comprehensive range of welfare services, it is convenient to discuss these in some detail since they predate and then coincide with discussions on the rights and needs of crime victims. Thus, while the 1834 Poor Law marks a somewhat repressive beginning to state welfare, the development of health and education provisions in the nineteenth century to some extent coincides with government co-ordination of the penal system (Frazer 1973). Then, as the penal system became remodified at the turn of the century, with the incorporation of the rehabilitative ideal into prisons, the introduction of probation, and the construction of the borstal system, Parliament passed legislation dealing with school medical inspection, the legal rights of children, pensions, and sickness benefit. The responsibility of the state for meeting the needs of 'victims of hardship' was thus firmly established.

These reforms provided a platform for the expansion of welfare services into the so-called postwar welfare state. The Labour government developed services aimed at tackling the problems associated with ill-health, inadequate housing, unemployment, and low incomes, and the 1944 Education Act provided universal coverage for the education of children up to age 15.

However, nowhere among these 'victims of misfortune' is mention made of crime victims. Thus the postwar reforms stemmed from the influential Beveridge Report in 1942. Using powerful rhetoric, with immediate appeal to the wartime population, Beveridge identified five giant evils of society, namely want, disease, ignorance, squalor, and idleness. Absent from this list, and unnoticed at the time, was the victim of crime. Indeed, as Taylor (1981) argues, the wartime and postwar concern over crime was focused not on individual victims but on society as the victim of black-marketeering. With minor exceptions (see below), crime victims were not seen as a concern of the *welfare*, as opposed to the *penal*, sector. A review of postwar political manifestos, dominated by the twin concerns of welfare and international relations, reveals no mention of crime victims until 1959 and, in the context of welfare, none until 1979. As a result, Charles Irving, a Member of Parliament closely associated with the emerging victims' movement in the 1970s, was able to ask, rhetorically:

> 'Where are the social workers employed by the State to look after the victims of crime? Where are the residential rehabilitation centres for disabled victims? Where are the special medical facilities they require? The answer is nowhere. Victims are the forgotten people of the welfare state; the people the state has failed to protect, and whose emotional and material needs are largely ignored.'
>
> (Irving 1977: 2)

This point is, of course, somewhat overstated. Within the apparatus of the welfare state those who, as the victims of crime, register needs appropriate to the major welfare agencies would be treated accordingly. The National Health Service, for example, provided free health care for those injured in crime, as for those injured for other reasons, and thus the unmet needs and expenses of victims were, from the 1940s at least, on a different level from that in many other countries. Similarly, income maintenance and unemployment policies covered those unable to work due to victimization, along with other illnesses and disabilities. Moreover, given the relatively large public-sector housing pool, compared with most capitalist societies, it was *possible* for those in public (council) accommodation to be rehoused if they experienced housing problems as a result of being the victim of crime. Nevertheless, as Irving rightly points out, there was no co-ordinated state welfare response to the needs of crime victims, and a review of social-work texts reveals no awareness that social workers might have any role to play in helping the victims of crime, despite the proximity of many of their needs to those of conventional client groups. Even in the case of child victims, who have been accepted as a responsibility of statutory and voluntary welfare services since the nineteenth century (Bready 1935; Hobhouse 1939), criticisms have been directed at social workers for *not* prioritizing the needs of the child but instead for seeing the interests of the family as paramount. As in America (Helfer and Kempe 1968; Kempe *et al.* 1962), in the context of the one area of victimology where welfare needs are recognized and distinguished, welfare agencies in Britain have been castigated in a series of inquiries beginning with that on the death of Maria Colwell in 1974 to the more recent case of Jasmine Beckford (Blom-Cooper 1985; Cook and Bowles 1980; Parton 1981).

In other respects, though, response to victims has been identified as part of the criminal justice system. The next sections therefore relate to the establishment of victim services as a penal rather than a welfare issue.

## The re-emergence of the victim

In this respect, Margery Fry emerged during the 1950s as the fairy godmother of Cinderella the victim. From a brief outline in her text on penal policy, published in 1951, Fry headed a campaign to gain compensation for victims which is widely acknowledged as formative in the development of criminal injuries compensation. This is true not only in Britain (Home Office 1959) but also abroad in countries like New Zealand and America (Edelhertz and Geiss 1974; Harland 1978; Meiners 1978).

In *Arms of the Law* Margery Fry (1951), having made brief

reference to reparation in her chapter on legal history, returns to it in a later chapter on fines and restitution. In fact, the bulk of the chapter relates to fines, but on the last three pages she notes with regret the fact that fines seem to have almost entirely replaced restitution in criminal law:

> 'It is noteworthy that the aim was to compensate the party aggrieved; the idea of punishment for a public crime came later. It is perhaps unfortunate that we have got so far away as we have from these primitive usages. ... The tendency of English criminal law in the past has been to "take it out of the offender" rather than to do justice to the offended.'
>
> (Fry 1951: 125)

Following publication of her book, Fry developed more systematic ideas on how compensation might be better incorporated in the criminal justice system. Recalling her own experience as the victim of a handbag snatch, which while unsuccessful shook her considerably, she attempted to fuse the twin concerns of the needs of victims (notably of violent crimes) and the advantages to the offender of incorporating a restitutive element in sentencing (Jones 1966). As in other countries (Cameron 1963; Edelhertz and Geiss 1974) she was aided by a notable case of injustice. In 1951 a victim who was blinded as a result of an assault was awarded £11,500 damages, at five shillings per week, leaving the offenders over four hundred years to pay off their debt and the victim without any practical means of receiving full compensation!

Fry outlined her plan for compensation to the Howard League in 1953, although 'The people in the Howard League did not catch fire' (Jones 1966: 233), and she was left to promote the idea on her own. It 'went public' in 1956 in a radio discussion and was followed by an article in the *Observer* in 1957. On a rather different level, she sought support from the Home Office and both Houses of Parliament. Her death, in 1958, brought a response from 'Justice' in *The Times*, suggesting that the adoption of a criminal injuries compensation scheme would be a fitting memorial. Private members' bills were subsequently introduced, unsuccessfully, to Parliament in the 1959/60 session by R.E. Prentice and in the 1960/61 session by C. Johnson.

In fact, by 1959 some form of compensation was an official part of Conservative Party policy. The White Paper, *Penal Practice in a Changing Society*, included in paragraph 25:

'It may well be that our penal system would not only provide a more effective deterrent to crime, but would also find a greater moral value, if the concept of personal reparation to the victim were added to the concepts of deterrence by punishment and of reform by training. It is also possible to hold that the redemptive value of punishment to the individual offender would be greater if it were made to include a realisation of the injury he had done to his victim as well as to the order of society, and the need to make personal reparation for that injury.'

(Home Office 1959: 7)

Subsequently, the Conservative Party manifesto for the 1959 general election promised that 'A scheme for compensating the victims of violent crime for personal injuries will be considered'.

Notably, by this time the emphasis had shifted from offender reparation to state compensation to victims. This was confirmed in the Home Office document, *Compensation for Victims of Crimes of Violence*, the report of a working party set up in 1959 (Home Office 1961). The first developments within the criminal justice system were thus defined in terms of compensation to the victims of violent crime, being financed from state resources.

## The introduction of criminal injuries compensation

The Home Office review began by positing two models for providing compensation. The first, a scheme for compensation on a weekly payments basis according to 'loss of faculty', was modelled on the industrial injuries system, and in fact followed Fry's proposal (Fry 1957). The other was based on a direct claim for lump-sum damages from the Home Secretary, to be administered by a board set up within the Home Office. The report did not come down in favour of either one model. However, it did provide a rationale for the provision of compensation which proved formative. Four points are crucial in this.

First, the committee rejected the claim that victims had a *right* to compensation. This argument, based on the claim that the state has a duty to protect its citizens from violence and is thus obligated to provide compensation where it fails, was refuted on the practical grounds that no government could possibly be expected to prevent *all* violent crime. Interestingly, a distinction was drawn here between 'ordinary' crime and 'political' riots, with some acceptance that the innocent victims of riot might have a right to compensation. Nevertheless, in general, 'The proposition that the State has a duty to protect its members from unlawful violence and that if it fails to do so it should pay compensation . . . seems to us to be both fallacious and dangerous' (Home Office 1961: 7).

Second, the committee pointed out *legal* anomalies. It accepted that the victim's common-law right to bring actions for damages against an offender was virtually useless, given the low detection rate and poverty of many offenders. Thus the state might accept responsibility for providing equity between different victims of violent crime, and between crime victims and civil litigants.

Third, the committee noted *welfare* anomalies. It therefore sought to provide equity between crime victims and others whose needs were met through the welfare state. Thus, noting that the state already made provision for other 'accidents and mischances of life' (Home Office 1961: 4), the committee saw precedents in welfare services. However, while postwar welfare services incorporated a mixture of rights and more discretionary provisions, the latter model was adopted here. Thus the state was seen as *gratuitously agreeing* to meet the needs of certain victims without accepting that it had any *obligation* so to do:

> '[We] think it could nevertheless be based on the more practical ground, already in the minds of its advocates . . . that although the Welfare State helps the victims of many kinds of misfortune, it does nothing for the victims of crimes of violence as such. . . . There is an argument for filling this gap, based mainly on considerations of sympathy for the innocent victim.'
> (Home Office 1961: 7)

Finally, and developing from this point, the committee chiselled in stone the distinction between the deserving and undeserving. Stressing that 'it must provide means of distinguishing the deserving claimant from the undeserving or fraudulent' (Home Office 1961: 7), it proceeded by including in the latter those who failed to report crimes to the police, those who provoked the crime, those of dubious character, and those with an ongoing relationship with the offender.

The working-party report was presented to Parliament in June 1961 and provoked reports from the Conservative Party and 'Justice' among others. The pressure on the government was, however, perhaps most noticeable from its own rank and file. Conservative Party annual conferences in succeeding years from 1961 to 1963

## State responses: criminal injuries compensation 43

carried resolutions in favour of the proposals. Nevertheless, by the time the next White Paper was published (Home Office 1964), New Zealand had already introduced a parallel scheme. Indeed, the speed of developments elsewhere was given as good reason why the scheme should be experimental: 'the Government consider it best to start with a flexible scheme which can be altered in the light of experience. This White Paper therefore proposes an experimental and non-statutory scheme' (Home Office 1964: 4).

In essence, the government rejected the Fry model and went for a scheme founded on executive rather than legal action (thus the use of the term 'non-statutory' in a strictly legal sense). It therefore set up the Criminal Injuries Compensation Board as a Home Office quango, financed by a 'grant-in-aid' from the general budget. As a result, the notion of victims' *rights* was rejected from the outset:

> 'Compensation will be paid *ex gratia*. The Government do not accept that the State is liable for injuries caused to people by the acts of others. The public does, however, feel a sense of responsibility for and sympathy with the innocent victim, and it is right that this feeling should find practical expression in the provision of compensation on behalf of the community.'
>
> (Home Office 1964: 4)

Membership of the board (originally five plus the chairman) was subsequently decided by the Home Secretary and the Secretary of State for Scotland. Awards were payable whether or not the offender was brought to justice, but only where injury was appreciable. (There was originally a minimum of £50 or three weeks' loss of earnings.) Compensation was based on common-law damages (except for the calculation of loss of earnings); in cases of fatalities spouses or dependants would be eligible; however, there would be no award for loss of expectation of happiness, or any element comparable to exemplary or punitive damages. Legal fees were not claimable, although witness expenses could be paid at the board's discretion. Crucially, following the 1961 model, claimants were excluded where the offence had not been reported to the police and where the offender was currently a member of the victim's household, and the board was directed to reduce compensation where any share of responsibility could be apportioned to the victim.

## The current position

Since its inception the Criminal Injuries Compensation Board has been subject to critical review (Miers 1978, 1980; Samuels 1973), it has published details of its operation in its annual reports, and it has been the subject of parliamentary review (Home Office 1978; House of Commons 1984). Its operations have also been scrutinized by researchers surveying the views of victims of violent crime (Genn 1984; Shapland 1984; Shapland, Willmore, and Duff 1985; Vennard 1976). Partly as a result of these, it has been modified; for example, following doubts raised by the board and the recommendations of the Home Office working party (Home Office 1978), the exclusion rule relating to violence within the family was modified. In other respects, changes have occurred *despite* criticism. Thus in 1983, as a cost-reducing exercise, the minimum award payable was raised to £400 (£500 for cases of violence within the family) to exclude minor claims, and the Home Office made clear to the Home Affairs Committee of the House of Commons that this increase was non-negotiable (House of Commons 1984).

The government has undertaken to bring in legislation to place the board on a statutory footing, and with this in mind an interdepartmental working party is, at time of writing, reviewing the current operation of the scheme. Given the likelihood of change, and the extensiveness of previous critiques (see especially Miers 1978), it is not proposed to detail the operation of the scheme. It is, nevertheless, important to provide some brief description of the current position and focus on problems associated with criminal injuries compensation.

In the year ending March 1984, the board received nearly 32,000 applications, nearly 27,000 from England and Wales. For England and Wales, 24,811 cases were resolved. Of these 3.3 per cent were abandoned, 88.5 per cent culminated in a single-member decision and 8.2 per cent involved a hearing. Excluding abandoned applications, 72.2 per cent resulted in full awards, 2.5 per cent reduced awards and 25.3 per cent nil awards, with £27,161,359 being paid in compensation, an average of £1,515 per successful applicant. Including Scotland, £32,820,772 was paid in compensation during the financial year, with the scheme itself costing an additional £3,854,344 (Home Office 1984).

This in fact represents the major part of the state's financial responsibility for crime victims. It is not, however, without its critics. At least three problems have been identified, relating to a mixture of procedural difficulties and issues of principle. At issue are the level of compensation, the accessibility of the system and the criteria of exclusion. Each has its equivalents in other areas of victim needs and services and the more general welfare debates.

First, there is the question of the level of compensation. In fact, one strong appeal of the original idea was its relative cheapness – Fry (1957) estimated an addition to taxation of one penny per adult taxpayer – and the restriction of compensation to victims of *violent* crime, the raising of the minimum award, and to some extent the ceiling on compensation for loss of income, reflect a government concern to save, leading Miers (1980) to describe the scheme as no more than a symbolic gesture. One question which is rarely considered, though, is whether compensation is in actual fact based on common-law damages. In this context, the Meah case is important.

Christopher Meah was convicted of the rape of two women in 1985. Although imprisoned, Meah's plea that the desire to rape was the result of injuries received in a car accident was accepted, and in a civil action he received £45,750 damages against the driver. As a result, Meah – unlike most violent offenders – had the means to compensate his victims, and a resulting civil action on behalf of the two rape victims ended in Mr Justice Woolf awarding the two women a total of £17,560. The low level of this award, compared with that made to Meah, caused a controversy, fuelled by the ironic coincidence that Mr Justice Woolf was responsible for both awards.

Whether or not the damages awarded to the rape victims were fair is a moot point. What is problematic, and what received rather less media coverage, was the comparison between the civil-law assessment of the 'cost of rape' and that of the Criminal Injuries Compensation Board. As was noted in the *Guardian*:

> 'The derided awards actually mean that the victims are significantly better compensated – judged purely in cash terms – as a result of a civil suit than they would have been under the existing criminal injuries compensation scheme. The experience of the two victims proves the point. They had already been awarded £3,600 and £1,000 respectively under that scheme. The Criminal Injuries Compensation Board normally starts its assessments in rape cases from a figure of £2,750. So the women have done much better in Mr. Justice Woolf's court.'
>
> (12 December, 1985)

It may be that levels of compensation are particularly low in cases of rape, compared with other offences (Samuels 1973; Shapland, Willmore, and Duff 1985). The 1984 guideline figure of £2,750 for a rape appears somewhat less than generous (Home Office 1984: 19). Nevertheless, the Meah case has raised unease where previously there was a commonplace feeling that the Criminal Injuries Compensation Board was comparatively generous.

The second problem identified is, however, less contentious – namely the question of access. Stemming partly from the notion of awards as *ex gratia* rather than rights, the onus is on victims to apply and, despite the efforts of the board itself, none of those with whom the victims of violent crime come into contact has a duty to make them aware of the scheme. Thus, in common with welfare benefits which are reliant upon claimant initiatives, take-up is low (Samuels 1973; Shapland, Willmore, and Duff 1985), due primarily to victims being unaware of the board and its applicability to their cases. From the original sample of Shapland, Willmore, and Duff (1985), for example, only 34 per cent actually applied for *any* form of compensation, and the chief reason for this low figure was lack of knowledge. In contrast, applications from those who have most knowledge of the board – victims who are police officers – make up a significant minority of cases (Samuels 1973).

Once a claim has been made, however, access through the system to a satisfactory outcome is not guaranteed. Unlike most American schemes (McGillis and Smith 1983), legal fees are not payable – nor does the claimant qualify for legal aid (in line with other tribunals in Britain). Yet, despite assumptions that legal representation is unnecessary (Home Office 1978), both this working-party review and Samuels (1973) acknowledge that where victims are legally represented at hearing, their success rate is twice that of unrepresented applicants. It thus appears that full access to the benefits of the system is prevented by lack of knowledge of its existence and, among those ending in personal hearing, by a lack of legal advice.

Finally, we can return to perhaps the key issue in critiques of criminal injuries compensation: the exclusion of the undeserving. Clearly, this was built in to the original scheme, and although provisions have been slackened in certain respects, allowing a victim who is related to the offender to apply where the relationship has been terminated, the board still interprets its role as including moral judgements. As Miers notes, 'It is clear that they look favourably upon those victims who exhibit the values and life-style that might be associated with the expression "law-abiding" ' (Miers 1978: 177). Moreover, the exclusion of claimants whose general life-style was dishonest (even where the crime was totally unrelated to this), introduced in 1969, demonstrates tightening-up of board policy.

Some writers have been more critical of the board's policy in this respect than have others (compare Miers 1978 with Shapland, Willmore, and Duff 1985, for example), and it is a point to which we shall return later in this chapter. At this stage, however, we should note that while the Criminal Injuries Compensation Board represents the first major attempt to meet the needs of a particular category of crime victims, it neither fully meets their needs nor, fundamentally, addresses their rights.

## The development of criminal injuries compensation abroad

New Zealand became the first Anglo-Saxon country to establish a criminal injuries compensation scheme, operational from January 1964. Elsewhere federal structures meant the introduction of schemes in some states rather than others. Thus the first scheme in Australia started in New South Wales in 1967, and at a similar time Canada's first scheme was initiated in Saskatchewan. In the United States, California had been the first state to implement a programme, approximately one year earlier, and while schemes are now found in most states, they are neither universal nor identical (Galvin 1986b).

In recent years a number of texts have focused on particular schemes or specific countries, most notably the United States (Edelhertz and Geiss 1974; McGillis and Smith 1983), Australia (Chappell 1970; Chappell and Wilson 1977), New Zealand (Brett 1964; Fahy 1975) and Canada (Burns and Ross 1973; Edelhertz and Geiss 1974; Miers 1978). Some of these, and others (e.g. Burns 1983), provide a comparative review. Two issues raised in this literature are of particular relevance here. First, almost all schemes, except the New Zealand one and the original California scheme, are based on legal rather than welfare systems. Second, again with the exception of New Zealand, criminal injuries compensation is designed to exclude victims defined as undeserving. Thus, where, as we have noted, the British scheme now allows some claims from victims related to offenders, within certain restrictions, compared with other schemes this is relatively generous.

However, the New Zealand scheme is worthy of mention, given its rather different focus. While the original scheme was similar to those developed elsewhere, the 1972 Accident Compensation Act eliminated the victim compensation programme and absorbed crime victim compensation within a comprehensive accident compensation scheme. Crime victims became subject to welfare compensation, where such compensation was theirs by *right*. The provision thus eliminated the problem of distinguishing between deserving and undeserving victims, although some have argued (Meiners 1978) that it has created the opposite injustice by providing, from the public purse, for those who do not deserve any compensation. Equally, it avoids the difficulty, cited in annual reports from the Criminal Injuries Compensation Board, of some crime victims receiving better treatment from the law than accident victims.

## The politics of state initiatives

At the beginning of this chapter we noted the variety of pressures behind the victims' movement. As is clear from our brief review of criminal injuries compensation, many different pressures apply to particular circumstances. Those supporting victims' initiatives may do so for very different reasons.

In Britain – in contrast with the United States – the emphasis on improving the efficiency of the criminal justice system as a basis for victim programmes has been minimal. However, to a greater or lesser extent, the other emphases which we cited are present in the initiatives under discussion.

The view of victims services as a response to the needs of victims finds expression through the discussions preceding the setting up of the Criminal Injuries Compensation Board. However, the responsibility of the state to meet needs was clearly prescribed – thus victims had no *right* to compensation, only deserving victims were included, and only victims of serious violent crime were eligible. Thus, while it may be true that criminal injuries compensation was geared to meet the needs of certain crime victims who appeared to have been ignored compared with offenders' needs or welfare recipients, equally, following Miers (1978), we can safely argue that a system designed with the chief priority of meeting the needs of crime victims would not have developed along this route.

What then of the other liberal interpretation of postwar victim legislation – that which sees it as in the interests of the offender? Although emphasized in *Penal Practice in a Changing Society*, it appears almost irrelevant in the context of criminal injuries compensation and can be left for further discussion in Chapter 4.

We have stressed these points because, with the exception of Miers (1978), most reviewers of postwar legislation have seen it very much as the result of humanitarian awareness and concern (see particularly Harding 1982). However, while Miers restricts himself to the criticism of criminal injuries compensation as a low-cost political response to the pressure for victim reform, we feel that there is rather more weight to this pressure than is openly acknowledged. The 1961 Conservative Party resolution well illustrates this concern that 'something ought to be done' about the crime problem and:

> 'That this Conference is concerned at the increase in numbers of murders and other crimes of violence, endorses the steps already taken to strengthen the police, increase penalties for young offenders, and provide more detention centres and calls for:
> (a) a swift implementation of the prison building programme and improvement of the staffing of penal institutions;
> (b) strict enforcement of sentences imposed in serious cases; and
> (c) immediate introduction of a scheme to ensure compensation for the victims of violent crime.'

Compensation indeed became adopted as a Conservative initiative. While the Labour Party Study Group Report, *Crime – A Challenge to Us All*, devoted only one paragraph to it (Labour Party 1964: 39), the 1964 Conservative manifesto proclaimed, 'we have taken measures to protect the public against lawlessness and introduced compensation for the victims of violent crime' and, in the context of increased policing and a review of sentencing, reminded its readers, 'Meanwhile, we have increased the penalties for malicious damage and the compensation to those who suffer from this form of hooliganism' (Craig 1975: 253–4).

While it is in no sense merely an 'anti-offender' measure, we would therefore argue that criminal injuries compensation, in demonstrating a concern for the innocent victim, neatly complements deterrent penal policies.

## Summary

In this chapter we have focused on the varied aspects of the victims' movement as this has manifested itself in state action, specifically regarding criminal injuries compensation. However, in discussing these developments, we have stressed that they are not merely addressed to meeting the needs of crime victims. The introduction of criminal injuries compensation reflects the views of those who saw the balance between the offender's needs and rights and those of the victim swinging too far towards the former. Legislation is thus a symbolic gesture, but one which has somewhat more political substance than Miers (1978) indicates.

But how have victims' interests been affected? First, clearly, the legislature has quite explicitly denied victims' rights, not merely to recompense but also to the information on which *rights to claim* might be based. Thus studies make clear both that victims have no legal right to compensation and that a majority of victims have no more than a vague idea of what possible avenues for compensation exist.

Equally, legislation applies only to a restricted series of victims' needs. Criminal injuries compensation addresses the needs of victims, at least victims of violent crime, but excludes those whose needs are not excessive (i.e. currently below the £400 or £500 minimum), rejects or adjusts down the claims of those who are considered 'in need' but 'not deserving', and avoids ensuring that those in need know of the existence of compensation.

The focus of the state on applying *financial* solutions to the needs of victims is thus restrictive, at least in the context of criminal injuries compensation, and with the exception of New Zealand a similar pattern has been identified elsewhere. However, the introduction of compensation orders in the 1970s, and the popularity of mediation and reparation more recently, provide other opportunities for state provision for crime victims. These are therefore the subject of the following chapter.

# 4 State responses to the needs of victims: compensation orders and reparation

**Compensation orders**

While Margery Fry's postwar initiative to provide compensation for crime victims resulted directly in the setting up of the Criminal Injuries Compensation Board, she was, as we have noted, concerned to introduce compensation in a much wider sense. Like Schafer (1960), she saw compensation *by* the offender as of benefit to both offender and victim.

That the board preceded these wider initiatives is ironic, given that requirements for offenders to compensate their victims were expressed already in a variety of legal systems, even if implementation of these requirements was patchy (Schafer 1960). In Britain, as in the United States, compensation was possible as a condition of probation, but it was also available in other circumstances. In 1969, for example, compensation was ordered in the criminal courts in 23,800 cases of selected indictable offences and 16,317 non-indictable offences (most especially vandalism related) (Home Office 1970a, App. E), involving a total sum of compensation of over £570,000.

These figures were produced in a report by the Advisory Council of the Penal System, instigated in 1966 by the Home Secretary, Roy Jenkins. Although this working party has been somewhat eclipsed by its twin chaired by Baroness Wootton (Home Office 1970b), the committee under the chairmanship of Lord Justice Widgery made a series of recommendations which were incorporated in the 1972 Criminal Justice Act, introducing compensation orders as a court order additional to sentence.

The context within which the working party operated is notable. While compensation orders could be justified as having an intrinsic moral value, or as a means of reform, their main appeal to the committee was as a means of preventing the offender enjoying the fruits of his crime; reparation was thus 'an essential element in the punishment of crime' (Home Office 1970a: 3).

Two major stumbling blocks – which the committee recognized – were, first, that a majority of offenders were not apprehended and, second, that of those who were, many were unable to fully compensate their victims due to poverty or the constraints of their sentences. Nevertheless, it was not in favour of compensation being confined within civil law, and also rejected the suggestion that the principles of criminal injuries compensation should be extended to cover property offences.

At a time when concern was being voiced at offenders (even those who were convicted) profiting from their crimes – the Great Train Robbers being a case to which the working party referred – the concept of punishment was paramount, and the committee toyed with two ways of expressing this: through bankruptcy proceedings and through prison earnings. In each case, reluctantly, the practical difficulties were considered too great to allow any immediate change in the law.

Nevertheless, the report concluded:

'The Council, however, believe that two factors would be such a powerful deterrent as to make it unlikely that anyone would again commit such an offence. These are, in the first place, a reasonable certainty of detection and secondly, reasonable certainty of loss not merely by the miscreants but also by their families, of the fruits of the criminal activity.'

(Home Office 1970a: 73)

In this context the recommendations for compensation orders appear somewhat of a reluctant acceptance of the practicable. Moreover, in making the recommendation, the working party invited judicial and magisterial discretion that had earlier concerned it in the context of current practice (para. 23):

'Nor do we see any advantage in making it a statutory requirement that the criminal courts shall always have regard to the possibility of ordering reparation, it is the duty of these courts to determine sentence in the light of all the circumstances of the offence and the offender, and it seems to us inappropriate to impose a statutory obligation to consider the possibility of making one particular type of order.'

(Home Office 1970a: 53)

This lack of directive to the courts proved costly. Early evaluations of the use of compensation orders in the Magistrates Courts (Softley

1978) and the Crown Courts (Tarling and Softley 1976; Vennard 1976, 1979) demonstrated a reluctance to impose compensation orders. This problem was compounded by the fact that victims are seldom aware of the possibility of compensation. Indeed, the possibility of imposing an order is not necessarily mentioned in court, and victims may indeed be refused the opportunity to make a claim on their own initiative (Shapland, Willmore, and Duff 1985).

A further problem exists where the offender is unable to pay compensation. This can arise due to lack of means (Softley 1978), a problem recognized by the original working party, which may result in courts not making orders, or in orders not being fulfilled (on which there is little evidence – see Shapland, Willmore, and Duff 1985). However, it may also arise because another decision of the court pre-empts it. Thus, Softley found that those who were sentenced to imprisonment were – not surprisingly – seldom required to pay compensation. Moreover, while fines were regularly combined with compensation orders, where the former was over £20 the proportion of orders decreased.

Finally, it appears that the courts have been reluctant to impose an order in cases of violence, as opposed to property offences (Softley 1978; Vennard 1979).

Many of these difficulties stem from the fact that 'what this approach failed to do was to provide any clear guidance for the courts on the place which compensation of the victim should assume among the aims of the penal system' (Wasik 1978: 602). In an attempt to redress this, the 1982 Criminal Justice Act allows the court to make a compensation order as a sentence in its own right. Alternatively, where the offender has insufficient means to pay both compensation and fine, the former is to be given priority.

Clearly, this does not solve all the problems: victims remain unclear of the possibility of compensation and they may forfeit any opportunity for compensation if the offender is not prosecuted (especially given the increased emphasis on cautioning, not only of juveniles; see Home Office 1985c). Furthermore, the emphasis on financial compensation restricts compensation by impoverished offenders, a limitation when so many defendants are in fact impoverished!

From the victim's perspective, moreover, clearly compensation orders are of marginal relevance. Not only are they applicable to only a small minority of victims, but the whole system is court focused, with victims having little opportunity to express their views on what compensation is appropriate. This problem is more openly addressed in recent initiatives towards reparation and mediation.

## Reconciliation: developments in North America

The idea that criminal justice systems in some sense dispossess victims of their crimes, and that there needs to be a return to a system where victims and offenders together negotiate a settlement of their conflict, is perhaps best expressed in Christie's (1977) presentation of 'conflicts as property'. Certainly, Christie was reflecting a growing interest during the 1970s in victim–offender reconciliation, expressed in initiatives in the United States and Canada (Dittenhoffer and Ericson 1983; Hudson and Galaway 1980; Umbreit 1985; Wright 1984).

The main impetus for these Victim Offender Reconciliation Programmes (VORP) came from the Mennonite community and most especially a group of Mennonite probation officers, 'rooted in their religious convictions to apply peacemaking at a very personal level as an alternative to the frequent depersonalization, frustration and trauma engendered by the criminal justice system' (Umbreit 1986a: 2). The VORP model was first applied in Kitchener, Ontario, in 1974, and was introduced to the United States in Elkhart, Indiana, in 1978. By 1986 it was operating in over thirty areas of Canada and some fifty communities across the United States (Umbreit 1985, 1986a).

The key elements of VORP incorporate the face-to-face meeting of victim and offender in the presence of a trained mediator. The mediator role is distinct from arbitration; the responsibility falls on the victim and offender to arrive at a solution acceptable to both. The process and the solution are thus both crucial:

> 'The primary goal of these Victim Offender Reconciliation Programs is to facilitate conflict resolution between the parties involved, by first allowing time to address informational and emotional needs, followed by a more practical discussion of determining a mutually agreeable restitution obligation (ie. money, work for the victim, work for the victim's choice of a charity, etc.).'
>
> (Umbreit 1986a: 3)

The advantages of such a model over criminal injuries compensation and compensation orders would seem to be twofold. First, the opportunity is available for offenders to appreciate the impact of their crime and provide reparation in a wider sense than is possible through compensation orders. Second, from the victim's perspective, victims have a greater involvement in the process and can gain a more realistic view of the offender and his motives than is possible in the court setting.

Of course, as with compensation orders, victims only stand to gain if offenders are caught. Additionally, though, despite the fact that VORP may be seen as an alternative to imprisonment (Dittenhoffer and Ericson 1983), not all offenders judged suitable are willing to participate, and equally many victims may be reluctant to become involved. For example, Galaway (1986) notes, in evaluating one project in Minnesota, that despite careful preparation and introductory meetings with those concerned, 34 per cent of referrals were lost by offenders refusing to participate, and of those remaining, 29 per cent were lost by victims refusing to become involved.[1] The problem of victims' reluctance to participate has, ironically, meant that some schemes are predominated by corporate victims – shopkeepers or insurance companies – such that the original philosophy becomes blurred. However, feedback suggests that victims usually find the outcome satisfactory and feel that VORP provides a desirable alternative (Galaway 1986; Umbreit 1986a).

The implementation of VORP however raises two issues which have found varying solutions in different projects; namely, in which cases is VORP most appropriate and at what stage of the criminal justice system should it be located? On the first point, it seems that despite initial attempts to use VORP as an alternative to imprisonment, referrals tend to be from the low end of the tariff, especially juveniles with few previous convictions involved in property offences (Dittenhoffer and Ericson 1983; Galaway 1986; Umbreit 1986b). Crimes of violence, or cases where victim and offender were linked in a pre-crime relationship, appear relatively rare, and indeed VORP is only now tentatively moving towards incorporating a significant number of violent crimes, and in so doing adjustments have been made to the original model (Umbreit 1986a).

The type of crimes and offenders that are referred to reconciliation programmes is interrelated to the question of what is the most appropriate point of access. As Karmen illustrates diagrammatically, in the American context the opportunity to make restitution may be arranged (1) prior to police involvement, (2) by the police as an alternative to formal action, (3) as an alternative to court proceedings, (4) prior to sentence, (5) as a condition of sentence, (6) during and as part of a custodial sentence, or (7) as a condition of parole (Karmen 1984: 181). As a general rule it seems that VORP is most frequently instigated either prior to sentence, where a successful outcome can subsequently be used to justify leniency in sentencing, or as a condition of a sentence such as probation. VORP is thus commonly *not an alternative* to more conventional sentencing procedures, *but a supplement* which allows greater victim involvement and the potential for the offender to gain a reduced sentence.

This is an important point to stress, in the context of the growth of reparation, conciliation, and mediation in Britain during the 1980s.

## Reparation and mediation in Britain

Recent developments in Britain have stemmed both from the North American experience and from Christie's (1977) influence (Harding 1982). At a time of crowded prisons and courts and of growing awareness of the problems faced by victims, a variety of pressures have led the government to support a number of experimental schemes, and have led to the emergence of the Forum for Initiatives in Reparation and Mediation (FIRM) as an umbrella organization. Some of these initiatives have been the subject of separate review (Blagg 1985; Walklake 1986; Wright 1983), but the most thorough accounts of the national picture are to be found in Marshall (1984) and Marshall and Walpole (1985).

Some of these, described by Marshall and Walpole (1985) as 'community dispute settlement', involve grass-roots participation in the handling of domestic and neighbourhood disputes, which in many cases are not reported to the police. Such schemes are in a minority and often deal with only small numbers of cases; they are, however, important in the context of the priority given by victims to offences committed by spouses or neighbours, noted in Chapter 2.

Nevertheless, most existing schemes focus on cases which have been referred to the police. In these cases, schemes may stress reparation, mediation, or both. Reparation is:

'the making of amends by an offender, either to his/her own victim ('direct' reparation) or to the victims of other offenders ('indirect' reparation). Reparation may take the form of compensation, atonement, restitution, or the performance of service for the victim.'

(Marshall and Walpole 1985: 65)

Mediation is one but by no means the only mechanism for determining reparation. It is:

> 'a method of settling a dispute or the aftermath of a crime with the help of a third party (who may be independent of, or related to, both parties) but without the imposition of a decision by the third party. If the principal parties cannot be brought to agree, the situation is left unsettled. There are 2 principal forms of mediation – *face-to-face* mediation, where the 2 parties meet together with the mediator, and the use of a *go-between* who visits each party separately to attempt to reach an agreement.'
>
> (Marshall and Walpole 1985: 64)

Schemes based on reparation and/or mediation are in Britain most likely to be located at one of three stages in the criminal justice process – prior to prosecution, prior to sentence, and as a part of the sentence. The first category is almost exclusively devoted to juvenile offenders, where the police, sometimes in conjunction with social workers or through juvenile bureaux, use reparation as an alternative to court action. One of the earliest initiatives in this area was the Exeter Joint Services Youth Support Team (Marshall and Walpole 1985), which started in 1979. Under the scheme, juveniles considered appropriate for cautioning might be incorporated in the programme, subject to voluntary agreement by the juveniles and their parents. Most are first-time offenders committing minor property crimes, and by contrast with the VORP model reparation is negotiated between the team and the offender before being presented to the victim.

Alternatively, reparation based on the principle of mediation may be attempted following conviction but prior to sentence. In such cases, adjournments may be used to allow the feasibility of reparation to be considered, and the power of the British courts to defer sentence provides a useful mechanism for postponing sentence to see whether an agreed outcome can be negotiated. In such cases, it is anticipated, the ultimate sentence will be influenced by the success (or otherwise) of mediation. The Coventry scheme described by Wright (1983) and the Leeds initiative are two examples of such approaches (Marshall and Walpole 1985).

Finally, reparation may be located as a feature of the sentence of the court. This is again evident in the Exeter experiment, where the flexibility allowed in the introduction of intermediate treatment (IT) following the 1969 Children and Young Persons Act provided the opportunity for probation officers or social workers to incorporate reparation as a condition of IT. As Marshall and Walpole (1985) note, IT has provided a convenient vehicle for reparation in a number of other areas. Equally, for older offenders reparation may be incorporated into the conditions of a probation order, while community service orders allow reparation in a rather wider sense (Harding 1982).

Without going into further detail here, it is clear that reparation initiatives have been developing rapidly in Britain in the last few years, although not all incorporate the principle of mediation. However, the variety of structures within which reparation operates is somewhat misleading when one considers the types of crime for which reparation may be a (partial) solution. Thus, as is indicated by the examples given, a majority of schemes focus on juvenile offenders and, as with VORP, non-violent property crimes are the norm. There are of course exceptions, and Wright (1984), among others, has advocated a more imaginative use of reparation and mediation for violent crimes, including those where offender and victim were known to one another prior to the offence. In this respect, it is interesting that while the recent development of schemes makes it difficult to provide an assessment of consumer feedback, the 1984 BCS does allow us to consider the views of victims in general.

## Victims' perceptions of reparation and mediation

Since many have criticized the criminal justice system for ignoring the interests of victims, it is surprising to find that some of those in the victims' movement, notably in the United States, have dismissed reparation without considering what victims themselves think. This is particularly true with respect to crimes of violence, where members of the President's Commission[2] and some participants in the refuge movement[3] have denied that mediation is appropriate. Equally, as we shall note later, in Britain some victims support schemes have been less than enthusiastic.

In this context the 1984 BCS is of particular interest since it provides the first comprehensive national data on what victims in general feel of the prospect of reparation and mediation. For the first incident form completed for each victim, respondents were confronted with the following:

'The Government is considering schemes in which victims and offenders would meet out of court in the presence of an officially appointed person to agree a way in which the offender could make a repayment to the victim for what he had done. Would you have accepted a chance of such a meeting after this crime?'

As many as 49 per cent of victims replied in the affirmative, with 45 per cent rejecting the idea and 6 per cent undecided. These latter two groups were then asked if they would have agreed to an out-of-court agreement where they would not have had to meet the offender. Under these conditions, the percentage willing to accept the proposal rose to 69 per cent of all victims. These were then asked whether they would want the offender to be prosecuted and punished as well, 20 per cent replying in the affirmative. Excluding these from the total we are left with 55 per cent of victims who saw some form of reparation/mediation as a sufficient and appropriate means to resolve their particular crime. Such figures are indeed encouraging to those concerned with extending the opportunities for reparation and mediation.

However, given the extent to which current initiatives have focused on non-violent crime, it is pertinent to ask how far the views of victims vary for different offences. If we make a distinction between household and personal crimes, not surprisingly victims of the former are more likely to be willing to accept reparation – 56 per cent compared with 30 per cent.[4] However, the fact that no less than 30 per cent of the victims of personal crime responded favourably is again encouraging for those involved in developing such schemes.

It might also be expected that responses would vary according to whether or not crimes become known to the police. However, differences were not excessive. For household crimes, 58 per cent of victims of crimes known to the police were in favour, compared with 55 per cent of other victims. For personal crimes, the figures were respectively 34 per cent and 28 per cent. Although reasons for these responses were not elicited, it thus seems that the proportion hostile to reparation because of its inadequacy is roughly balanced by the proportion who feel that official action of *any sort* is unnecessary.

What then of other characteristics of the offence situation which affect attitudes towards reparation? Using BCS data we are able to consider how far attitudes varied according to characteristics of the victim, the offender, and the victim–offender relationship, controlling for offence type and, where appropriate, for whether or not the crime was known to the police.

Taking first victim characteristics, it seemed that for personal crimes, attitudes towards mediation varied only slightly for different subcategories of victim, the most notable difference being by income level, with high-income groups least receptive to the idea. For household crimes there was more variation, with separated/divorced victims, males, and middle-income earners most favourably disposed, and the widowed, female, and elderly least so. For the widowed and those aged 60 or more, this was especially pronounced where only reported crimes were considered, but even here 34 per cent of widowed victims and 41 per cent of the elderly were in favour of reparation.

Turning to offender characteristics, rather large differences emerged. Personal crimes involving one offender, females, and offenders aged 26 or more were *least* likely to be considered suitable for reparation; crimes involving four or more offenders and males were most likely to be seen as suitable. Interestingly, victims of personal crimes by school-aged offenders were relatively likely to favour reparation, but not when only reported crimes were considered. Victims of household crimes committed by one offender were also less inclined to favour reparation than were victims of four or more offenders. However, for reported crimes, victims were most likely to favour reparation where the offender was female or aged 26 or more.

This somewhat confusing pattern is at least partially explained if we consider variations according to the victim–offender relationship. For personal crimes, victims were most likely to favour reparation in the small number of cases where the offender was completely unknown, and this was true even where unreported crimes were excluded. This finding is perhaps indicative of the overrepresentation of thefts from the person in this category. For the rest there was little variation according to whether the offender was a stranger, a casual acquaintance, or well known, except that among victims who reported the crime, those who knew the offender well were least in favour of reparation. Where the offender was a neighbour, victims were especially likely to reject reparation, whether or not the incident was known to the police. For personal crimes involving spouses, it seemed that victims of unreported crimes were often in favour of reparation, but the small number of incidents covered which were reported makes further generalization hazardous.

The pattern for household crimes was clearer. Victims of crimes by offenders known to be strangers were least likely to favour reparation – 43 per cent for all crimes, 50 per cent for reported crimes. At the other extreme, 75 per cent and 71 per cent, respectively, of victims of crimes by casual acquaintances were receptive to the idea of reparation.

Consideration of variations according to victim or offender characteristics, or the victim–offender relationship, thus reveals a number of differences but no clear-cut patterns. To some extent, this reflects the complexity of the crime situation. Additionally, though, it suggests that a wide variety of incidents are *possibly* amenable to reparation, depending on the particular mix of circumstances. There is certainly no evidence that reparation initiatives should focus exclusively on young offenders, impersonal crimes, or crimes by strangers, although there is an indication that personal crimes between neighbours may present a challenge to neighbourhood mediation initiatives.

One other point is also worth making here. While reparation may be an alternative to traditional prosecution in a number of reported crimes, a similar number of victims of unreported crimes responded positively to the idea. This may be a cause of concern to those who see dangers in the net-widening potentials of reparation (Dittenhoffer and Ericson 1983). However, it also suggests that many who see few advantages in reporting crime to the police feel that other actions may be more appropriate than no action at all. While this is not an issue we would wish to pursue here, it does have implications for the range of incidents which we considered in Chapter 1 could most appropriately be labelled as inconveniences or nuisances rather than problems. Moreover, it implies solutions in a rather different direction to those suggested by current moves to criminalize public nuisances. In any event, practical responses to victims cannot, on this evidence, be exclusively directed at those who report crimes to the police.

## Discussion

To date, criminal injuries compensation and compensation orders provide the major involvement of the state in helping victims of crime. Yet, as we have stressed throughout this and the previous chapter, they touch only the tip of the iceberg; they reach only a minority of victims and in no way adequately address victims' problems. They provide inadequate financial solutions to some victims' problems; in no sense do they either promise or deliver justice.

In this context the gradual growth of reparation and mediation initiatives is a promising development, partly because it widens the criteria on which reparation might be assessed, partly because it addresses the issue of justice more directly. For these reasons it heralds a shift in approach.

In Chapter 3 we suggested that the political appeal of criminal injuries compensation lay in its providing a balance to a law-and-order platform. Here, in reviewing compensation orders, we have focused more directly on their appeal to punitive values. Thus the 1966 Conservative election manifesto promised as part of its 'War Against Crime' to 'Make offenders pay restitution for injuries and damage they have done' (Craig 1975: 289), and this emphasis on deterrence was reinforced in the 1970 manifesto: 'We will also change the law so that the demonstrator who uses violence, or the criminal who causes personal injury or damages property, will be obliged to compensate his victim in addition to fines or other punishments' (Craig 1975: 341). Such a view, as we have detailed, was expressed in the tenor, if not the recommendations, of the 1971 working-party report.

We are not suggesting that this was the only pressure towards compensation for victims, nor that the Conservative Party was alone in its campaign. Nevertheless, we would argue that concern over the crime problem and the deterrent appeal of compensation by offenders provided a powerful impetus towards the introduction and development of compensation initiatives, all under Conservative governments.

If we are correct, reparation and mediation initiatives have a distinctly different pedigree. While partly inspired by a desire to reduce the prison population, they more fully reflect a willingness to balance the interests of offenders and victims, possibly, but not necessarily, as an alternative to penal measures. To this extent they provide advantages to victims, by allowing greater victim involvement in the process, and to offenders, who may receive less severe sentences. However, despite the positive approach of the Conservative government in Britain to experimental schemes, they do sometimes attract criticism from the right, where offenders are seen as 'getting off lightly'.[5] Equally, despite the positive response shown in North America by victims who have participated, and the generally favourable response of many victims in Britain, there is

### State responses: compensation orders and reparation 63

some scepticism from victims organizations, which argue that such initiatives are *not necessarily* in the interests of victims.[6]

Reparation and mediation are, however, of recent origin and have as yet had little impact on the vast majority of crime victims. They do, nevertheless, reflect one aspect of growth within the voluntary sector, where some schemes are run by voluntary organizations or use volunteers. They thus provide a bridge to Part III, where we shall focus in more detail on the role of voluntarism as a response to those problems experienced by victims, for which the state accepts little or no responsibility.

# PART III
# *The response of the voluntary sector*

# 5 The community and the voluntary sector

Just as kin in pre-industrial societies retained considerable responsibility for the restitution following a 'crime', so welfare in its widest sense was the responsibility of family and community. Just as critiques of modern criminal justice systems have harped back to community conciliation, so the current anti-statism vogue in welfare policy decries the alleged death of individual responsibility. On the boundaries of social and penal policy, the Kitty Genovese case illustrates a concern that individuals rely over-much on state services and are unwilling to become personally involved as 'good samaritans'.

Of course, the reasons why bystanders do or do not want to become involved to help crime victims, or others clearly in need of help, are more complex than this (Mawby 1984). However, behind the rhetoric is an ideology which embraces self-help and idealizes community responsibilities.

Unfortunately, however, the community Utopia, first confronted in the context of crime by Jane Jacobs (1961), is part myth, an idealization of past societies. Equally, interpersonal relationships are a complex feature of social structure and cannot be disentangled and revitalized at will. The shift from mechanic to organic solidarity, from community *Gemeinschaft* to society *Gesellschaft*, the increased division of labour, reflect theoretical specifications of changing social structures (Nisbet 1966), where the role of kin is inevitably weakened. Social and geographical mobility, key features of urbanizing and industrializing society, left the individual more at the mercy of social forces and more in need of formal state intervention in regulating an increasingly complex society.

In a formative article, Abrams (1977) specifies the optimal conditions within which communities might be expected to meet the needs of their members. On an attitudinal level, empathy and obligation (a sense of duty) encourage interdependence. On a structural level, community self-help might flourish where external resources are unavailable *and* where there is social homogeneity, generational diversity and stability of residence:

'But none of these factors or others that could be listed can be counted on, on their own or in combination with others, to produce an acceptable level of care, or even a reliable flow of information about needs for care to public agencies. We have, in sum, no recipe for adequate community care *by* the community and must therefore concentrate attention on the possibility of eliciting and sustaining care *in* the community from without.'
(Abrams 1977: 134)

While community involvement is *possible*, in most cases, moreover, 'the effective social bases for community care are kinship, religion and race, not community' (Abrams 1977: 133). In these contexts the extent to which needs are met informally should not be underestimated. The health service, for example, is dependent upon primary care being provided by the family (Taylor 1979). But even here problems arise where help from the family means, in practice, care by women (Finch and Groves 1980).

Similarly, the work of Waller and Okihiro (1978) in Canada and Shapland, Willmore, and Duff (1981) in Britain indicates that some psychological and service needs of crime victims are met by kin and close neighbours. Conversely, as we have shown in Chapter 2, those who evidence the most problems in coming to terms with crime tend to be isolated from the community or living alone, problems only becoming manifest where there is no primary-level support available.

Nevertheless, despite glib assumptions that family and community can take over more responsibility for community care, it is more widely accepted that public participation requires organization. Thus much of the effort in moving away from state involvement is directed at an expanded role for the voluntary sector. That is, governments have encouraged *voluntary organizations* to take on more responsibility, and both voluntary and statutory bodies to involve *more volunteers*. This is just as true of the criminal justice system as it is of welfare services. For example, Neighbourhood Watch – community supervision under the careful eye of the police – is one current vogue. Equally, in the context of crime victims, the role of the voluntary sector has received considerable attention. Indeed, given the minimal role of statutory services in meeting the needs of crime victims, the voluntary sector appears to have developed amidst much more favourable circumstances than where it is aimed at replacing state services. Before focusing in more detail on the role of the voluntary sector *vis-à-vis* crime victims, however, it may be useful to briefly review the place of voluntarism on a more general level.

## The voluntary sector

Statutory organizations may use volunteers as well as salaried employees. Equally, voluntary organizations exist which use volunteers and/or paid workers. While there is no clear-cut definition of a voluntary organization, commentators tend to accept, as an ideal-type model, that it should have five characteristics. It should be formed independently of the state, not be controlled by the state, receive at least some finance from independent sources, be non-profit-distributing, and not restrict its clientele to the fee-paying (Brenton 1985; Hatch 1980; Johnson 1981).

Voluntary organizations of this ilk first developed on a wide scale in Britain in the late nineteenth century, where the identification of a series of problems in urban industrial society and the resulting fear of unrest coincided with middle-class concern (or guilt) over social conditions and the opportunity for middle-class women to identify an active role for themselves in the socio-political fabric. In such conditions, organizations like the YMCA, Barnados, the Waifs and Strays Society, and the Salvation Army flourished, combining the messages of self-help and moral improvement with a concern to save the weak and deserving.

However, while in America increased state responsibility for welfare became translated into state subsidy of voluntary bodies, which retained major responsibilities for providing services (Brenton 1985), in Britain the gradual involvement of the state in the provision of welfare superseded that of the voluntary sector. As state services expanded through the twentieth century, the voluntary sector correspondingly became less significant. In part as a reaction, by the early 1970s voluntary bodies were becoming more co-ordinated, more specialist, and more dependent upon state subsidies. Then, as government spending became identified as a key issue, anti-collectivist governments in Britain and the United States promised to roll back the boundary of state intervention. Voluntary bodies, alluringly a more independent and apparently cheaper alternative, were back in fashion, allowing governments to demonstrate concern without financial obligations.[1]

Financial issues, although paramount, were not the only advantages cited for an expanding voluntary sector. The Wolfenden Committee, for example, saw advantages for the consumer in a mixed economy of welfare, where services were offered by the state, the voluntary sector, the private market and the family and community (Wolfenden 1978). From a rather different ideological perspective, those concerned at the growth of professionalism and welfare bureaucracies saw advantages in self-help groups, which grew in number in the 1970s. Moreover, academics writing on the voluntary sector – most of whom are committed to the concept of voluntarism (for a critique, see Brenton 1985) – cite the advantage of the voluntary sector in terms of allowing innovation and pioneer work, the importance of an independent voice, the role of voluntary bodies as pressure groups, and the integrative potential in voluntarism as community involvement.

Unfortunately, as Brenton (1985) notes in one of the few dispassionate analyses of the voluntary sector, some of these advantages are unproven, and while voluntary effort is beneficial it is not on its own sufficient. Moreover, voluntary bodies experience considerable difficulties which undermine their efficiency and perhaps explain why they were originally superseded by statutory services. Thus, voluntary bodies have become more dependent upon state finance (Wolfenden 1978), which of course limits the financial advantages of the voluntary sector to the government and limits the extent to which voluntary bodies provide an independent voice. But it also *creates* difficulties where government funds, through MSC or Urban Aid grants, for example, are short-term and at low rates of pay (Kingsley 1981), since voluntary bodies may both have their stability undermined *and* devote much of their time and energy towards meeting government funding requirements rather than client need (Mills, Mawby, and Levitt 1983). Similarly, other problems exist, like, for example, the distribution of bodies according to availability of volunteers rather than consumer need, as indeed was so graphically illustrated by the research carried out for the Wolfenden Committee:

> 'The tendency for there to be an uneven goegraphical distribution of voluntary organisations is exemplified by the CPAG. The location of its branches correlates highly with the presence of universities, particularly those with departments of social administration, but not with data indicative of the presence of families with low incomes.'
>
> (Wolfenden 1978: 57)

The advantages and disadvantages of voluntary provision are well documented by Brenton (1985), and we shall return to them in more detail in the context of victim services. Here, though, it is important to note that an increased role for the voluntary sector is advocated not necessarily on grounds of efficiency, or even cost-effectiveness, but is dependent upon ideological considerations. However, as has been implied, voluntarism is multifaceted. Thus, as we go on to consider voluntary services for crime victims, it might be useful to locate these within a typology.

## The ant and the elephant

Referring to voluntary organizations, the Wolfenden Report commented, 'They are as different from each other as the ant is from the elephant or the whale from the hermit crab' (Wolfenden 1978: 189). It is not surprising, then, that classifications of voluntary organizations have been varied. Leaving aside those statutory organizations which utilize volunteers, perhaps the most useful distinction between voluntary bodies is that provided by Hatch, based on three levels of questions. Hatch divides organizations in terms of whether the work is primarily carried out by volunteers or paid staff. For the former, he then subdivides them according to those which provide services for their own members (so-called 'mutual aid associations') and those which provide a service for a distinctly separate group, the clients ('volunteer organizations'). For those employing paid staff, he distinguishes according to source of income – whether it is almost exclusively government grant funded or relies to a considerable extent on donation and charges (Hatch 1980: 35).

These distinctions ignore other criteria; for example, the main function of the agency may be service-orientated or political. Equally, some of the distinctions are not clear-cut: funded charities vary in their use of volunteers in addition to paid staff, and special agencies use volunteers. Perhaps most importantly, the distinction between mutual-aid associations and volunteer organizations may be more useful in ideological than practical terms; thus some organizations will consciously seek to minimize the barrier between helper and helped, others use volunteers who are distinct from clients.

For our purposes in categorizing voluntary services for crime victims, we have opted for four issues, on each of which voluntary bodies can be located on a continuum. While these issues incorporate most of the distinctions made elsewhere, they do, we would argue, have the advantages of including statutory organizations using volunteers within the same model *and* of allowing us to make rather more subtle distinctions between agencies which might otherwise be categorized together. The four issues are, respectively, the relationship to conventional statutory agencies; source of funding; goals; and the relationship between helper and helped. *Figure 5.1* illustrates the classification. At one extreme lie conventional statutory welfare agencies; they are appeasing (by definition), state financed, focus on social-provision goals and provide distinct criteria for distinguishing between professionals and clients. The antithesis is an agency which provides a radical critique of statutory provision, is self-supportive,

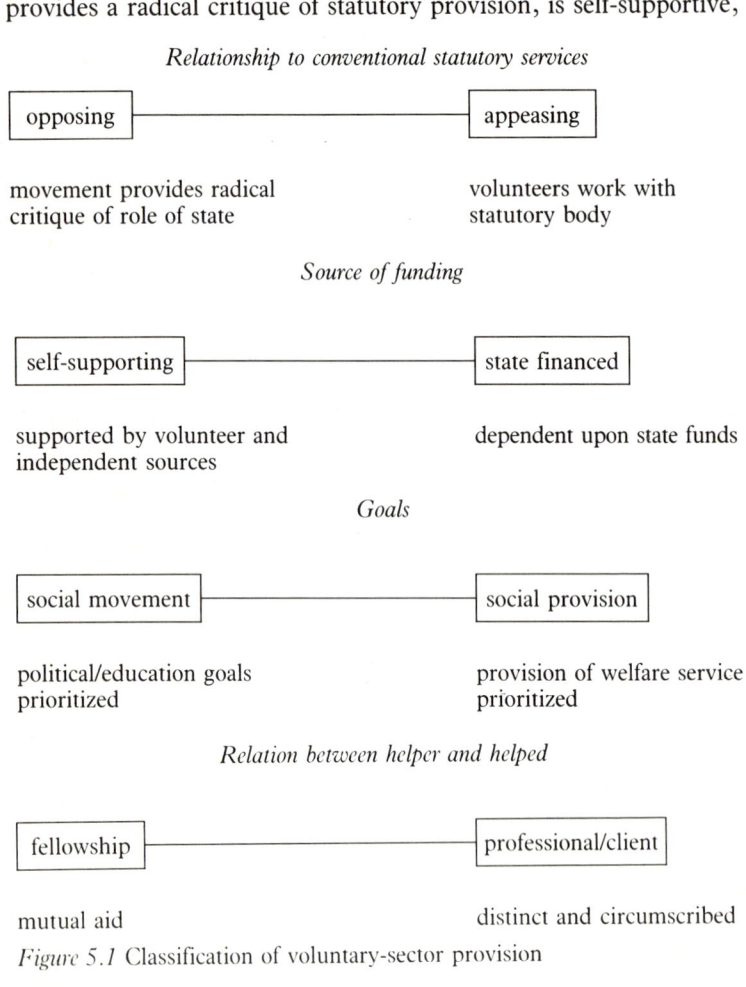

*Relationship to conventional statutory services*

| opposing | —————————————— | appeasing |

movement provides radical critique of role of state

volunteers work with statutory body

*Source of funding*

| self-supporting | —————————————— | state financed |

supported by volunteer and independent sources

dependent upon state funds

*Goals*

| social movement | —————————————— | social provision |

political/education goals prioritized

provision of welfare service prioritized

*Relation between helper and helped*

| fellowship | —————————————— | professional/client |

mutual aid

distinct and circumscribed

*Figure 5.1* Classification of voluntary-sector provision

prioritizes social-movement goals and is based on mutual aid. However, while most state welfare workers would deny the typicality of the former combination, so, as we shall show, the latter is perhaps even rarer.

To illustrate the categorization here, we shall first consider each issue in turn, and then focus on voluntary agencies for victims which allegedly fall to the left of the classification, namely Refuges for Battered Women and Rape Crisis Centres.

1. *Relationship to conventional statutory services* Here we wish to distinguish between, at one extreme, voluntary bodies which are shaped by a fundamental critique of state involvement (ultimately defining the role of the state as either compounding or creating the problem) and at the other, voluntary services which complement statutory services. Near the 'opposing' pole of the continuum come many Refuges for Battered Women and Rape Crisis Centres. At the 'appeasing'[2] pole are voluntary services which are actually provided within statutory services, and thus aim to supplement them; in the context of the criminal justice system, for example, we have in mind probation volunteers and police special constables, and some victim services in the United States (see Ch. 7). Somewhere between these extremes lie those voluntary bodies which, while stressing their distinctness from the state, define their role as supplementary, and indeed interrelate with and perhaps co-ordinate alternative statutory services. The degree to which this incorporates critical review of state services will, of course, vary. As we shall show in subsequent chapters, victims support schemes in Britain can be placed broadly in this middle ground.

2. *Source of funding* Clearly, as we have already noted, source of finance has implications for the relationship to conventional statutory services, and organizations which seek state funding may be required or may 'choose' to modify their ideological stance. Nevertheless, it is useful to distinguish between the two issues, as we shall later illustrate in the context of Rape Crisis Centres. At one extreme are agencies which are self-supporting, depending on volunteers' free time or independent sources of funding. At the other are voluntary agencies which are entirely dependent upon state grants, like many Nightshelters, what Hatch terms 'special agencies' (Hatch 1980). Between these

extremes, of course, lie a large proportion of voluntary bodies which are dependent upon the state to fund the organization and its administration and upon volunteers to provide the bulk of client contact.

3. *Goals* Here, using Pahl's (1979) terminology in a rather more specific sense, we wish to distinguish between agencies which see their role as essentially political ('social movement') and those which see their primary role as providing a service for those needing help ('social provision'). Again, in practice, many distinctions lie in the middle ground. Thus we shall argue that in Britain victims support schemes have been 'social provision' orientated, whilst the American victims' movement has a stronger political focus. In contrast, as we shall illustrate later in this chapter, Women's Refuges and Rape Crisis Centres in Britain are more frequently found towards the 'social movement' end of the continuum than their American counterparts.

4. *Relationship between helper and helped* For those agencies which do provide a service, we can make a fourth distinction according to the relationship between those providing and those receiving the service. At the pole typifying professional–client relationships, many services in voluntary organizations are provided by professionals where there is a clear distinction between professional and client, reinforced by the terms themselves. At the other extreme, as has been incorporated in Hatch's (1980) model, lie a variety of mutual-benefit or self-help groups, emerging in the 1960s and 1970s, where the distinction is minimal. Alcoholics Anonymous is one early example of this. However, for our purposes it is perhaps more useful to make comparisons within the middle ground. Nearer to the professional–client pole lie those voluntary agencies or statutory bodies which rely on volunteers who, while not professionals in the context of the help provided, are distinctive from the agency's clients. Towards the fellowship pole lie agencies which stress fellowship on an ideological level, although helper and helped may be different in terms of social characteristics, experience of the problem, and so on. Here we are thinking of Rape Crisis Centres and most Refuges for Battered Women in Britain, with their concept of 'sisterhood', contrasted with the more traditional victims services, where there is a clearer distinction between volunteer and victim.

These four issues are not exhaustive. However, the importance of categorization is in its practical application. We shall therefore use it in describing alternative victims service – in this chapter Refuges for Battered Women and Rape Crisis Centres and in subsequent chapters victims support schemes. We shall argue that the four continua help us to distinguish between these different manifestations of the victims' movement and, indeed, between subcategories of each.

## Refuges for Battered Women

Although the extent of violence within the family was raised as a problem by early feminists, contemporary concern over domestic violence grew from two quite separate traditions. On the one hand, research on the discretionary role of the police identified a number of incident types where the police rarely used their discretion to arrest the offender (Parnas 1967), and following this tradition researchers on police decision-making have identified domestic incidents within the context of studies of everyday policing. On the other hand, given the real needs of the victims of domestic violence, activists sought, through social and political involvement, to confront the problems head-on.

In the United States, feminist concern was at the root of a number of such initiatives in the 1970s. However, it is generally accepted that the development of refuges was at that time most pronounced in Britain, and we shall thus concentrate on these developments here, returning to a consideration of the position in the United States later.

The problems faced by battered women and their children and their need for accommodation which is inaccessible to their spouses are, of course, far wider than the issue of police inactivity. The shape of welfare service development, with its focus upon welfare for the family unit, meant that the provision of services by social workers, housing, and income maintenance services are inimical to the needs of the battered wife. Women may find little protection from their husbands should they seek help from the police; equally, social workers may define their responsibilities as preserving the family unit, housing services are reluctant to provide additional accommodation, and social-security services present numerous bureaucratic obstacles for women not legally separated from their spouses.

The first refuge aimed at meeting the short-term needs of battered women was set up in Chiswick, London. In 1972 a group of women associated with the Women's Liberation Movement were campaigning for price restraints, when they became aware of the extent of violence against the women they met. Their willingness to identify with the victim, avowing fellowship in the name of sisterhood, is illustrated in Rose's account:

'Sensitized by the critique of family life developing within the movement and the patterns of power and domination in male/female relations, together with a philosophy of sisterhood which commits movement women to seeing other women's problems as their own problems, the Chiswick group found no difficulty in recognizing the personal problem as a public issue.'

(Rose 1978: 528)

As a result, the first refuge, the Chiswick Women's Aid, was founded, with Erin Pizzey (1974) the foremost campaigner on behalf of battered women, using the media effectively and ultimately, through her book *Scream Quietly or the Neighbours Will Hear*, putting the issue on the political map. Indeed, by the time of the first national meeting in 1974, there were twenty-five groups either operating or in the process of being formed, and by the following year this had grown to over eighty (Rose 1978).

However, by this time a split was emerging between Chiswick and the national federal structure, between Pizzey and the feminist influence. Partly it was a clash of personalities; more importantly a conflict of ideologies. In her first book, for example, Pizzey (1974) wrote with concern about the dangers of refuges run democratically, which could exclude applicants deemed 'undesirable'. She was, moreover, more concerned with explaining the incidence of domestic violence in its own context, as early research at Chiswick by Gayford (1975) illustrates, rather than focusing in general terms on each man as a potential batterer and domestic violence as endemic to sexist societies. Her second book, concentrating on women who were attracted to violent relationships (Pizzey and Shapiro 1981, 1982), merely confirmed that the split was permanent. National Women's Aid, which had already established a London base, continued to grow, and most new refuges conformed to its blueprint. By 1978 there were 150 refuges catering, at one time, for some 1,000 women and 1,700 children (Binney, Harkell, and Nixon 1985).

Nevertheless, refuge provision and wider policy initiatives have never approached the level of need. Despite the *Report from the Select Committee on Violence in Marriage* (House of Commons 1975), which criticized the role of police, housing, social workers, and DHSS, and called for widespread provision of refuges as emergency accommodation, changes have been inadequate. Legal changes have been largely ineffective (McCann 1985), refuge provision is only a fraction of that recommended (Binney, Harkell, and Nixon 1985), and a range of studies across the country show continued dissatisfaction with the responses of different welfare agencies to battered women (Binney, Harkell, and Nixon 1985; Dobash and Dobash 1979; Pahl 1978).

In the light of this unwillingness or inability of statutory services to meet the needs of battered women, refuges attached to the National Federation of Women's Aid Groups adopted their own style. Although dependent on government funding (largely from short-term MSC or Urban Aid money but also from Local Authority Housing) (Binney, Harkell, and Nixon 1985), they combined self-government with voluntary support from the feminist movement. Pahl's (1978) study was of only one refuge, the Kent Women's Centre, but it well illustrates these key principles of self-help, mutual support and power-sharing. Equally, the focus on battering as endemic to society provides both a moral justification for excluding men from the shelter and its management structure and a point of identification between those women who have and have not been victimized. It also provides the basis for the focus of the refuge movement as political and educational as well as service-orientated. In terms of the four issues we identified, then, the refuge movement in Britain has balanced somewhat precariously between an oppositional relationship with conventional statutory services and a dependence on state grants for funding. While not exclusively committed to political and educational goals, it is, in Pahl's terms, a social movement (Pahl 1979). Thus:

> 'The high degree of motivation of the workers meant that they did not welcome outside interference. They did not see the women's centre as just another social service, nor did they just see themselves as ordinary voluntary workers. They were motivated by ideas about the position of women in society, about the nature of family life, and about the position of women within marriage; this ideological basis for their work 'fitted' with the problems brought to the refuge.'
>
> (Pahl 1978: 60)

The implications of this ideologically were that while not all helpers were victims of domestic violence themselves, or indeed shared the social class or ethnic background of those requiring help, barriers between helper and helped were minimized and refuges adopted co-operative styles: 'The staff see themselves and are seen as co-workers, not wardens. The women themselves make the decisions about their lives and the way the refuges operate' (Daniels 1977: 10). However, even within the Federation refuges vary, in terms, for example, of the use of paid staff with clearly defined authority. Moreover, whereas the 'social movement' refuge has been the subject of considerable research, 'social provision' refuges have received far less attention. Yet, as Gill notes in one of the few studies of refuges of this type (Gill 1986a), the emphases are markedly different.

Thus one of the refuges in south-west England described by Gill had close relationships with conventional statutory services (in fact, incorporating a management committee of welfare 'experts'), was funded through government grants, focused on the provision of a welfare service to the almost total exclusion of political or educational goals, and incorporated through its rules and residents' perceptions of those rules a clear distinction between staff and residents. Most markedly, on an ideological level, reflected in relationships with conventional statutory services and goals, the refuge staff identified the causes of violence within the family relationship, not as a feature of gender relationships in the wider society.

Clearly, the federation model and Gill's (1986a) alternative reflect extremes, where in reality other refuges fall somewhere between. Of crucial importance, however, is the viability of the former, where it is dependent upon state funding and co-operative relationships with at least some other statutory welfare agencies from whom it receives referrals and requires co-operation for women in or leaving the refuge.

These same influences appear to have had a more predictable effect in the United States, where refuges are more akin to Gill's example. Thus the pressures of funding and the need to maintain links with police and other statutory bodies have led to more professional refuges. For example, the Refuge House of Leon County in Tallahassee, Florida, began life in 1972 as a programme of the Women's Centre, concerned mainly with rape, with a major focus on political activism and community education. The Refuge House programme developed in the late 1970s and by 1985 it was operating with an annual budget of $160,770, with eight paid staff and some twenty volunteers serving a refuge which, during the year, had provided accommodation for 120 women and 186 children for an average of twelve nights each. The Spouse Abuse Shelter in Clearwater, in contrast, is one of those founded in the 1970s under the auspices of Religious Community Services. Operating with an annual budget of over $100,000, it relies on five full-time staff, three part-time staff and over thirty volunteers to provide short-term refuge to over 300 women and children each year.[3]

At the very least, then, there appears to be a greater diversity in the types of refuge operating in the United States, a point we shall consider further. Before that, however, it is perhaps appropriate to review provisions for rape victims, where a similar divergence is evident.

## Responses to rape

As with spouse battering, responses to the problems of the rape victim emerged as part of a wave of feminism in the 1970s. However, the pressures were slightly different. Whereas the refuge movement gained momentum in Britain and has been less influenced by the North American situation, Rape Crisis Centres were founded in America and imported to Britain (Gilley 1974). Furthermore, whilst Women's Aid focused on the inadequacies of state responses to the needs of battered women, critiques of official responses to rape were even more critical of the role of agencies such as the police, health services, courts, and so on, arguing that the victim was, in fact, twice victimized, once by the offender, once by the system. Thus state agencies, far from ignoring the problem, were accused of exacerbating it.

Indeed, early criminological or victimological studies of rape, by identifying the issue of victim-precipitation (Amir 1971), provoked further response (see, for example, Clark and Lewis 1977; Weis and Borges 1973). In the early 1970s a succession of authors, criticizing the way states defined the raped as 'the legitimate victim' (Weis and Borges 1973), argued that rape and fear of rape helped to maintain sexist relationships in society. In one early critique, for example, Le Grand asserted:

'In hundreds of ways, large and small, a woman's life is shaped by the persistent threat of rape: women hesitate to venture out at night without male escort; to live alone; to hitch-hike; to stay late at the office to work alone; to take certain jobs. . . . The fear of rape not only inhibits the freedom of women, it also exaggerates the dependency of women upon men. The law concerning forcible rape and the way it functions both influences and is influenced by the relationship between men and women in our society.'

(Le Grand 1973: 919)

Given such definitions of the problem, it seemed only natural to define the response in terms of developments outside the statutory services, provided by women, for women. In the United States, two women's groups, the National Organization for Women (NOW) and the Women's Political Caucus (WPC), were instrumental in putting the rape issue on the political agenda; the Second Wave of Women's Liberation followed through by negotiating state funding for specific Rape Crisis Centres (Hafer 1976). As more centres were founded, the idea spread to other countries, such as Canada (Clark and Lewis 1977) and Britain, where the Rape Crisis Centre was opened in March, 1976, in London. The project, operating a 24-hour counselling, legal, and medical advice service for women, had dealt with 629 cases by September, 1978, under one-third of which had been reported to the police (RCRP 1979). By mid-1983 there were twenty-six Rape Crisis Centres or Crisis Lines throughout Britain (London Rape Crisis Centre 1984: 136–7).

The working basis of Rape Crisis Centres in Britain – expressed through the annual reports of the Rape Counselling and Research Project (RCRP), evidence to the Royal Commission on Criminal Procedure (RCRP 1979), and a recent book (London Rape Crisis Centre 1984) – is perhaps best summarized through five issues.

First, following the original American feminist response, rape is defined as a feature of sexist societies, within which all men are potential rapists:

'Once we see that rape is not an abnormal act, but part of the way men . . . treat us as women, we realise that we cannot make a distinction between "normal men" and rapists. The silence around rape and the myths that obscure the reality have prevented women from realising that rapists are not recognisable as such. While men may choose not to commit rape, they are all capable of it and know this. When women know this too, we can stop relying on men for protection, start being angry and begin to find our own strength.'

(London Rape Crisis Centre 1984: 7)

Second, following from this, the police and courts ultimately act against the interests of women, because they reflect societal norms of male domination, compounded by the fact that they are inevitably run by men.

Third, in response it is necessary for women to redress the problem themselves – it is only this way that women can develop the social awareness by which they can see the 'real' basis for rape. The London Rape Crisis Centre was, therefore, 'run by and for women' (London Rape Crisis Centre 1984: ix).

Fourth, it follows from this that the role of centres is to a large extent political, 'committed to educating and informing the public about the reality of rape, to refute the many myths and misconceptions which distort and deny women's experiences' (London Rape Crisis Centre 1984: ix), and this takes place through bringing direct pressure on governments (e.g. the presenting of evidence to government committees), providing information and research to the public, and through public protests.[4]

Finally, though, given the immediate problems faced by the rape victim, the centres' primary function is to provide services for victims: 'Our primary aim is to provide a place where women and girls who have been raped or sexually assaulted can talk with other women, at any time of the day or night' (London Rape Crisis Centre 1984: ix). In order to do this, centres provide emotional support, accept the accounts given to them unquestioningly, give counselling and provide women with help in dealing with any official agencies, such as police or medical services.

The model presented is akin to that for Women's Aid, where fellowship-based services, under a women's caucus, and providing political and educational goals as well as a welfare service, have developed outside and to some extent against state services. Moreover, while an alternative model for refuges, outside the feminist framework and involving structured and co-operative links with statutory agencies, emerged only slowly in Britain, alternative models of rape service provision are more evident elsewhere.

This is particularly the case in the United States, where programmes based on professional services, linked to police or medical facilities, were common even in the mid-1970s (Arbarbanel 1976; Adleman 1976; Hirschel 1978). It was, however, accentuated by the dependence of programmes on funding and thus the need to balance political radicalism against financial security. While even the more radical centres appeared to have relatively close links with other agencies, 'As interest in anti-rape projects grew, professionals and community leaders became involved and implemented more conventional structures' (O'Sullivan 1978: 50). Formal structures developed, with committees incorporating professional representatives of other agencies such as mental health services and the police, and volunteers' services were supplemented with those of paid staff, who took over more responsibilities and more closely distinguished the helpers from the helped. O'Sullivan's survey of those working (paid or voluntarily) in centres demonstrates the resulting ambiguity; while most were women (93 per cent) and in their twenties (62 per cent), students and professionals were overrepresented and members of ethnic minorities drastically underrepresented (O'Sullivan 1978). Volunteers were thus in some respects scarcely representative of the typical rape victims.

O'Sullivan also found considerable variations in funding. Of eighty centres providing information, approximately half spent less than $100 monthly, while five operated on over $4,000 per month. Most of the better financed were receiving support from the Law Enforcement Assistance Administration (LEAA),[5] although finance was also forthcoming from other local and national sources. However, given that most of these grants are short-term, and renewed funding is uncertain, centres face many of the problems common to other voluntary organizations, which we noted earlier: independence may be sacrificed for what turns out to be carrots for only one meal.

Funding aside, it is clear that services for rape victims have developed along a variety of pathways in North America. Amir and Amir, for example, comparing a number of schemes in Canada and the United States, place them on a continuum from political to treatment- or service-orientated centres (Amir and Amir 1979). The political schemes are distinctive in terms of both ideology and structure, illustrated in this quote from the Toronto Rape Crisis Centre:

'An idea becomes a movement,
The movement becomes an organisation,
The organisation becomes an institution,
And there lies the death of an idea.'
(Amir and Amir 1979: 255)

However, on these terms a number of rape services have 'died' in order to survive. By the end of the 1970s there were over a thousand rape-related programmes in the United States, with consequential heterogeneity:

'Since this growth began, the "definition" of the rape crisis centre has been radically altered, the nation-wide pool of rape crisis centres has changed from the small homogeneous core to a large, fluid and enormously diverse group of programmes. . . . Today, approximately a decade after the anti-rape movement began, the original "model" of the rape crisis centre is virtually extinct.'
(Gornick, Burt, and Pittman 1985: 250–51)

Thus centres may provide 'direct services' or community 'education and action', or a mixture of each. The former, which may be based in hospitals or police stations or separate buildings, may provide a 24-hour hot line, emergency assistance, face-to-face crisis intervention, and/or counselling. The latter may focus on public education, target relevant agencies in the criminal justice system, prioritize political lobbying, or encourage direct political action (Gornick, Burt, and Pittman 1985). Add variations in the extent to which centres rely on volunteers and paid employees, and the alternatives multiply further.

Nevertheless, Gornick, Burt, and Pittman (1985) distinguish four general types, which can be adequately described using our four continua:

1. Those resembling the original feminist collectives of the early 1970s – ideologically distinct from state services and financially relatively independent, fulfilling both a political/education and a service goal, where service ideology stresses minimal barriers between helpers and helped.
2. Those resembling mainstream social-service programmes – closely linked to state and other voluntary agency services, using both paid staff and volunteers, and providing a social service to a distinct client group, while maintaining a political orientation.
3. Those embedded in a welfare agency – and thus closely identified with state services, especially community mental health, providing a long-term service given by professionals to a distinct client group.
4. Hospital-based or emergency-room-based programmes, similar to the above, but less distinct from other services provided in the unit (in terms of personnel, finance, etc.) and focusing more on short-term crisis work.

An example of the second category is the Hillsborough County Rape Crisis Centre in Tampa, Florida. This began in 1974 as a grass-roots movement providing short-term crisis work and education services. However, by 1985 it had developed into an 'independent' agency (dependent upon county and state government funding), taking referrals from welfare agencies and the police as well as self-referrals, and providing in addition nurse education and consultancy work. An emergency call from the police is responded to by a nurse and a counsellor (usually a volunteer); long-term counselling, where considered necessary, is usually provided via groupwork by professional staff. There is also an offender group. The annual budget for the centre is currently in excess of $300,000.[6]

It is useful to make these distinctions both in order to illustrate that Rape Crisis Centres are not all 'ants' rather than 'elephants' (in Wolfenden's terms) and to show how alternatives have emerged in America while in Britain Rape Crisis Centres are more akin to their feminist roots. Of course, there are variations in Britain; Blair, for example, cites contrasting relationships between centres and police authorities (based on police perspectives) (Blair 1985). West Midlands Police, for example, apparently enjoy a good relationship with the Birmingham centre, whereas the London centre 'has been stridently and persistently critical of rape investigation in the Metropolitan Police area, and at present will not enter into dialogue with police' (Blair 1985: 34).

Given the difficulty of receiving funds, for example through Urban Aid, where organizations continue in the radical/political model, centres in Britain have determinedly stuck to their principles. In the current climate, where rape is becoming more widely condemned and identified as a serious social problem, it could indeed be that centres will, in the long term, be successful in maintaining their principles and receiving government grants. However, the ambivalence with which funding applications are met is well illustrated in a recent controversy in Plymouth, where the Conservative leader of the city council commented that the local Crisis Line was too radical to receive local authority funding. He subsequently was forced to withdraw his remark. Notably he had felt safe to make it. Equally notably, his political judgement proved wrong, although we feel he could have safely made the same remark two years earlier.

On the other hand, it is also likely that, faced with the politically embarrassing accusation that they are not doing enough to help rape victims, the government will channel funds into more politically acceptable organizations, in much the same way as it has seen Citizens Advice Bureaux as more acceptable alternatives to Law

Centres. Thus the first of nine much-heralded rape examination suites, housed away from police stations, was opened by the Metropolitan Police in early 1985, and it seems probable that funds will be made available for the police to improve their own services. At the same time, there is encouragement from the Home Office (if not all chief constables) for victims support schemes to increase their involvement in rape cases, a move not surprisingly welcomed by the National Association of Victims Support Schemes (NAVSS), and future developments may well widen the variety of provisions available for rape victims, to some extent following the American model.

**Summary**

In this chapter we have noted how the voluntary sector had, in the financial stringencies of the late 1970s, been accorded renewed approval by governments eager to cut public spending. The coincidence of this re-emphasis at a time when the needs of crime victims were only just being recognized, and the restriction of statutory provisions to the financial and (in Britain) medical needs of victims, has provided the opportunity for considerable voluntary-sector development.

Yet such developments are by no means unitary, and in distinguishing different forms of voluntary provision we have focused on the role of the feminist movement in the spread of Refuges for Battered Women and Rape Crisis Centres, and the subsequent development of alternative structures for delivering services to these groups of women. At the same time, we have implied that victims services in general have emerged in different form and that services in Britain and North America are distinct from each other.

Referring back to our original classification, we have argued that in Britain Rape Crisis Centres and most refuges can be defined in terms of an opposing relationship to conventional statutory services, espousing social-movement as well as social-provision goals, and defining the helper–helped relationship as one of the fellowship – this, despite some dependence upon the state for funding. There are, as Gill has illustrated, variations from this ideal type (Gill 1986a), and one advantage of our classification is that it allows one to identify contrasting examples and any changes which take place over time. Most notable, though, is the contrast between Britain and the United

States. In the latter case, as we have illustrated, many refuges and shelters are heavily financed by local or national governments, and partly as a consequence of this have closer relationships with conventional statutory agencies, prioritize social-provision goals and make clearer distinctions between helper and helped.

However, such marked differences are not confined to developments which were inspired by the feminist movement. A review of wider victim issues suggests that help for the victims of crime in general has taken equally different forms. To illustrate this, in Chapter 6 we shall focus on the emergence of victims support schemes in Britain, and in Chapter 7 look at equivalent developments in the United States.

# 6 Victims support schemes in Britain, 1971–87

Although victims services developed in the United States and Britain at a similar time to the spread of Women's Refuges and Rape Crisis Centres, the directions which the British schemes took were different from both their American equivalents and the feminist-based refuges and centres.

Accounts of the development of victim services in Britain, interestingly, make only limited reference either to refuges or to the American situation. The idea of victims support schemes arose quite separately, allegedly, over an evening drink in a Bristol pub between the chairman of the Bristol Association for the Care and Resettlement of Offenders (BACRO) and the National Association (NACRO) area organizer (Rankin 1977). As a result, BACRO set up a study group in the Bristol area in 1971, involving representatives of the police, prison service, probation service, and magistracy. Then, following a regional conference on the issue, a formal working party based in Bristol met between December 1972 and the summer of 1973. Subsequently, the decision was taken to launch a pilot project covering the Bristol area.

The pilot scheme which emerged contained four elements which have remained as key ideals of schemes. First, the creation of an independent organization, utilizing community resources and engendering the support of statutory agencies such as police and probation, was seen as crucial. Second, it was felt that a full-time administrator (a co-ordinator) should be appointed, ideally being 'a qualified social worker, with administrative skills' (Rankin 1977: 5). Third, the brunt of service provision would fall on a group of carefully selected and trained volunteers. Finally, it should be an immediate crisis service agency.

One crucial aspect of the pilot scheme was the opportunity to unveil a level of need which had previously gone unrecognized. Thus the project team's estimation that it would receive ten referrals per week proved an understatement, with demand some three times that, leading the team to exclude certain crime types (notably car-related thefts) and recruit more volunteers. In the meantime, an article by the Bristol team publicized the needs of victims and the consequent importance of victim services (Gay, Holton, and Thomas 1975).

However, despite the apparent success of the scheme in targeting in on an area of unmet need, the Bristol initiative failed to gain secure funding, and services were suspended in September 1974 so that publicity could be concentrated on providing a secure financial base. Although it was only partly successful, enough was raised for the scheme to reopen in April 1975, and indeed expand.

The creation of similar schemes in other areas was facilitated by the publicity focus of the Bristol scheme. In 1975 the BBC 'Open Door' programme included a feature on victims support. Following enquiries from various parts of the country, a day conference was arranged, resulting in two interrelated developments. First, a number of schemes were initiated in other areas. Second, the need for some national co-ordination of effort was accepted. NACRO provided administrative support, and by 1977 guidelines for setting up victims support schemes had been published (NAVSS 1981: 17). Later that year, separate regions were defined and regional secretaries nominated; this led in 1978 to the formation of a national committee and the birth, in 1979, of the National Association of Victims Support Schemes (NAVSS). By the publication of the first annual report there were sixty-seven schemes in operation. According to the NAVSS, a majority (thirty-seven) had been formed following initiatives by probation officers, with twelve more stemming from voluntary organizations and ten from church personnel (NAVSS 1981: 22). By the end of 1980 these schemes were dealing with approximately 14,000 referrals. Two years later, the number of schemes had doubled and referrals risen to over 41,000, and the growth continued. Thus, by March 1985, 256 schemes were operating across the country (see *Figure 6.1*), dealing with over 125,000 referrals annually; one year later there were 293 schemes and some 185,000 referrals (NAVSS 1986a: 19). Not surprisingly, then, victims support has been described as the fastest growing area of voluntary-sector provision.

Nevertheless, only a very small proportion of those who are victimized and who report the crime to the police are ever referred to a victims support scheme. The British Crime Survey (Hough and Mayhew 1985: 31) estimated this at about 1 per cent in 1983. Similarly, in arguing for an expansion in services and resources, the NAVSS in successive annual reports (NAVSS 1983, 1984, 1985) has pointed out the substantial gap between crimes known to the police

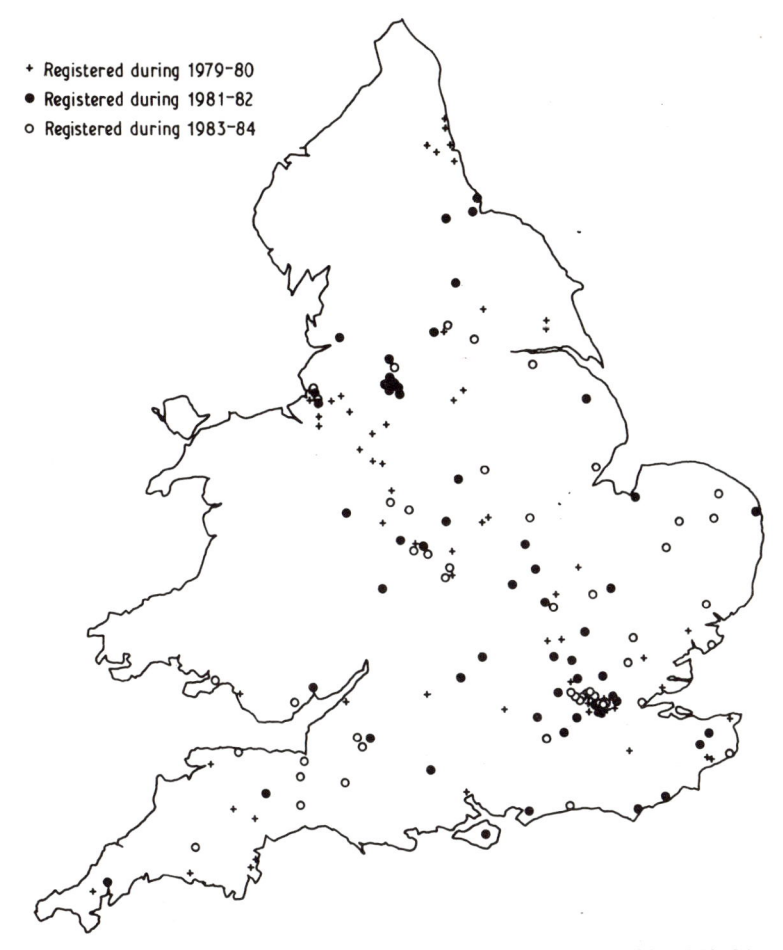

+ Registered during 1979–80
● Registered during 1981–82
○ Registered during 1983–84

*Figure 6.1* Victims support schemes registered with the NAVSS, 1979–84

and those referred to victims support schemes.

This gap varies according to different offence types. The British Crime Survey, for example, allows one to estimate that a greater proportion of those reporting burglary (19 per cent) and theft from the person (15 per cent) and rape (16 per cent) subsequently are referred to victims services (NAVSS 1985: 11), compared with other offences.

This is, of course, partly the result of policies adopted by individual schemes to exclude certain offences and thereby concentrate resources, partly the result of police referral practices based on informal and often unsubstantiated perceptions of which victims require services. This point has been made forcefully in NAVSS annual reports, and will be considered more fully later.

What, then, are the essential features of victims support schemes operating in Britain today? In providing an overview we shall begin by describing the structure and function of victims support and then locate schemes in terms of the four continua we discussed in Chapter 5. We shall here re-emphasize the point we have already made in the context of Women's Refuges and Rape Crisis Centres, namely the extent of individual variation, and subsequently illustrate this through an analysis of patterns of area provisions in England and Wales. Throughout we shall refer to a number of sources of data, principally records and reports provided by the NAVSS (including returns from 104 schemes for 1984) and annual reports provided for us by a number of schemes in metropolitan, urban, and rural areas,[1] as well as published sources such as the Home Affairs Committee Report (House of Commons 1984; Home Office 1985b) and the recent survey by Maguire and Corbett (1986).

## The structure of victims support in Britain

On a structural level, most but not all victims support schemes are affiliated to the NAVSS.[2] For administrative purposes, England and Wales are then subdivided into thirteen regions,[3] each with a representative on council and each with a regional chairperson and communicator. Regions are then, for convenience, often subdivided by county. Some rural areas have a management committee for the county and are affiliated to the NAVSS as a 'county scheme'. Most individual schemes, however, have their own management committee. Taking a national sample of the first 104 schemes submitting annual returns to the NAVSS for 1984, the average size of this committee was twelve.

The constitution requires affiliated schemes to submit details of the committee membership to the NAVSS and to include on the committee at least one representative each from the police, probation or social services, a voluntary organization or church, and (since 1985) the scheme volunteers. The idea behind the management committee, which is central to the scheme's function and means (see below) is that it should involve 'a panel of experts, covering a wide range of professions' (NAVSS 1981: 16) and so be able to give professional or technical advice to volunteers and offer more comprehensive services for victims. The scheme co-ordinator, who might be a volunteer, be employed on a full- or part-time basis, or be paid an honorarium (see NAVSS 1985: 25), also advises on the committee[4] and provides the critical link between the committee and volunteers, who provide the direct resource to referrals. On average the schemes in our national sample each had eighteen volunteers.

Exceptionally, victims services in some schemes may be provided by paid staff. This appears to be the case in a small number of metropolitan schemes where volunteers are difficult to recruit and where some funding of low-paid workers is possible, for example on MSC schemes. However, in the large majority of schemes contact with victims is made only by volunteers, and indeed there is some evidence that where paid staff are involved other than as co-ordinators this is sometimes the source of friction (Maguire and Corbett 1986).

The commitment to voluntary-sector provision is a consistent one. Voluntary services are preferred on the grounds that such services can be better provided by the community than by an agency of the state, and that voluntarism provides the opportunity to balance and integrate statutory agencies with rather different priorities. However, in practice these arguments for community involvement and agency integration are difficult to separate.

The advantages of community participation stem partly from a critique of complex bureaucracies, partly from an ideological commitment to the principles of self-help (or community self-help) and the contrasting dangers of stigma where services are provided by welfare bureaucracies. This perspective was endemic to the original Bristol scheme and has been maintained as a first principle ever since. It is based on the ideal that 'Victim Support at a local level is very much a community response' (NAVSS 1985: 7): 'The use of volunteers as visitors was not just a money-saving device but a very positive aspect of the scheme – a clear message that fellow-citizens *do care*' (NAVSS 1981: 15). Thus, the involvement of the community in the criminal justice system, and indeed the wider helping process, is an end in itself: 'Individual members of the community have an opportunity to participate constructively in helping to seek some solution to crime' (Reeves 1984: 7).

Additionally, though, the voluntary base is seen as crucial for the cementing of the responses of a variety of statutory agencies, each with its own priorities. A specialist voluntary organization is thus seen as an essential means of maintaining balance, both providing a more comprehensive service and serving to integrate the work of various statutory agencies:

> 'By co-ordinating local resources, it can be demonstrated that the offer of support is from the whole community, which includes members of the criminal justice system, rather than from a separate or partisan agency. . . . By promoting balanced committees, no one agency is able to dominate Victims Support policy and no one agency would become accountable for the work. This ensures that Victims Support is the priority of the Committee and not a subsidiary interest to other agency priorities. . . . There is a bonus in that agencies who would normally have very little contact are able to work together in a positive way, with mutually agreed aims.'
> (Reeves 1984: 7)

Commitment to a community-led service is perhaps best summed up in an earlier annual report of the NAVSS:

> 'No single existing agency could provide all the knowledge and skills needed but spread throughout our communities all the necessary resources already exist. Victims Support Schemes provide organisation and structure which allow interested individuals and a wide range of agencies or professions to work together to provide a service as and when it is needed. The Schemes aim to co-ordinate, not to compete with existing services. Working in this way avoids the need to set up separate specialist departments designed to cater for all victims' needs. This would be inappropriate, removing yet another area of responsibility from the community and turning ordinary citizens into a new problem group as "clients" of the new agency. People do not necessarily need long-term support or professional help following crime, but basic advice and immediate reassurance. Those who do need extra help should be given easy access to the agencies which already exist but which are often inaccessible to the majority of citizens.'
> (NAVSS 1982: 22)

Such independence is illustrated by the fact that most schemes are run from private addresses (NAVSS 1985: 23). It also distinguishes the British model from many North American counterparts (Dussich 1976), and thus fits better the community-based rather than the system-based model of American schemes (see Ch. 7).

However, while a community service may be detached from local agencies and thus able to offer an integrative service in a way that system-based schemes may not, there is some evidence from research in the voluntary sector that integration of statutory agencies is difficult for voluntary bodies to maintain. For example, one recent study of a Plymouth nightshelter run by the voluntary organization, the Council for Christian Care, demonstrates the difficulty that a voluntary agency without power to enforce policy outside its own brief has in attempting to provide a continuity of services which are dependent upon statutory agency co-operation. Thus, Mills, Mawby, and Levitt (1983) found that the nightshelter had difficulty co-ordinating with the probation services over the provision of 24-hour cover (a problem of continuity) and difficulty co-ordinating with the Housing Department over the provision of appropriate accommodation for those no longer needing nightshelter accommodation (a problem of staged progression).

In the context of staged progression, the NAVSS sees schemes as ideally referring clients in need of long-term counselling to specialist agencies (NAVSS 1981: 16; Reeves 1984), although whether or not this occurs is difficult to assess. For example, in their study Maguire and Corbett (1986) found that in practice volunteers played a more active role, possibly acting as an intermediary or advocate. However, most discussion has centred on how victims get to be referred to victims support schemes in the first place.

Here again there are considerable variations between schemes. Some, like Wolverhampton VSS, receive a number of self-referrals. Others take referrals from a variety of agencies. For example, Wigan VSS also receives referrals from CAB and social-services departments, and Rochdale VSS notes in its annual report that it has received referrals from a local MP, Age Concern, the Salvation Army, CAB, a health visitor, a tenants association and MIND! In contrast, some schemes actually discourage referrals other than those which come from the police.

Nevertheless, it seems that the vast majority of referrals come from the police. The role of the police as gatekeepers to victims services is therefore crucial. Here two alternatives emerged. First, following the Bristol model, a number of schemes operated on an automatic-referral policy, where the police referred all cases, or all cases for agreed offence-types, to the victims support scheme. Alternatively, as schemes were set up in different areas, it became common practice for the police to screen cases and refer only those considered in need to the local scheme.

As we shall stress in Chapter 9, this discretionary policy has been severely criticized, notably due to the lack of referrals in some areas and an alleged reluctance by the police to refer victims other than 'obvious' cases like the elderly and women living alone. Accepting this, a number of police forces, like the Metropolitan Police (House of Commons 1984: 97), have shifted to a version of an automatic-referral policy. It now seems that slightly over half the schemes operating in the mid-1980s receive automatic referrals (Maguire and Corbett 1986), although in our experience variations between schemes in what is considered 'automatic' may mean that this is an overestimate.

Where the police do operate an automatic-referral policy, clearly the number of victims with whom schemes are confronted increases dramatically. Thus, ironically, schemes themselves are faced with the question of how to ration their services. Again, a number of options exist, which have been described extensively by Maguire and Corbett (1986). At one extreme, schemes may visit all those victims who are referred, or decide whom to visit on the basis of information provided by the police. In other cases, schemes contact some or all referrals by letter or telephone and follow up all positive responses with a personal visit. As in other areas of welfare (Foster 1983), however, the operation of rationing depends on the agency making the decision, the criteria on which the decision is based, and ultimately, on resources. In any case, it is quite clear that if we relate policies to victims' responses in the British Crime Survey, there is a considerable amount of unmet need.

**The function of victims support**

The functions of schemes are to provide short-term help for crime victims. Within this general statement it is recognized that victims vary in their needs and that services should not be exclusively for those experiencing extreme distress; moreover, the precise needs may vary, from emotional to practical, resulting directly from the crime or as a consequence of the subsequent law-enforcement process (Reeves 1984).

The precise functions do, however, vary according to different schemes, and we can make a distinction in terms of responses to two questions: which victims and what sort of help?

Undoubtedly, the initial focus of victims support was on victims of certain types of property offences, especially burglaries. However, as we have already noted, the Bristol scheme almost immediately excluded car-related thefts from routine consideration and some other schemes followed suit from the outset. Nationally, then, victims support is heavily concentrated on certain types of crime. In 1984–5, for example, the NAVSS estimated that 79.5 per cent of referrals were victims of burglary, 10.9 per cent other property offences, and 8.4 per cent violence, with 1.2 per cent of referrals being for non-crime victimization (NAVSS 1986a: 20). The corresponding figures for 1985–6 are 78.6 per cent, 10.9 per cent, 9.5 per cent, and 1.0 per cent, respectively. We followed this up for a sample of schemes by considering data available for the first 104 schemes submitting annual returns to the NAVSS for 1984. Excluding twenty-seven newer schemes which had not operated for the whole of 1984, we found that the 'average' scheme had dealt with approximately 807 referrals of which 618 were for burglary and sixty-six for robbery. Full details are contained in *Table 6.1*. It is notable that schemes on average dealt with about ten referrals per annum which were not crime related, for example those following fires or traffic accidents.

Three areas of contention here are worthy of more comment, namely involvement with domestic incidents, rape cases and non-crime victims. In the former case, Maguire and Corbett (1986) note a considerable reluctance to become involved in domestic disputes because of the imminent presence of the offender, and

Table 6.1 *Referrals per scheme, by offence type, 1984*

| offence type | mean per scheme | percentage of all referrals |
| --- | --- | --- |
| burglary | 618.2 | 76.6 |
| theft from person | 36.4 | 4.5 |
| other theft | 30.3 | 3.8 |
| fraud | 7.8 | 1.0 |
| criminal damage | 17.4 | 2.2 |
| robbery | 66.2 | 8.2 |
| homicide | 0.3 | 0.0 |
| rape | 1.8 | 0.2 |
| indecent assault | 9.0 | 1.1 |
| other crime | 9.5 | 1.2 |
| non-criminal incidents | 9.8 | 1.2 |
| total | 806.8 | 100.0 |

national statistics confirm that such cases are only infrequently included. Yet, as we shall note later in this section, many victims of such incidents who were interviewed in the BCS felt that victims support would have been helpful. This thus raises the point of whether victims services are avoiding involvement in an area where demand might be considerable, including cases where the police were not called, and whether for *some*, victims support schemes might be seen as more appropriate and helpful than Refuges for Battered Women.

A second issue arises in the context of rape, which is covered more fully by Maguire and Corbett (1986). Traditionally, victims support schemes were not seen as appropriate agencies for helping rape victims, partly due to the lack of specialized training for volunteers but also because of the focus of schemes on impersonal crimes and short-term work (see below). However, where suitable volunteers were available, schemes have provided help for rape victims, and given the present ideological conflict between statutory agencies and Rape Crisis Centres, which we discussed in Chapter 5, schemes have been encouraged to expand this aspect of their work. This is particularly so in the London area, with the Islington scheme having dealt with some thirty rape cases by 1984, according to Superintendent Harley (House of Commons 1984: 105). Indeed, in London as in some other metropolitan areas the NAVSS and local schemes have co-operated with the police and have arranged a series of training sessions for volunteers, so that specific volunteers can be called on by the police where rape victims are concerned. Thus, while this is a relatively new departure, the involvement of victims support schemes in work with rape victims is likely to increase.

A rather different issue concerns the involvement of victims support schemes with non-crime victims. As noted above, a small minority of referrals fit this category, and the constitution indeed allows for this.[5] However, at national level the feeling tends to be against non-crime referrals, although the advantages *and* disadvantages of such involvement are appreciated.[6] Thus some schemes reject non-crime referrals because of lack of resources, others because they feel that rather different specialist skills are required, and others through a fear of becoming identified as a general welfare service for the police.

On the other hand, schemes may accept non-crime referrals through a desire to help all those with problems, or to provide work for under-used volunteers. To quote from individual schemes,

Southwark VSS accept victims of racial harassment (whether or not these are crimes or have been so defined by the police), Eastleigh VSS include fire and cot-death cases, and the 1985 annual report from Cumbria Victims Aid notes that there were 'an unusually high number of non-crime referrals including fire, car accident, cot death and bereavement'.

This relates to the second question, namely about the types of services victims support schemes provide. Maguire and Corbett (1986) note that most visits are short term, providing advice, emotional and practical help (such as contacting an agency on the victim's behalf). However, even this disguises a wide range of services which are offered, as the following examples illustrate. The Medway Towns VSS has a Victims-in-Need Fund. Similarly, in the county scheme in Cheshire, each co-ordinator is provided with a sum of £20 to give 'immediate financial help . . . when help is needed but official Departments are not readily available' (such as at weekends). Wolverhampton VSS have managed to help a whole street containing mainly elderly residents, who were being harassed (including burglary and vandalism) by local children, by setting up a community association and Community Watch Scheme. Lambeth VSS is but another scheme keen to forge closer links with Community Watch.

Coventry VSS's help to victims extended to providing a good door lock for one client and digging up a tree in a garden for another. Calderdale VSS trained three people for a Bereavement Support Group and subsequently assisted at the Bradford fire disaster. Rochdale was one of the many schemes which have helped clients to obtain compensation for their injuries from the Criminal Injuries Compensation Board. Indeed, in their 1986 annual report, Rochdale note that since they began operating, the total amount successfully claimed on behalf of victims from the board exceeds £60,000.

In this context, clearly not all victims support work is short-term crisis intervention. Maguire and Corbett (1986) note that while three-quarters of victims receive only one visit, 13 per cent of burglary and 34 per cent of violence victims receive at least one further visit. Again, though, there are considerable variations between schemes at both the level of policy and the provision of services. For example, while Tamworth and Lichfield VSS restrict their volunteers to only three visits, this original policy at Barnet VSS had to be revised because of the needs of some victims for long-term help.

So, just as it was illustrated earlier that there can be a number of agencies referring victims, so it is true that schemes are involved in a wide variety of work extending beyond crime victims, to 'victims of circumstance', mediation work and even the befriending of offenders. We shall reiterate these points at a later stage via our own research in south-west England. Here, we merely wish to draw attention to the considerable difference of policy and practice reflected by the autonomy of individual schemes. This will become increasingly evident in the context of our model for voluntary-sector involvement.

Before leaving this discussion of function, however, it might be appropriate to briefly refer to data from the 1984 British Crime Survey. Here victims[7] were asked a series of questions about victims support schemes. Just under one-third (31 per cent) of victims said they had heard of their existence, but when told what they did 40 per cent said they thought *all* victims of crime should be contacted by victims support and a further 25 per cent felt that the victims of serious crimes should be contacted. Asked specifically about their own experience as victims, only 19 per cent said they would have liked to have been contacted by a victims support scheme, but over twice that number (41 per cent) said they would have accepted assistance from a scheme had it been offered. Quite clearly, then, consumer 'demand' far exceeds current supply.

But does victim demand correspond to the crimes or groups targeted by schemes? In some senses the answer is Yes. For example, victims who reported incidents to the police and victims of robbery and burglary offences were relatively likely to respond favourably. However, so were the victims of 'threats' and damage offences, less likely to be seen as typical clients of victims support schemes. Moreover, slightly more victims of personal offences than victims of household crimes were inclined to say that they would have liked or accepted help from a victims support scheme, and among victims of personal crimes those who had suffered at the hands of their spouse/cohabitee (or former spouse/cohabitee) or neighbour were most likely to respond positively. For example, 76 per cent of the former and 50 per cent of the latter said they would have accepted help from victims support. Yet these are some of the groups the early schemes specifically avoided. Clearly, then, if we use a demand-based definition of need (Nevitt 1977), victims support schemes could offer a service to a much wider range of victims, given adequate resources.

The question of resources is one to which we shall return at various points in this and subsequent chapters. Here it is most appropriate in the context of the second of the four criteria we have used to describe voluntary services. In the next four sections, then, we shall focus on these in some detail, in order both to identify the characteristics of victims support schemes in general *and* to identify variations between schemes.

## Relationship to conventional statutory services

The means by which victims support schemes operate are essentially a product of their structure and functions. Thus they are a community resource which co-ordinates the services of other agencies while ensuring that service provision is not duplicated (Reeves 1984). The relationship with statutory services is thus one of appeasement not opposition. Moreover, as we have noted above, schemes are dependent upon the police for the majority of their referrals, and this necessitates good relationships with police forces.

However, as already stressed, the NAVSS sees strength in schemes being independent of statutory agencies, and the balance between police and probation or social services, for example on management committees, is considered one means of maintaining independence.

Schemes are thus not service-based in the way that many of their American equivalents are. Consequently, when the Home Affairs Committee recommended closer administrative and organizational links with probation services (House of Commons 1984: x), this was greeted with surprise by the NAVSS and gave the government the chance for a note of dissent which, perhaps alone in its response, received widespread support:

> 'In the Government's view the victims support movement rightly values the independence of local schemes and the spontaneity and enthusiasm of the local voluntary effort on which they depend. We are inclined to agree that, from the standpoint of preserving and promoting these vital features of the movement as it now exists, the creation of close official links with a statutory agency such as the probation service would be counter-productive.'
> 
> (Home Office 1985: 1–2)

Thus, despite an 'appeasing' relationship with statutory services, victims support schemes claim independence by taking a position *between* agencies with very different priorities and perspectives. As we shall indicate in the following chapter, this makes them distinct from many equivalent services in the United States. Nevertheless, the balancing act is a precarious one, which we shall consider in more detail in our local study. Thus, in Chapter 9 we shall focus on relationships with the police, in Chapter 10 relationships with the probation service, and in Chapter 11 the ideologies of volunteers compared with police and probation volunteers.

**Sources of funding**

Victims support schemes, quite clearly, developed in full accord with the voluntary ideal. However, while some have maintained their commitment to voluntaristic principles to the extent that they have no paid members of staff and volunteers receive nominal or no expenses, the demand for services has led to a recognition that voluntary efforts are no longer sufficient.

However, the expansion of schemes has occurred at precisely that time when public donations to voluntary bodies have declined in importance (Wolfenden 1978), illustrated by the poor response to the NAVSS public appeal on BBC television in 1983.[8] This is not to denigrate the role of the public and private charities; in 1985–6, for example, the NAVSS received some £33,000 from trusts and charities (NAVSS 1986a: 36) and local schemes gained approximately £88,000 from trusts and public appeals (NAVSS 1986a: 27). Nevertheless, a review of annual reports suggests that schemes were often dependent upon the probation service for providing office accommodation and secretarial services and the police for grants from property funds, charity balls and barbecues, and in some cases for administrative and clerical assistance.

This is, however, insufficient, and victims support schemes have become more reliant upon central and local government funds. However, once again the timing has been inopportune, with the government attempting to cut its welfare budget. Thus here, as in other areas, the government has offered considerable encouragement but few resources. To quote the Under-Secretary of State for the Home Office:

> 'The Government has seen its role, in relation to the victim support schemes, as one of encouragement, of financing the headquarters of the National Association of Victim Support

Schemes, so that the impetus is given from that central point to the development of schemes throughout the country. But the local organisation is seen by the Government as a matter for voluntary effort, and I do not think it would be feasible to think of the Government taking on the sort of financial responsibilities that would be needed for local schemes to be aided directly by public funds.'

(House of Commons 1984: 32)

Clearly, the lack of financial obligations may be seen by government as one of the advantages of encouraging the voluntary sector. But are voluntary organizations cheaper? In so far as they are served by volunteers, this may be so, although as Haxby (1978) notes for probation, the training and supervision of volunteers may itself be a costly exercise. Moreover, it is sometimes misleading to assess volunteers' time, unclaimed expenses, and so on, as a nil-cost resource:

'It has often been said that Victims Support Schemes are extremely cheap to run, the average Scheme spending little more than £500 a year apart from any salary or honorarium paid to the Co-ordinator. A very limited survey . . . suggested that 63 per cent of the potential costs of salaries and expenses were met by the Co-ordinators who worked voluntarily and by the Volunteers who did not claim their out-of-pocket expenses. . . . Taken over all, the Schemes were having to meet only 42 per cent of the costs they would have incurred without the voluntary subsidies of their members. It is uncertain how long this situation can continue.'

(NAVSS 1983: 14–15)

On a national level, the NAVSS was originally funded by the Voluntary Service Unit of the Home Office, the DHSS, and some private trust grants (NAVSS 1981), as well as receiving support in services and accommodation from NACRO. In the financial year 1985–6, £126,000 of its income of £171,912 came from the Home Office (NAVSS 1986a: 36).

On a local level, at least fifty-seven schemes were indirectly sponsored by other agencies providing them with accommodation. In addition, at least eighty-two received Urban Aid, Inner City Partnership, Opportunities for Volunteering or MSC funding, and 116 county council or local authority grants.[9] However, the grants total of just over £1 million, although about one-third more than in the previous year, was considered by the NAVSS as both unevenly distributed and no more than a fraction of what was required (NAVSS 1986a: 26–7).

We thus arrive at the ironic situation where victims support is highly dependent upon state funds, but where a paltry amount of the budget for the criminal justice system is devoted to victims, and most of this goes to the Criminal Injuries Compensation Board, leading the Home Affairs Committee to note:

> 'We see a marked lack of consistency in the Home Office expressing "great admiration for the work of the volunteers who devote their time and energy to this very worthwhile cause", if they are not prepared to ensure that they possess the basic resources necessary for long-term survival.'
>
> (House of Commons 1984: ix)

As we noted earlier, however, the problem of finance is wider than this. Where schemes are funded through Urban Aid, MSC money, and so on, funding is on minimum salaries for a specified time period. Neither factor is conducive to recruitment of the best staff, committed to long-term development. Moreover, schemes may be required to waste valuable resources campaigning for more resources and devote time to making further grant applications, putting additional pressure on co-ordinators (Maguire and Corbett 1986). These financial pressures, combined with the problems specific areas may have in recruiting volunteers (see below), result in severe strain in particular schemes.

Although the government has recently provided more for 'contingency funding' local schemes,[10] it is, however, evident that victims support schemes are currently concerned to increase state financing, especially to pay co-ordinators. While the government has resisted a shift away from the 'self-supporting' pole of our continuum, the announcement of extra funding over the period 1987–90 marks a U-turn in government thinking and a possible change in the structure of the organization (see Ch. 12).

### Goals of the NAVSS

Moving on to the third dimension of our model, the goal of the organization, it is indisputable that victims support in Britain has adopted a 'social provision' rather than a 'social movement' emphasis. While the National Association has played an important role in publicizing the needs of crime victims, and the need for more appropriate funding for victims services, the service dimension has remained paramount. Most especially, the danger inherent in becoming involved in debates as the victim advocate and critic of current sentencing policies has been well recognized. There are, of course, exceptions. Thus the first president of the NAVSS had earlier argued that in developing victims services 'the money should come from some of the vast amounts currently devoted to the care of offenders' (Irving 1977: 4). However, in early debates, and leading to the formation of the National Association, an unambiguous policy emerged:

> 'In considering the wider implications of our work, we were aware that on occasions some people have sought to link the growth of the Victims Support movement with the growth of violent crime and comments regarding stiffer penalties for offenders. One of the Council's earliest decisions was a clear and unambiguous agreement that it was not appropriate for NAVSS to concern itself with or to express opinions upon matters concerning the penal system, sentencing policy or other aspects of the criminal justice system except where it may be *directly* relevant to the needs of victims, such as compensation or restitution.
>
> All members agree that we would wish to attract public support for our work but we consider that we have a responsibility not to spread unnecessary fear and distress in doing so. Our hope is that people will adopt sensible precautions to crime, see the problem in perspective and then get on with life.'
>
> (NAVSS 1981: 3)

Two subsequent examples further illustrate the application of this policy. The first refers to the 'Victims of Violence' controversy, the second the involvement of the National Association with the World Society of Victimology.

Victims of Violence, an organization based in Merseyside and Leeds, was established in the mid-1970s to 'bring help and comfort to the many seriously injured victims of criminal assaults in Merseyside'.[11] Although focused on the needs of victims and a concern for victim-orientated policies, in so doing the organization emphasized the threat of crime, especially to the old, in Britain, contrasting with the NAVSS, which has always sought to avoid dramatizing crime and needlessly increasing people's fears. Thus, when in 1980 the BBC 'Man Alive' programme based on Victims of

104  *Crime Victims*

Violence focused on crimes against the elderly, the NAVSS combined with Age Concern and Help the Aged in condemning a film, which, while using statistics which were 'in fact highly questionable and may well exaggerate the position', could 'lead to unnecessary anxieties and fears'.[12]

In this case the NAVSS distinguished between meeting needs and campaigning for victims, though stressing the seriousness of the crime problem. A similar distancing is evident over the victims' rights issue.

As we shall note in more detail in Chapter 12, the World Society of Victimology has campaigned for a charter of victims' rights through the United Nations, and in so doing has argued for increasing the influence of victims at the sentencing and post-sentencing stages. Partly as a result of this, the NAVSS withdrew from membership of the World Society, and in a clarification of its position, Helen Reeves (1985) argued the case for concentrating on victims' needs and avoiding policy statements about the wider sentencing structure.

In conclusion, then, while the NAVSS does act as a pressure group on victim-specific issues, it clearly and unambiguously avoids involvement in wider issues of penal policy.[13] It is in this sense distinct from the feminist-based services in Britain which we described in Chapter 5 and also, as we shall stress in the next chapter, from many victims services in the United States.

## Relationship between helper and helped

Turning to the fourth of the criteria we have used to describe voluntary organizations, namely the relationship between helper and helped, we are immediately struck by the lack of discussion on this point. As has been noted, the NAVSS has eulogized the *community response* to *its* crime problems, but there is little evidence of who volunteers are, or what the most desirable volunteer–victim relationship should be. Thus, while the importance accredited to training might be seen as necessitating a divide between helper and helped, in the current, and otherwise excellent, training manual, the 'ideal' volunteer is outlined in the following paragraph:

> 'They are ordinary members of the community who provide a confidential service to victims of crime. The primary characteristics required are caring, trustworthiness, stability, calmness,

friendliness, concern, sensitivity, understanding, ability to learn and seek help and ability to stand back from the victim's distress in order to maintain objectivity.'

(NAVSS 1986b: 1)

Such statements aside, it seems that victims support is not based on ideals of fellowship which characterize Women's Refuges and Rape Crisis Centres in Britain. However, we have little information on whether volunteers do share the social characteristics of their clients, or more specifically, whether volunteers who have themselves been victimized in the past are seen as having advantages. We shall therefore focus on these unanswered questions in our own survey, notably in Chapter 11.

## The classification of victims support schemes

Referring back to our original classification, the position of schemes appears unequivocal on two of the four criteria we suggested. In terms of their relationship to conventional statutory agencies, schemes can be located at the 'appeasing' pole of the continuum, although they attempt to maintain independence through their relationship with *different* statutory agencies, notably police and probation. In terms of their goals, they clearly can be located towards the social-provision pole. However, on the other two criteria there is some ambivalence. Considering the relationship between helper and helped, schemes seem to be more appropriately located towards the right of the continuum, where the relationship approximates that of professional and client, although national policy is certainly not in favour of professionalism as such. In terms of source of funding, the ambivalence is found on two levels. First, there is conflict between government and the NAVSS, where the latter would like to move towards further state funding while maintaining independence. Second, there is variation between schemes, with some resisting any sacrifice of the principles of voluntarism.

This raises the question of how far schemes vary from one another. We have already noted that schemes differ markedly in their structures and functions. It is perhaps appropriate to consider variations in resources by considering differences between schemes in their finances and, most especially, the availability of volunteers.

## Area variations

In Chapter 5 we noted a number of the disadvantages of voluntary-sector provision which have been raised in previous writings. Here we wish to concentrate on one of them: the problem of area inequities.

Of course, territorial injustice is not exclusively a problem of voluntary services (Davies 1968). Indeed, numerous studies of state welfare services have demonstrated that despite the optimism that welfare provisions in the postwar period would even out provision between regions, considerable disparities remain – in health (Black 1980), services for the elderly (Davies 1971) and children (Davies, Barton, and McMillan 1972), and domiciliary services (Weir and Simpson 1980) for example. Nevertheless, where the state ultimately accepts responsibility for service provision, area variations can be minimized, given the political will. In contrast, where services are provided by the voluntary sector, distribution may reflect more the availability of volunteers than the extent of need, as we have already noted.

Despite this, there is actually very little evidence on the maldistribution of voluntary resources. True, the Wolfenden Committee Report cites variations between northern industrial cities and volunteer strongholds in cathedral cities like Exeter (Wolfenden 1978), but much of this evidence is drawn from a somewhat limited survey of the distribution of listed voluntary bodies in urban areas, and in no way demonstrates urban–rural contrasts. In this context, interestingly, the urban areas of the South West, including Plymouth, are identified as volunteer strongholds (Hatch and Mocroft 1977).

We have been able to test this assumption elsewhere in the context of police and probation volunteers. Using national data on police specials in each police authority, for example, it is easy to demonstrate that while police paid manpower varies in relation to need (i.e. the distribution of crime), police specials are more common in rural authorities with lower crime rates. Similarly, from a brief questionnaire sent to probation services, it seems that the distribution of probation volunteers does not match demands on the service. Thus, just as we can consider how far volunteers working for victims support schemes are or are not typical of local communities, so we can ask whether victims support schemes are more likely to emerge in particular areas. On the basis of earlier writings on volunteers, and our own research on police and probation volunteers, we might hypothesize that schemes would be more prevalent in rural, low crime rate areas compared with metropolitan areas with high crime rates.

It is possible to test this in two ways, by looking at victims support schemes in terms of their date of origin (approximated to year of registration with the NAVSS) and the current number of volunteers.

Taking first the date of origin of the different schemes, we have already mapped the number of schemes registered with the NAVSS at three points in time: 1980, 1982, and 1984. Further consideration of *Figure 6.1* suggests, with few exceptions, that schemes have developed *fairly evenly across the country*. Perhaps most notable is the early development of schemes in Cheshire and the South West and the spawning in 1981–2 of schemes in East Anglia, the Midlands, and the mid-West, resulting in a concentration within a band from South East to North West. In order to investigate this further, we considered the schemes registered at these three points of time according to other criteria of need – whether or not they fell in police authorities with high or low recorded crime rates or areas designated as urban priority. We also considered the growth of victims support according to volunteer potential by using area data on police and probation volunteers.

Such an analysis is admittedly crude, given that schemes may be formed in pockets of extreme need within larger areas where deprivation is less in evidence, or *vice versa* (Bentham 1985). Bearing this in mind, however, the following points emerged.

First, there was no particular tendency for victims support schemes to originate in areas of urban deprivation, but equally some of the early schemes were to be found there. Thus eighteen of the victims support schemes established by 1980 fell in one or other of the forty-eight areas designated as such by the Department of Environment (Bentham 1985), as did a further eleven established in 1981–2. However, clearly many of the early schemes were started in 'less deprived' areas, and we thus considered the data, reclassified by police authority, to test out further patterns according to need as defined by population density and crime.

Controlling for population in each authority, we correlated the number of victims support schemes started by 1980, in 1981–2, in 1983–4, and for the overall total with the population per hectare and the recorded notifiable crime rate. In no case was there any indication of a relationship. We therefore categorized police authorities according to their offence rates in 1982, comparing the twelve forces with rates of 6,000 or more per 100,000 population, the nine with rates of between 5,000 and 5,999 and the twenty-one with rates below 5,000. These authorities accounted, respectively, for 45 per cent, 20 per cent, and 35 per cent of the population of England and Wales. Of schemes established by 1980, 40.3 per cent were in high crime authorities, 9.7 per cent in medium-rate areas and 50 per cent in low-rate areas, showing that victims support schemes were significantly more common in low crime authorities ($x^2 = 7.76$, $p< 0.05$). However, schemes were not markedly underrepresented in high-rate authorities, the difference being largely accounted for by the lack of schemes in medium crime rate authorities. Although the 1983–4 period saw the rapid spread of schemes in metropolitan areas such as London, Manchester, and Liverpool, this overrepresentation of low-rate areas at the expense of medium crime authorities was maintained. By early 1985, 46.8 per cent of schemes operated in high crime authorities, only 13.2 per cent in medium-rate authorities, and 40.0 per cent in low-rate authorities ($x^2 = 8.03$, $p< 0.05$).

We then turned to consider the development of victims support according to rates of probation and police volunteers. Considering each police authority separately, there was a slight, but not statistically significant, tendency for schemes to be more common in areas with higher rates of special constables (overall, $r = +0.265$, $0.05<p<0.1$), although there was no pattern according to the distribution of probation volunteers. Again, we continued by dividing authorities into three categories, according to their involvement of police specials or probation volunteers. For the former, 17 per cent of the population lived in authorities with high rates of special constables, 28 per cent in medium-rate areas and 54 per cent in low-rate areas. However, victims support schemes started by 1980 were overrepresented in the former (29.0 per cent) and underrepresented in the latter (43.6 per cent), although the difference was not statistically significant ($x^2 = 6.36$, $0.05 <p<0.1$). By early 1985 the difference was even less – 20.8 per cent of schemes were in authorities with low rates ($x^2 = 3.67$, $p>0.1$). In no case was the availability of probation volunteers in an authority related to the emergence of schemes.

It thus seems that while the spread of victims support schemes across the country has been slightly uneven, it is by no means unrelated to area needs. Nor does it appear as closely linked to volunteer potential as other voluntary-sector studies might suggest.

Rather, we would suggest the ambiguous pattern reflects the pull of these two opposite forces. Schemes developed *both* in areas with high crime rates and poor volunteer potential *and* in areas with low crime rates but active volunteers. In contrast, areas with intermediate crime rates were less likely to see the development of victims services.

In terms of the creation of schemes, then, the argument that voluntary groups would form most readily in areas where needs were least (i.e. with low crime rates) is not borne out. However, this says very little about the operational requirements of schemes once formed. That is, do schemes in certain areas experience particular problems recruiting sufficient volunteers? We thus turned to our second criterion of provision, the current volunteer status of different schemes.

On the basis of annual returns from the seventy-seven schemes from our national survey, the average scheme in 1984 had approximately eighteen volunteers and dealt with 807 referrals. However, these average figures, not surprisingly, hide a considerable degree of variation. Many schemes operated with under ten volunteers, some with fifty or more; many dealt with under 200 referrals, three with more than 3,000. Moreover, while there was a significant correlation between number of referrals and number of volunteers ($r = +0.417$, $p<0.001$), there were also enormous variations. In order to illustrate this, we divided referrals by volunteers for each of our sample of schemes running throughout 1984. Details of each were included for seventy-two schemes, producing a mean of 49.5 referrals per volunteer. At one extreme, two schemes had over 200 referrals per volunteer (i.e. each volunteer would have some four referrals per week); at the other extreme, five schemes had less than four referrals per volunteer per year.

Of course, where the referral–volunteer ratio is particularly high due to a large proportion of crimes being referred by the police, it is arguable that the needs of these 'extra' referrals will be less severe than in schemes where referrals are selective. Additionally, as Maguire and Corbett (1986) note, schemes may operate their own forms of rationing. Consequently, the increased workload on volunteers will be less than the numerical increase in cases suggests. Similarly, rural schemes covering larger geographical areas may require proportionally more volunteers. Moreover, pressure on volunteers will to some extent vary according to the amount of time volunteers have to give – retired, unemployed, or otherwise unwaged volunteers may be better able to deal with more referrals than those in full-time employment, for example.

Despite these notes of caution, however, it seems probable that many victims support schemes suffer from either one of two problems. On the one hand, some schemes may be unable to recruit enough volunteers to provide an adequate service to victims referred to the scheme. On the other hand, some schemes may find themselves with volunteers who feel under-used, with consequent implications for morale: 'A low referral rate and an underused set of volunteers was never off the mind of a frustrated Management Committee. There can be no doubt in that time we lost many potentially excellent volunteers because they felt their services could be better used elsewhere.'[14] With this in mind, we considered the characteristics of areas where schemes had either very high or very low rates of referrals per volunteer. In contrast to the case of the *formation* of schemes, clear patterns emerged, with urban, particularly metropolitan area, schemes having higher rates. Consideration of referrals and volunteers separately suggested that this was *partly* because of the higher number of referrals in these areas, with some rural or small-town schemes having very few referrals in 1984; however, it also appeared that metropolitan schemes had only marginally more volunteers to deal with the very high numbers of referrals. For example, taking all returns to the NAVSS for 1983 and our sample for 1984, the numbers of referrals per volunteer for the West Midlands was 66.4 and 84.4 and for London 45.7 and 66.6. In contrast, Somerset had rates of 12.0 and 10.3, Norfolk 21.0 and 19.1, and Devon and Cornwall 11.9 and 28.3. Other areas where sufficient data were available only for 1983 included Essex (21.0) and Kent (10.0). It thus appears that while the introduction of victims support schemes has not been markedly skewed by area characteristics, schemes in urban, particularly metropolitan, areas experience more difficulty recruiting sufficient volunteers, while ironically, more rural schemes may find referral levels too low to keep volunteers busy.

To illustrate this, we correlated referral–volunteer ratios in each police authority with our other variables. A clear pattern emerged, with ratios higher in more densely populated areas ($r = +0.480, p<0.01$) with higher crime rates ($r = +0.378, p<0.05$). Controlling for other variables, the offence rate became less decisive, and although the subsequent regression equation accounted for only 22 per cent of the variance, it demonstrated the influence of *both* density *and* proportion of police specials on the ratio.[15] The fact that there was no relationship between the ratio and measures of probation volunteers suggests that victims support schemes recruits may be less typical of these than of police specials, a point to which we shall return – on a local level – in later chapters.

That aside, it appears that the criticism that voluntary developments are not evenly spread according to need has some justification. While victims support schemes were initiated in high crime rate areas, as well as areas with good volunteer potential, the former, especially the metropolitan areas, seem under most strain due to lack of volunteers to cater for needs. These conclusions mirror those of Maguire and Corbett (1986) based on a somewhat different analysis of national data. They are also illustrated in the manpower problems raised in many annual reports from metropolitan schemes, illustrated in at least one case by intra-metropolis 'commuting': 'There is, however, still an imbalance between the geographical locations of volunteers and those areas of high crime and this is something we shall need to address ourselves in the year ahead.'[16]

An alternative to the importing of volunteers is a greater reliance on paid staff, as either co-ordinators or service providers. Unfortunately, closer analysis of variations suggests that although metropolitan schemes were more likely to have paid co-ordinators, and many rural schemes may have little funding for co-ordinators, the differences were not excessive.

The situation is made more complex by the fact that while many schemes have one, or even more, full-time co-ordinators, others have part-time staff and many more give an 'honorarium' to the co-ordinator. Moreover, in 1983 the amount of this 'honorarium' varied from £50 to £1,500, more than was paid to some part-time co-ordinators. Considering victims support schemes both individually and within regions, it seemed that the average metropolitan scheme was paying out some £2,000 to £3,000 to its co-ordinator or co-ordinators, while rural regions may provide either nothing or a few hundred pounds. However, within the areas of London, the West Midlands, Manchester, and Liverpool, for example, there were enormous variations, and some town or small-city schemes had succeeded in getting external funding, which meant they were financially better off than metropolitan schemes. For example, in 1983 Handsworth paid only an honorarium while Hastings had a full-time co-ordinator; within Liverpool, Toxteth had one full-time worker, while south Liverpool had two full-time and two half-time workers.

Where victims support schemes have to rely on Urban Aid or similar funding, their success will depend on a number of factors, including the availability of funds to the area and their place in the priorities pecking order within, say, a metropolitan authority. As a result, the distribution is inevitably haphazard, and while, in general, funding is more readily available in areas of most need, there is no overall rationale which allows resources to be distributed most equitably.

It is this problem of maldistribution of voluntary resources which the government sought to address by providing money directly to the NAVSS in 1986 to distribute to individual schemes. It was, however, based on the assumption that the need for such central funding is the exception rather than the norm, and temporary rather than permanent. Moreover, the additional funding was in no way sufficient to allow existing schemes to provide services for a more varied sample of victims, certainly not on the scale which victims themselves feel helpful or – in the context of rape for example – the government considered appropriate. The resulting change of policy has implications for the future of schemes, which we shall consider in Chapter 12.

At the same time, clearly not all schemes require paid co-ordinators, and indeed some may reject the idea as a matter of principle. This sometimes happens in metropolitan areas where an inadequate supply of volunteers struggle to handle large numbers of referrals while maintaining the voluntary ideal: Handsworth is a case in point. Most commonly, it is rural areas with good volunteer potential which may find their volunteers under-used, with subsequent implications for morale. It is, nevertheless, not a problem exclusive to victims support schemes, but rather an issue common to many services based on the use of volunteers. As Stockdale has pointed out in the context of probation, 'there is no simple answer to the problem of how to have just the right number of properly-prepared volunteers available for all the tasks and no more' (Stockdale 1985: 27).

**Summary**

As we have noted in this chapter, victims support schemes have developed in relative isolation from victims services in the United States and from services for battered women and the victims of rape. Not surprisingly, then, the form of voluntary services is distinctive.

Using the criteria we introduced in Chapter 5, victims support schemes typically have close relationships with statutory services, often depend on state finance (however inadequate this may be), emphasize social-provision rather than social-movement goals, and distinguish between helper and helped to a far greater extent than do British Rape Crisis Centres and Women's Refuges.

In fact, NAVSS definitions of the distinctive features of victims services in Britain prioritize two issues subsumed within this model – the close relationship between schemes and statutory agencies and the extent to which volunteers, if distinct from victims, are at least representatives of the communities from which victims are drawn. We shall, therefore, devote special attention to these in later chapters, concentrating in Chapters 9 and 10 on the relationship between victims support and the police and probation, and in Chapter 11 reviewing the social characteristics of volunteers. Nevertheless, because our local study is concentrated on the South West, we have devoted the last section of this chapter to area variations, especially concerning the availability of volunteers and the extent of dependence on external funding.

We have argued that the distribution of victims support schemes is not as uneven as earlier writings on voluntary bodies might have suggested, possibly because schemes developed *both* in areas where volunteers were readily available *and* in areas where needs (in terms of crime rates) were evident. However, area variations are marked in terms of the pressures under which schemes operate, with urban schemes generally having higher referrals per volunteer than rural schemes. Despite this it is possible to argue, as Helen Reeves has done in the context of the South West, that 'The difference between a city scheme and a rural scheme is not that great.'[17]

The problem of schemes where volunteers are under-used is one which we shall reconsider further in the context of many schemes in the South West. However, where schemes clearly have difficulty in recruiting sufficient suitable volunteers, external funding becomes crucial. It is therefore a sad irony that where government support for victims services is enthusiastic it has not been matched by adequate funding. Victims support schemes are insufficiently funded, even in relation to the small amount spent on compensation (see Chs 3 and 4). Moreover, the operation of state finance, through Urban Aid, the MSC and other individually approved short-term funds, in no way adequately addresses either the appropriate level or the appropriate distribution of state finances. It is thus appropriate at this juncture to

## 114  *Crime Victims*

draw comparisons with services in the United States, where services are both better funded and more closely integrated with statutory agencies.

# 7 Victims services in the United States

**Ideologies in the victims movement**

In the United States, as in Britain, the 1970s saw a growing recognition that the victim was unjustly excluded from the criminal justice process, and thus that the system was not necessarily in the victim's interests. However, just what these interests are, and how they are best represented, are the subject of debate. In Britain there appear to be two major foci – on women's rights, which we have identified with Refuge and Rape Crisis Centre developments, and on victims' needs, which we have seen as the priority of victims support schemes.

However, in the United States the victims movement is a more complex conglomeration of issues and ideologies. In addition to those factions which prioritized women's rights and victims' needs, there are at least four other major influences on the development of policies. We have labelled these the offender-focus, the system-efficiency priority, the law-and-order emphasis, and the victims' rights lobby.

The first of these we have already discussed at some length in the context of the development of reparation and mediation. We shall not spend any further time on it, except to emphasize that, for many, an interest in the victim is secured through the perspective that offenders will benefit from a greater awareness of the impact of crime on the victim. While this perspective has recent parallels in Britain, as we have noted, the other three concerns are less in evidence here, and are consequently worthy of attention.

First, much initial interest in victims' treatment by the criminal justice system was engendered by a concern with system-efficiency. That is, lack of co-operation from victims or witnesses was seen as undermining the operation of the system; the public appeared unwilling to report crimes to the police, and even more reluctant to co-operate in court, through appearing as witnesses. The system of deposition hearings, where the defence has the opportunity to question the victim in closed session prior to prosecution, tends to aggravate the situation, leading to a common view among victims that they are alone and defenceless in court (Carrington 1975; President's Task Force 1982).

The law-and-order focus has a certain amount in common with the above perspective. Essentially, it is based on a zero-sum equation, alleging that in the interests of offenders' rights the interests of victims have been disregarded. There is thus considerable emphasis on the alleged inadequacy of law-enforcement agencies to effectively deter offenders, and on crime as out of control (President's Task Force 1982; Schembri 1976).

This perspective is, however, most forcefully expressed by Carrington in one of the earliest texts, *The Victims*: 'It is an elementary proposition that if there were fewer criminally inclined individuals at liberty to victimize the innocent, there would be fewer victims of crime' (Carrington 1975: 120). To this end, he argues for a reversal of the Miranda decision and on expanded use of capital punishment:

> 'No others more clearly display an utter disregard for the victims of crime than the advocates of the abolition of the death penalty. . . . We must place the sanctity of human life in its proper context – that of the innocent victim. If the life of *one* such victim can be saved through the deterrent effect of the death penalty, then its usefulness has been established – except perhaps to those whose philosophy shuns the victims of crime completely.'
>
> (Carrington 1975: 182–99)

Policies and policy-makers are thus divided into two camps – those who have the interests of the victim at heart and those who favour the offender:

> 'In recent years the lines have been drawn generally into two schools of thought regarding the treatment of those accused, or convicted, of criminal acts. The first of these is the hard-line or victim-oriented viewpoint; the second is the permissive or criminal-oriented approach.'
>
> (Carrington 1975: 124)

We have focused on Carrington because he has been so prominent in the victims movement. He was, for example, chairman of the Victims Committee of the American Bar Association, is executive director of the Victims Assistance Legal Organization in Virginia Beach, and he served on the President's Task Force (1982) on victims of crime. He was also formerly executive director of Americans for Effective Law Enforcement, a national organization founded in 1966 which operated as a pressure group to Congress, advocating severe sentences and capital punishment and helping to defend police officers accused of 'bending the rules' in the interests of gaining convictions.

Carrington is, however, by no means exceptional. Thus, for example, the 'Citizens for Law and Order' in Oakland, California, operated a 'court watcher' programme and published attacks on judges considered lenient. As will become clear subsequently, the influence of the law-and-order faction in the victims movement is considerable. It is also linked to the final influence we wish to note here; that which prioritizes victims' rights. Here the emphasis is on the rights of victims to be heard, in terms of making known their feeling about the crime and its impact *and* their views of the appropriate sentence for offenders. In this context, victim impact statements are becoming a more common feature of the courtroom process, allowing for the victim to provide for the court's consideration details of the effects of the crime. In addition, some groups have attempted to influence the court through direct intervention by those victimized within a neighbourhood or by the employment of a victim advocate to represent victims in court, who might demand 'higher bonds, fewer continuances, and harsher penalties than the prosecutors themselves' (Du Bow and Becker 1976: 157).

Clearly, these last three influences overlap, having in common a concern that offenders receive better treatment from the criminal justice system than do victims. Equally clearly, despite our comments in Chapters 3 and 4, they have no obvious equivalents in Britain. Nevertheless, it is important to stress that they are only part of the victims movement, which is extremely complex. Thus, as Karmen (1984) notes in the context of proposals for federal criminal injuries compensation, in the United States support has come from more radical politicians, with conservatives more concerned with the financial implications of legislation. Moreover, prioritizing victims' needs, women's rights, or offenders' interests provides rather different perspectives on victim policies.

Nevertheless, following Smith (1984), we are concerned to tease out the variety of perspectives which form the base for victim policies. In the following section we shall therefore consider the development of services in the 1970s and the creation of the National Organization for Victim Assistance (NOVA). We shall then review the variety of victim programmes, before concentrating on those which provide services similar to the ones in Britain.

## The development of victims services

Concern over crime victims, voiced in 1967 by the President's Commission on Law Enforcement and the Administration of Justice, led to the creation in the early 1970s of the Law Enforcement Assistance Administration (LEAA) programmes to sponsor projects to improve the handling of victims and witnesses by the criminal justice system. As well as administering the National Crime Panel, the LEAA provided funds for local projects, and between 1970 and 1975 had spend over $22 million on victim-assistance programmes (Lowenberg 1981; Schneider and Schneider 1981). Criticizing the criminal justice system, Donald Santarelli, administrator of LEAA, agreed that 'the odds are better than even that any citizen who comes into contact with the system will come out of that experience with a sour taste in his mouth, with his or her confidence eroded' (quoted in McDonald 1976a: 30). It was this 'sour taste' that LEAA funds were directed to cure. However, incorporated in the initiative was a concern to use improvements as a *means*, the ends being to encourage victims and witnesses to co-operate with police and prosecutors (Bolin 1980).

Meanwhile, many other programmes to help victims emerged independently of LEAA funding. Others, for example, grew out of the Commission on Victim Witness Assistance created in 1974 by the National District Attorneys Association with funding from the US Department of Justice (Lynch 1976). Thus, by the mid-1970s a variety of victim programmes emerged, from Rape Crisis Centres to citizen protection associations, from centres for dispute settlement to crisis services, from child abuse programmes to court-focused services (McDonald 1976a).

The suggestion for a national organization for those working in these various agencies apparently arose in 1972, when a number of American academics and practitioners prepared for the First International Symposium on Victimology, which was to be held in Israel.[1] It was developed by John Dussich during the organization of a national conference on victim advocacy in 1974, funded by the LEAA. Then in 1976 Dussich co-ordinated an *ad hoc* board of directors, including Santarelli from the LEAA, Carrington, Joe Hudson, Ann Burgess, Emilio Viano, Marlene Young, and Duncan Chappell. Between them these represented a variety of perspectives; for example, Burgess was prominent in the rape policy field, Chappell was involved in analysis of criminal injuries compensation, and Hudson is best known in the context of reparation and mediation. By the end of 1976 NOVA was operating as an umbrella organization, and during the next five years it expanded to serve as a national clearing house of information and as a co-ordinator for hundreds of victim-service programmes (Carrington and Nicholson 1984). The NOVA (1985) *Program Directory* illustrates the extent and variety of services covered. It lists between 1,500 and 2,000 affiliated services. In California alone ninety-nine organizations are cited, including Victim/Witness Assistance Programs, Rape Crisis Centres, Parents of Murdered Children, a Children's Self-Help Project, Community Against Violence and a Domestic Violence Coalition. Florida had at the same time 147 affiliated organizations, including Citizens Crime Watch, Mothers Against Drunk Drivers, a Missing Children Help Center, Victim Assistance Programs, a Sexual Assault Family Emergency Center, Spouse Abuse Centers, Victim Advocate Programs, Parents of Murdered Children, Crime Against the Elderly, and a Bureau of Crimes Compensation.

The impact of NOVA and the bodies which are affiliated to it cannot be underestimated (Smith 1984). 'Crime Victims' Weeks' are proclaimed annually by the president of the United States, and in 1982 the president instigated a Task Force on victims of crime. Chaired by Lois Herrington, the commission, which reported in December 1982, was heavily influenced by NOVA, which welcomed its recommendations.[2] It is thus worth pausing to consider it in some detail.

The report is best described as falling into two sections. The first of these, some twelve pages in length, presents an image of crime and victims in the United States; the second covers a series of proposals. The central concern of the first section , 'Victims of Crime in America', is the harm crime causes to its victims, and the unfair ways in which victims are treated by the criminal justice system. This leads to a series of proposals to increase victim services and improve victim rights, which have been welcomed by the victims movement.

However, in presenting its case, the commission constructs an image of crime strikingly different from that presented in British parliamentary reports and in marked contrast to the presentation of the 1982 British Crime Survey (Hough and Mayhew 1983). The scene is set in the opening sentence: 'Before you, the reader, can appreciate the necessity of changing the way victims are treated, you must confront the essential reality that almost all Americans, at some time in their lives, will be touched by crime' (President's Task Force

1982: 2). True; but while, as we have stressed in Chapters 1 and 2, serious crimes are less common (even in the United States), the Task Force provides a series of examples which suggest that murder, kidnap and rape are commonplace, and that victims are routinely victimized by the system. The result is an image of the typical crime victim as devastated by serious crime and abused by a police and prosecution system which is constructed with the offender's interests at heart. Even a 'disclaimer clause' in the final paragraph does little or nothing to mar such an image:

> 'Having survived all this, you reflect on how you and your victimizer are treated by the system that is called justice. You are aware of inequities that are more than merely procedural. During trial and after sentencing the defendant had a free lawyer; he was fed and housed; given physical and psychiatric treatment, job training, education, support for his family, counsel on appeal. Although you do not oppose any of these safeguards, you realize that you have helped to pay for all these benefits for the criminal. Now, in addition and by yourself, you must try to repair all that his crime has destroyed; and what you cannot repair, you must endure.' (President's Task Force 1982: 13)

Not surprisingly, then, the resulting proposals include within the same package a series of initiatives which would improve conditions for victims, while also advocating the abolition of the Miranda exclusion decision, making it an offence for schools not to report certain crimes to the police and mandating public access to parole hearings.

The extent to which victim policies in the United States impinge upon wider penal policies is an issue to which we shall return. At this juncture, however, it is important to stress that the Task Force accepted many of NOVA's suggestions, at a time when LEAA funding was being phased out. As well as providing a series of legislative proposals which would improve victims' legal rights, then, the report laid the foundations for a new structure for funding new and existing victim programmes.

In fact, by the early 1980s federal support for criminal justice innovations, including those programmes for victims and witnesses, was being scaled down, and NOVA was anticipating a shift towards dependence on private funding (Young 1981). The Task Force Report, with its backing for NOVA, was thus crucial in creating the climate for new federal funding initiatives.

The first of these was the Justice Assistance Act 1982, which allowed Justice Department funds to be used for a variety of criminal justice programmes, including those providing victims services. However, no funds were specifically set aside for victim programmes, and although the position has now altered, it appeared at first as though few funds were being allocated to victims services. Appreciating this difficulty, the President's Task Force (1982) recommended that a Federal Crime Victims Fund be created, and this was the centrepiece of the Victims of Crime Act 1984. The revenue for the fund comes from fines and penalties collected from federal criminal offenders (up to a maximum of $100 million). Up to 5 per cent of the fund may be used for federal initiatives, up to 50 per cent for state victim compensation, and at least 45 per cent for local victims assistance programmes. Although recent proposals to cut government spending have threatened the extent of federal funding, the 1984 Act thus provides for a series of local victim-service initiatives, similar in some respects to Urban Aid money in Britain. As we shall note later, however, the situation in the United States differs in so far as many services have been incorporated within statutory bodies and thus are funded directly by state or county budgets. To a greater extent than in Britain, then, grants such as those provided by the LEAA programme have been used to initiate services which subsequently became funded locally. This is well illustrated if we review the types of victims assistance programmes which developed.

## Victims assistance programmes

The range of services provided for victims of crimes is, as we have already stressed, considerable. It is therefore useful to categorize them in some way. Following Ziegenhagen and Benyi (1981) we might distinguish six categories: victim compensation, offender restitution, neighbourhood justice, victim/witness, victim advocacy, and crisis intervention. The first three of these we have referred to in earlier chapters, and it is thus most appropriate here to focus on the others, namely victim/witness services, victim advocacy programmes and crisis-intervention work.

Considering first victim/witness services, these were, as we have shown, a priority of LEAA initiatives. They were fuelled by a concern that victims were treated badly by the system and a perhaps greater concern that this had implications for the willingness of victims or witnesses to co-operate with police and courts. As a result, a series of programmes were funded by LEAA, providing information and support to crime victims, most notably if and when a suspect is identified and prosecuted. It is thus a service restricted to a minority of crime victims.

Victim/witness programmes generally provide for witnesses to be kept informed of progress on the case, dates of court hearings, and so on, and if necessary may act on witnesses' behalf if dates are inconvenient. Such initiatives may also include improving facilities for witnesses in court and supporting victims or witnesses during the deposition or court proceedings (Schneider and Schneider 1981).

Victim advocacy programmes, in contrast, focus on victims' perceived problems rather than assuming that, with regard to some policies, victims' and court interests are synonymous. For example, plea bargaining as a strategy for ensuring quick convictions is in the interests of the prosecution but may be against the wishes or indeed the interests of the victim. Victim advocacy thus provides victims with opportunities for them or their representatives to make a contribution to the decision-making process.

The mechanisms for this are threefold. First, in some cases, lay people, usually friends or neighbours of the victim, have acted in concert to make an informal impression on the court. For example, Du Bow and Becker describe how, following gang harassment in a Chicago neighbourhood, the 'Early Ardmore Group' exerted its presence on the court:

> 'They pressed more than half a dozen cases against members of the gang. When there were hearings on these cases, the group would muster a carload or more of neighbours to accompany the victims. On several occasions over 40 residents appeared in court. When gang related cases were called, the residents would rise and move to stand at the railing separating the audience from the working court area. Their presence was obvious.'
> (Du Bow and Becker 1976: 152)

An alternative method of presenting victim advocacy is for the victim to be represented in court by counsel. Again, Du Bow and Becker (1976) illustrate this with an example from Chicago. Here a lawyer was employed to act on behalf of victims, not only in the court but also in the context of crime prevention and the post-sentencing stage. As we have already noted, in such cases the advocate frequently demanded more severe sentencing.

The third form of advocacy, which has achieved widespread acceptance, is the victim impact statement. Here victims may be assisted or encouraged to complete a form stating the impact of the crime, which may subsequently be produced in court prior to sentence, along with the social-enquiry report. Although victim advocate forms are becoming common, practices vary. For example, in some areas victims have a right to complete one, in others it is mandatory, in others it is more flexible. Similarly, the agency responsible may be variously probation, police, or victim services specialists. Finally, it is notable that some but not all states allow victims to include a recommendation on sentence.

The final types of service provided for victims we have, for convenience, termed 'crisis-intervention work'. These services are more akin to victims support schemes in Britain. They provide a broad range of services to victims, including support and counselling, information on other services, advice on claiming compensation, crime prevention advice, and information on progress of the case (NOVA 1983; Young and Stein 1983). However, the services provided are if anything even more diverse than their British counterparts. Dussich (1976), for example, concentrates on the variety of locations for services. Most services appear to be based in statutory agencies, what NOVA term 'system based'.[3] However, the agency involved may be the police, the prosecutor's department, or a probation department. Others are more community based, being located in hospitals, religious organizations, or with voluntary organizations.

Again, services provided within similar agencies may vary. For example, those based within police departments may operate according to a 'co-operation model', where the police furnish a list of crime victims; a 'collaboration model', where counsellors are brought immediately to the scene of the crime; or a mixture of both (the 'comprehensive model') (Aurora Associates Inc., undated: 26). However, even where schemes are located with the police, it is interesting to note that referral problems are not eliminated:

'Relying solely on referrals from any source is problematic for two reasons: the referral agencies may not trust the victim program and therefore make few (and often inappropriate) referrals; and, even where there is trust in the ability of the victim service agency to be of real help, the diagnostic abilities of untrained agency personnel may effectively bar many needy victims from getting help. Typically, it is only the hysterical victim whom the agency staff refers on for help, not perceiving that tears are not the sole indicator of crisis.'

(Young and Stein 1983: 52)

Victims services also vary in other respects. In terms of clientele, some focus on specific offences, with sex offenders, including rape and child molestation, most notable; others focus on specific victim categories, like the elderly. Some respond personally to all referrals, some respond to many by letter or phone. In terms of service, some concentrate on immediate response, others on less immediate short-term crisis work, others on long-term counselling; some include more emphasis on victims' rights, including perhaps victim advocacy, legal assistance, or pressure-group activities. A number of individual schemes are described in the literature, for example by Chesney and Schneider (1981) and Friedman (1976). Here, we wish to illustrate variety in the following four sections by describing rather different service models. First, we shall focus on three examples from the state of Florida, where services are based in police agencies, but where use of volunteers varies between programmes. Then we shall describe a programme run independently in Pima County, originally funded by an LEAA grant, but dependent upon police collaboration. Third, we shall describe the role of a larger voluntary organization, the American Association of Retired Persons, in providing services for the over 50s by volunteers aged over 50. Finally, we shall consider the growth of Mothers Against Drunk Driving as an organization prioritizing both social-movement and social-provision goals. We shall then reconsider victims services in the United States using the four criteria we introduced in Chapter 5.

## Police-based services: examples from Florida[4]

Three examples of police-based services can be taken from the state of Florida, to illustrate rather different approaches to the use of volunteers.

The Victim Advocacy Program in Clearwater is located in the Police Department, where it is staffed by a Deputy Victim Assistant, on call twenty-four hours every day. All cases of rape, homicide, suicide, and accidental sudden death are referred to her automatically. For other cases, she is dependent upon her police colleagues, who will call her where they feel a victim would benefit from the services of the Victim Assistant. The combination of police discretion, reliance on one staff member, and general perceptions of, for example, burglaries as creating few problems for victims, means that such cases are likely to be confined to the elderly, or women living alone. Victims of domestic assaults who are seriously injured are usually seen, and other cases of aggravated battery or domestic violence are sent a letter informing them that services are available should they require any. In general, though, services are focused on victims of violent crime, where short-term help and referral to appropriate agencies for long-term assistance are the major forms of intervention.

A similar system operates through the Orange County Sheriff's Office in Orlando, although here a team of assistants are employed. Again, though, pressure on resources means that Victim Assistants concentrate on the more serious crimes of violence, and in many cases contact with victims is by phone only. What best distinguishes the Orange County service from that in Clearwater, however, is the development of a largely autonomous volunteer programme dealing with elderly victims. The Victims of Crime Assistance League (VOCAL) operates through the Sheriff's Office, with volunteers regularly sifting police reports. All victims identified in the reports as aged at least 55 are then contacted by phone by volunteers, and are later visited if this is considered necessary.

A more integrated volunteer programme is provided through the Seminole County Sheriff's Office. Victims services in the Sanford area were started in 1978 on the instigation of the mayor and, as in Clearwater, are primarily the responsibility of a Deputy. She is responsible for a public-speaking and schools' programme, and responds to referrals from her colleagues during working hours. In contrast to Clearwater, calls at other times are covered by a pool of some twelve volunteers. These include nurses, teachers, and housewives, and are mostly drawn from former students at the Police Academy who do not subsequently join the police. They are trained by the Deputy and meet monthly to discuss approaches to cases. Even with this larger pool of volunteers, however, help is usually restricted to serious violent crime and is otherwise dependent upon the discretion of the referral officer.

**The Pima County Victim/Witness Program**

A rather different model for providing a range of services for victims is described by Bolin (1980) (see also Aurora Associates Inc., undated; Lowenberg 1981). The Pima County Program began in 1975, partly financed by an LEAA grant, to enhance services for victims and witnesses, encourage their co-operation with the criminal justice system and reduce police involvement in 'social work' functions. In 1978 its funding was taken over by the county, which voted the programme an annual budget of $191,000. Services were provided to victims by a regular staff of eight and some thirty volunteers.

Victims are put in touch with the programme through a variety of agencies, but most are referred by the police. Most are crime victims, with domestic disputes accounting for about one-third of referrals, but non-crime victims were also incorporated in the programme in response to police requests. These include potential suicides, abandoned children, victims of extreme poverty or age-related disabilities, and relatives of accident victims.

Perhaps the most distinctive aspect of the service is the emergency-response provision, with staff providing 24-hour cover and having use of an unmarked radio patrol car between 6 pm and 3 am, when most welfare agencies are closed. However, as well as providing an emergency crisis response, the Pima County Program follows up victims by letter to update them on case proceedings, provides a court alert system, and manages a conflict resolution service for domestic or neighbour disputes.

### Voluntary agency services: the AARP[5]

When Dr Ethel Percy Andros formed the American Association of Retired Persons (AARP) in the late 1950s, she could hardly have anticipated the enormous growth in the organization that was to take place in the following twenty-five years. Based on the motto, 'To serve, not to be served', the AARP has spearheaded a greater understanding of the problems confronting the elderly population, and at the same time encouraged those aged over 50 to play a part in improving the quality of their lives, especially through voluntary activity.

There are a number of dimensions to the work of the AARP. It has initiated a variety of programmes, including Health Advocacy, Tax Aide, Widowed Person's Support and Mature Driving Guidance. In each case it has produced easily comprehensible documentation, frequently supplemented by audio-visual aids, on how to operate schemes.

Of particular relevance here, though, is its work within the criminal justice system, which again is varied. Some programmes, such as those of victims assistance, have involved the elderly as volunteers helping elderly victims. Others have been designed more to involve those over 50 in the criminal justice system. A prime example here is Crime Analysis, such as that operated by the Colorado Police Department. By analysing crime trends on behalf of the police, the programme has enabled more informed decisions to be made about the deployment of personnel, and enlightened understanding of community problems.

On a rather different level, the AARP has inspired a wider appreciation of the problems of criminal victimization of the over 50s (indeed, one programme was designed to reduce the risk of other persons being victimized). In 1973 seminars with law-enforcement administrators and trainers within the criminal justice system were conducted to brief them on the particular problems of the elderly.

By 1976 this had developed into the first course on 'Law enforcement and older persons', which is now used in law-enforcement academies throughout the United States, and in a number of foreign countries. So, by initiating and directing schemes at administrators and professionals on the one hand, and the over 50s on the other, they have sought to improve the lives of a particularly disadvantaged group of people.

## Mothers Against Drunk Driving

Perhaps one of the nearest North American equivalents in structure at least to British victims support schemes is Mothers Against Drunk Driving (MADD).[7] It was formed in 1980 in California by Candy Lightner following the death of her daughter in an accident caused by a drunken driver. Although at the time there was one other pressure group active in the field, Remove Intoxicated Drivers (RID), Mrs Lightner introduced an alternative which combined pressure group activity with direct help for individual victims. By mid-1986 MADD had 385 chapters in forty-nine states, each chapter averaging some sixteen active volunteers (Harris Lord 1986).

The aims and strategies of MADD are fourfold. First, MADD focuses on a campaign of public education, to make people aware of the dangers of driving while under the influence of drink. This campaign takes the form of speeches, stalls, advertising, and candle-light vigils. Second, and allied to this, MADD puts direct pressure on the legislature to tighten up the laws on drunk-driving, provide information and courtroom facilities for victims and to bring some consistency to the sentencing process. Third, it acts on behalf of individual victims, in offering advice and advocacy in particular cases. This can take the form of gaining a personal interview with the probation officer writing a social-enquiry report on an offender, helping the victim to make a victim impact statement, or gaining access to parole hearing.

Finally, MADD focuses on the needs of individual victims. Stressing the loss felt by relatives of the bereaved, and particularly their lack of preparation for their loss, MADD identifies the range of emotional and practical needs expressed by relatives (Harris Lord 1986) and provides individual and group counselling to meet those needs.

Partly due to its pressure-group activities, MADD is practically independent of government funding, although it does get donations from private companies as well as the public. It thus has few paid staff, largely occupying administrative roles, and is dependent upon members and volunteers. Members contribute financially to the movement; volunteers provide services.

Given the nature of the MADD organizational structure, policies vary between different chapters. In some, for example, only past victims will be used as volunteer counsellors, and other volunteers will be employed in fund-raising and pressure-group activities. In others, non-victim volunteers provide counselling. Overall, some two-thirds of MADD chapter leaders are themselves either survivors of drunk-driving incidents or relatives of fatally injured victims (Harris Lord 1986).

While the structure of MADD, at national and local level, is very similar to that of victims support schemes in Britain, it is in marked contrast in terms of our classification. Given its pressure-group emphasis, with a balance of social-movement and social-provision goals, it is largely self-supporting and relatively critical of conventional statutory services. In terms of the relationship between helper and helped, it is also clearly distinctive, indeed, embodying more of the mutual-aid principles than even Women's Refuges and Rape Crisis Centres.

## Classifying victims services

Given the variety of victim-assistance programmes which exist in the United States, it is appropriate to consider, in the context of our model, differences within the United States and contrasts with British services. Again, we shall consider the four dimensions of our model in order, namely relationship with state agencies, funding, goals, and helper–helped relationship.

Taking first the relationship between service providers and state agencies, there are, as we have noted, marked variations, with some services being system based and others community based. However, by and large, examples of oppositional relationships with statutory services are few. Just as many feminist-inspired services modified their stance to gain LEAA funding, so wider victim services which began on LEAA grants have tended to become incorporated into state agencies. In some cases, services are the responsibility of state organizations using only government employed personnel. In others, state agencies provide services via volunteers, in similar ways to the use of volunteers by, say, the probation service in Britain.

Perhaps the best example of victim services located towards the oppositional end of our continuum is MADD. Here, agency policies are critical of official practices, *vis-à-vis* sentencing the drunken motoring offender, but given the powerful drink lobby, MADD has rather less government support than do many others in the victims movement. Nevertheless, overall services in the United States appear more towards the right of our continuum than do those in Britain.

To a certain extent, as the example of MADD further illustrates, this is closely akin to the question of finances. Although some victims services in the United States are low cost, highly dependent upon volunteers, and/or dependent upon private donations, most services are in marked contrast to those in Britain, with local or central government money prominent. This is partly the result of different welfare traditions in the United States, where services have commonly been provided by the voluntary sector on behalf of government, with appropriate grants, and where specific taxation is often explicitly tied to financing specified programmes. For example, some fines collected by the criminal justice system are directed towards victim services, while in some states marriage taxes contribute towards the costs of Women's Refuges. Overall, then, again victims services in the United States appear more dependent upon government funding than do those in Britain.

Third, differences are again marked in terms of the goals of the agency. In Britain, as we have noted in the previous chapters in this section, most Women's Refuges and Rape Crisis Centres have prioritized social-movement as well as social-provision goals, partly through an emphasis on women's rights. However, victims support schemes have focused more on *needs* than on *rights* and have explicitly avoided involvement in sentencing issues. Not so in the United States. There, a much greater emphasis on victims' rights has, almost inevitably, led victims' organizations into discussions over offenders' rights. Clearly, in many but not all respects, the balance of victims' and offenders' rights is a zero-sum equation: gains for victims are often at the expense of offenders.

A number of examples, some already cited, will serve to illustrate the point. At various times victims' programmes in the United States have campaigned for the mandatory arrest of suspects in certain offence categories (e.g. domestic violence); greater use of imprisonment and longer sentences; less use of bail; restrictions on parole; the right of victims to make recommendations to the court *vis-à-vis* sentence, bail or parole; greater powers for the police; and so on. Moreover, the greater emphasis on the threat of crime and the prevalence of the crime problem, an issue avoided by the NAVSS in Britain, itself lends potency to policies aimed at toughening the criminal justice system. We have already noted this in the context of the President's Task Force (1982), but it is also applicable to victims' organizations. Take, for example, the NOVA document *Campaign for Victim Rights: A Practical Guide, 1985* (Edmunds *et al.* 1985). In it the authors offer advice on how agencies can best get across their message to the media, including the suggestion that some victims might be willing to address a press conference on the impact of crime on themselves. The document ends by providing as an example an edited text of a speech by its director, Marlene Young, where the following image of crime in modern America is presented:

> The brutal fact is that crime is still rampant around us, its casualties grow in number, and only a few of them are accorded the compassion and justice due them from their fellow citizens and their institutions of democratic government.
>
> For these facts remain part of the social landscape of this country:
> – Every minute there are fifty thefts.
> – Every minute there are thirteen burglaries.

- Every minute there are nine assaults.
And these are indicators of the state of our union today:
- Every day there are fourteen hundred children abused.
- Every day there are four hundred women raped.
- Every day there are fifty-five people murdered.
(Edmunds *et al.* 1985, unpaginated)

The result is precisely what is avoided in the British Crime Survey analysis by Hough and Mayhew (1983) and by the NAVSS. The crime problem is presented in some abstract notion of rate per minute or day. In order to stress the inadequacy of services for victims, inferences on wider policy matters are invited.

To some extent, NOVA would deny that it is directly involved in advocating tougher sentences, and although, as we have noted, NOVA has enthusiastically welcomed the similar-styled conclusions of the President's Task Force (1982), there is some truth in this. Given that NOVA acts as an umbrella organization for an enormous variety of programmes, it is difficult for it to speak on behalf of the victims movement on issues which are not specifically victim related. There are thus factions within the movements which tend to look to different allegiances in respect of particular policy goals. For example, the National Coalition Against Sexual Assault operates as a distinctive pressure group, and more specific coalitions may be formed in certain circumstances (Stowers and Snair 1986). Moreover, NOVA's catholic approach can be illustrated in its current prioritizing of the problems crime causes for racial minority groups, lesbians and gays, not causes likely to invite enthusiastic commitment from the political right.[8]

Nevertheless, while it is simplistic to label the victims movement in the United States as exclusively devoted to a law-and-order platform, two points are evident from the above discussion. First, the emphasis on rights rather than needs and the presentation of victims problems as part of a law-and-order problem have resulted in NOVA, and many victims programmes, engaging in political dialogue to a greater extent than their British counterparts. Second, where there are disagreements, these tend to be over the *nature* of political goals. That is, agencies within the NOVA umbrella may disagree on the content of the political agenda, but they are almost equally likely to have one.

To a certain extent this is ironic since, as we have already noted in Chapter 5, services for raped or abused women tend to be less politicized than their British counterparts. Thus, while victims support schemes in Britain are distinctive in prioritizing welfare goals, services in the United States appear to vary between a centrist position on our spectrum and one towards the social-movement pole.

Finally, then, what of the helper–helped relationship espoused by victims services? Two points are of particular relevance here. First, services in the United States have tended to emphasize the long-term effects of victimization (Young and Stein 1983) to a greater extent than have services in Britain (Maguire 1984); there is thus a correspondingly greater emphasis on specialist professional counselling. Second, while community services are acknowledged as valuable, and indeed in some volunteers may be recruited specifically to help similar categories of victim (see the case of AARP above), community voluntary or grass-roots services have not been eulogized to the same extent as in Britain. Correspondingly, the idea of services being provided by professionals, possibly assisted by volunteers, is more openly expressed and is sometimes seen as increasing credibility with other agencies (Aurora Associates Inc., undated). Again we must stress that there are considerable variations between programmes. Nevertheless, in general, it appears that the helper–helped relationship is more closely identified with that of professional–client than is the case in Britain.

In attempting to generalize, we are conscious that we have underplayed the extent of variation between services in the United States. Consequently, in *Figure 7.1* we have located victims services in Britain and the United States across ranges on the four criteria we identified. On each, there are points of overlap. Nevertheless, in general we have suggested that our model is useful as a means of distinguishing between programmes in the two countries.

**Discussion**

Overall, we have identified a number of differences in the directions taken by developing victims services in Britain and the United States. Two of these have tended to dominate our discussion. First, services in the United States have been more explicitly concerned with political issues, generally but not exclusively presenting an image of crime as a problem, the criminal justice system as inadequate, and the need for tougher measures against offenders. Second, and partly related to this, victims assistance programmes, especially victim/witness programmes but also victim crisis services,

*Victims services in the United States* 133

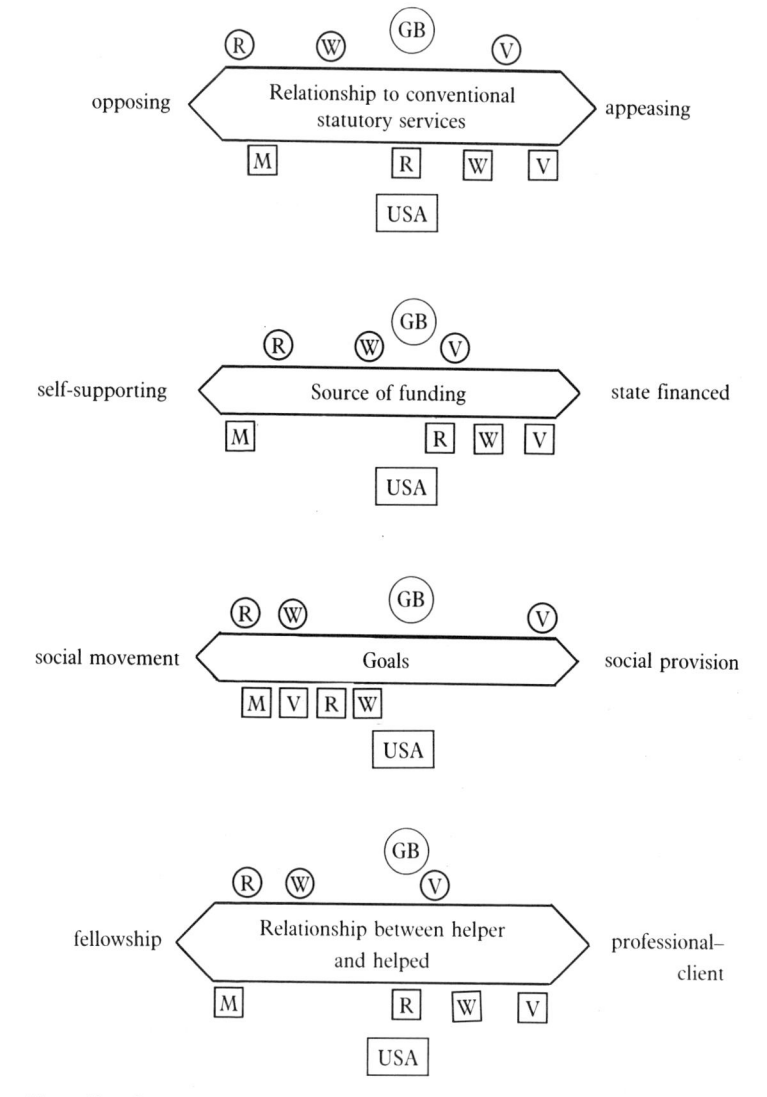

Key: R – Rape Crisis Centre
W – Women's Refuges
V – Victims support schemes or equivalent
M – MADD

*Figure 7.1* Classification of voluntary-sector provision: Britain and the United States compared

are more likely to be agency-based, and especially more likely to be located in police agencies.

There are some advantages in this for the victim. Services are, for example, likely to be better funded, and are more likely to engage co-operation from crucial figures, notably the police as gatekeepers. Nevertheless, as we have illustrated, problems of referral practices have not been eliminated.

However, the result of these developments is that the victims movement is much more closely identified politically, and is more readily seen as an extension of police services. While this latter point has much to commend it, especially where the police in Britain have been criticized for not prioritizing victim issues (Shapland 1984), it does of course create problems where victims who are suspicious of the police may be reluctant to utilize services.

We shall return to this issue in the final chapter. Here, though, we have provided an additional dimension to consideration of victims support schemes in Britain by drawing comparisons with the United States, where services are less committed to the voluntary ideal. In the next section we shall focus on our own detailed study of victims support schemes in the South West of England, where, as we shall stress, voluntarism is prioritized. Then, in the context of these rather different examples, we shall discuss possible future policy directions.

# PART IV

*Victims support schemes in the South West*

# 8 Victims services in a rural area

## The emergence of victims support in the South West

The South West of England, defined here as the two counties of Devon and Cornwall, is largely rural. Plymouth, the largest city, with a population of some 250,000, is the exception, with its main industries centred around the Naval Dockyards. It is some three times the size of the administrative centre for Devon, Exeter. Although the Tamar Valley, which links the counties of Devon and Cornwall, was previously a patchwork of rural mining communities, and small industries are scattered through the South West, tourism is the most important local industry. Victims support schemes may thus be seen as more typical of rural than of many urban schemes. The South West, as a whole, has a below-average recorded crime rate (although Plymouth is not atypical of similarly sized cities) and, as we have already noted, the South West has been defined elsewhere as a traditionally good recruiting ground for volunteers. Nevertheless, rural areas should not automatically be assumed problem free. For example, of the seventeen travel-to-work areas in England with unemployment rates of more than 20 per cent in mid-1986, no less than seven are in Devon or Cornwall.[1]

That said, the early development of victims services in the region owed much to the proximity of Bristol, the model there being readily transferable, especially to the local probation services. The first scheme in Devon emerged in Exeter, a relatively small cathedral city identified by the Wolfenden Committee as good volunteer country (Wolfenden 1978). More important at this initial stage was the commitment provided by local agencies. The probation service was especially enthusiastic, with the Assistant Chief Probation Officer, John Harding, already committed to community developments within the criminal justice system and later to spearhead reparation initiatives (Harding 1978, 1982). It was supported by the local churches and an already-established Christian voluntary body involved in welfare projects, the Council for Christian Care.[2]

By 1978, schemes were also operating in Plymouth, Barnstaple (a small market town to the north-east of the region), and Torbay, a holiday resort and popular middle-class retirement centre. In each of these schemes the probation service played an initiating role and the

138  *Crime Victims*

police provided full co-operation. In Barnstaple and Plymouth, as in Exeter, the Council for Christian Care was an additional stimulus. In Plymouth, the Guild of Community Service, a volunteer bureau, provided further impetus and a base for the scheme. By 1980, schemes were also operating in Crediton and Teignbridge, and the first scheme in Cornwall opened in Camborne and Redruth. The initial impetus of schemes in the South West has been maintained, with by mid-1986 nineteen schemes operational in the region. As *Figure 8.1* illustrates, there are nine schemes in Devon (Crediton; Exeter; Exmouth; North Devon; Plymouth; Tavistock; Teignbridge; Tiverton; and Torbay), and ten in Cornwall (Bodmin, Wadebridge, and Padstow Area; Camborne and Redruth; Helston and District; Liskeard Area; Newquay; North Cornwall; Penwith; South-East Cornwall; St Austell; and Truro District). In addition, there are plans at the time of writing to complete services to all parts of the two counties by initiating schemes in, first, Falmouth and then the South Hams districts. When these start operating, all parts of the South West will be covered except for the eastern extremity.

However, the research focus of this and the following three chapters is on twelve of these schemes. At the time the study began, fourteen were operating in all, but two schemes were reluctant to

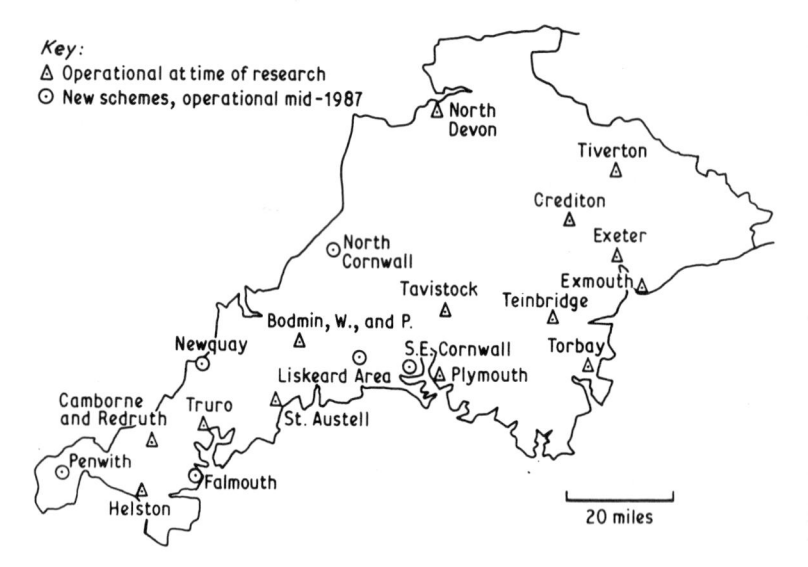

*Figure 8.1* Victims support schemes in the South West

participate fully in the project, although one of these did subsequently agree to allow us to attend meetings and provided information on the service offered. Before going on to describe the research in more detail, it is perhaps worth pausing to note the main features in the schemes which differ from the overall national picture.

First, given the low crime rate for the South West, and the relatively large numbers of schemes in the area, the number of referrals per scheme is relatively low, as *Figure 8.2* displays for twelve of the fourteen schemes. While it is not surprising that two cities, Exeter and Truro, should receive more referrals than most other schemes, that Plymouth (approximately three times the size of Exeter, and fifteen times that of Truro) should receive so few is worthy of additional comment here.

At the time of the research, Plymouth VSS was facing something of a crisis. It was unable to find a co-ordinator, and responsibility fell upon the local Guild of Community Service. This arrangement suited neither party. The representative from the Guild was too busy to dedicate time to co-ordinating responsibilities, and consequently the scheme suffered. The volunteers did not hold meetings, and in any event there were so few volunteers that they were frequently unable to fulfil police calls for assistance, despite a selective referral policy.

Plymouth, however, was not alone in relying on selective referral. Indeed, there was considerable confusion in Devon and Cornwall over different referral policies. One scheme, for example, claimed it worked on automatic referral on the grounds that the police automatically contacted them when they considered a case was worthy of VSS attention. Nevertheless, it was common for the co-ordinator to contact the police daily to receive referrals. It was simply that in Truro and Exeter it was agreed that *all* cases would be referred, and as national (Maguire and Corbett 1986) and local (North Tyneside and Blyth Valley VSS 1984) evidence suggests, the result is a dramatically greater rate of referrals. We shall, however, return to the issue of referrals and police involvement in the following chapter.

Given the lower crime rate coupled with the selective referral policy, it is perhaps not surprising to find that, generally speaking, schemes involved rather fewer volunteers than nationally. Again, Plymouth is striking, especially since four of the seven volunteers had only joined a month before the data were collected and therefore had not received any referrals, a further reflection of the

140　*Crime Victims*

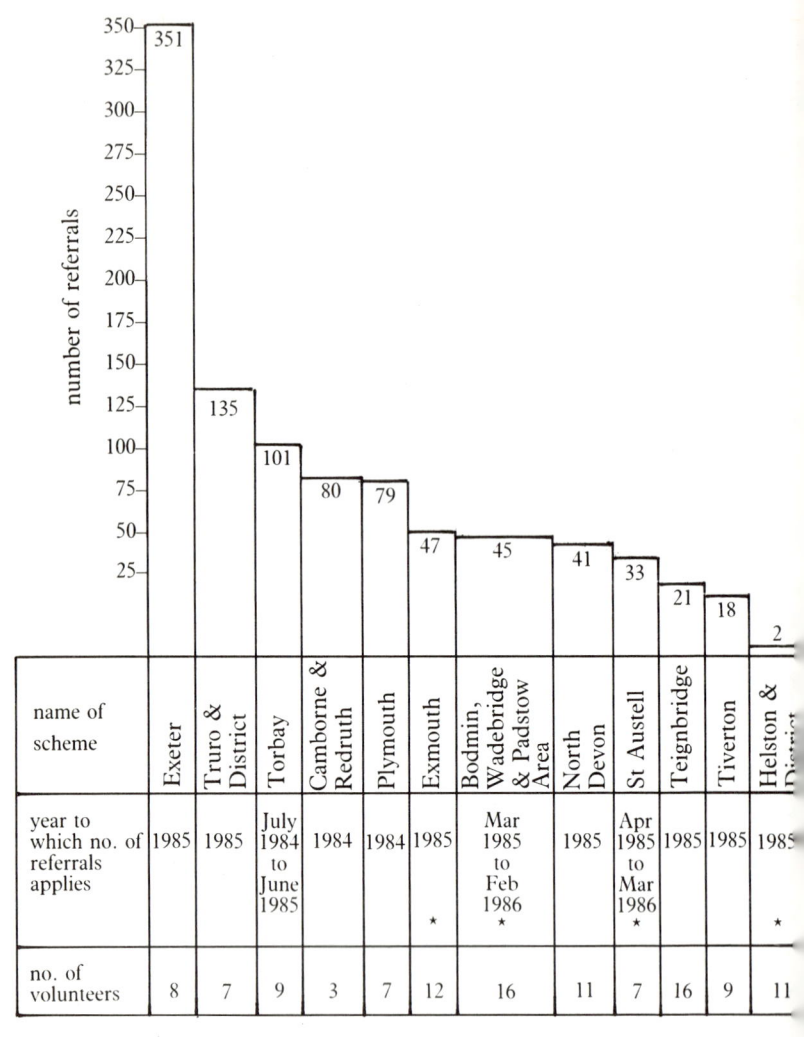

| name of scheme | Exeter | Truro & District | Torbay | Camborne & Redruth | Plymouth | Exmouth | Bodmin, Wadebridge & Padstow Area | North Devon | St Austell | Teignbridge | Tiverton | Helston & District |
|---|---|---|---|---|---|---|---|---|---|---|---|---|
| number of referrals | 351 | 135 | 101 | 80 | 79 | 47 | 45 | 41 | 33 | 21 | 18 | 2 |
| year to which no. of referrals applies | 1985 | 1985 | July 1984 to June 1985 | 1984 | 1984 | 1985* | Mar 1985 to Feb 1986* | 1985 | Apr 1985 to Mar 1986* | 1985 | 1985 | 1985* |
| no. of volunteers | 8 | 7 | 9 | 3 | 7 | 12 | 16 | 11 | 7 | 16 | 9 | 11 |

*Note:*
*Schemes in the first year of operation when referrals are likely to be lower.

*Figure 8.2* Number of referrals per scheme for stated year, and number volunteers per scheme in 1985

disorientated position, which, at the time of writing, is under review. The scheme appears to have entered a spiral where low rates of referral lead to low volunteer morale, leading to fewer volunteers less able to respond should referrals be increased.

*Victims services in a rural area* 141

Other schemes were distinct, however, for their high number of volunteers per referral. Bodmin, Wadebridge and Padstow Area VSS, Helston District and also North Devon have large (rural) areas to service and therefore involved more volunteers in order to have at least one within easy access of each part of their catchment areas. Teignbridge VSS, on the other hand, felt that it needed a large force of volunteers in order to cover emergencies should they arise. In any event, what is important to emphasize is that the geography of Devon and Cornwall results in the need for schemes to service large areas, which in many cases dictates the need for high numbers of volunteers.

There is one other characteristic of schemes in the South West which requires emphasis here, that is the question of autonomy. Nationally, the NAVSS has attempted to provide leadership, improve standards and encourage uniformity. Yet schemes in the South West are highly sceptical of the need for affiliation. Despite the fact that all but one scheme were affiliated (or anticipated being affiliated) to the NAVSS, many expressed reservations about the benefits of this. Indeed, the continued affiliation of some owed much to their healthy financial position (unlike other parts of the country; see Maguire and Corbett 1986). As a result they could afford to reaffiliate, but added that should their financial status change, then affiliation would be seriously questioned. This ambivalence towards affiliation was reflected in a strong feeling registered at the 1984 regional conference against any attempts to restrict the activities of unaffiliated schemes.

Part of the scepticism about some schemes related to the perceived advantages of affiliation to a national organization in what was generally considered a local service. We have already stressed that the NAVSS has always encouraged schemes to see themselves as accountable locally, through wide community representation on the management committee. The irony here is that such was the strength of commitment to the local community that some felt sceptical towards any other allegiances. For the same reasons, the idea of a county scheme (involving the amalgamation of all local schemes) was treated with hostility when the idea was floated at the 1985 regional conference.

In fact, there was considerable scepticism about any regional co-ordination. Regional meetings were not held twice annually as NAVSS guidelines suggest, because of lack of commitment from individual schemes. True, where they were held, meetings were well attended, with most sending their co-ordinator, and possibly their chairmen and a police (or other) representative. But most viewed the meetings as fact-gathering exercises and sought no personal involvement beyond this. There was certainly a reluctance to stand for regional office. So, too, were schemes hesitant to contribute to the expenses of the regional chairperson. Indeed, at one regional meeting the details of the regional chairperson's expenses were outlined in the context of applying for central government aid. However, not only was central government assistance rejected out of hand, but a levy of £5 per scheme to help defray the expenses had not been received from *any* scheme six months after it had been agreed. It was quite clear that many schemes expressed a jaundiced view of any level of bureaucracy beyond the individual scheme.

Regional meetings did, however, provide an opportunity for schemes to exchange experiences and become aware of similar problems (e.g. the low rate of referrals). They were able to learn of one another's fund-raising experiences, and of the latest developments within the victims movement. This was considered a strong reason for remaining affiliated to the NAVSS, as one representative to a regional meeting argued: 'Despite my reservations about National, I think it would be a mistake not to reaffiliate, because we need to tap into the mainstream of activity. We don't know everything down here, and we do need to know some things otherwise we become insular.' Nevertheless, there was a prevalent belief that the NAVSS needed them more than they needed it. As one representative contended at its regional meeting when the merits of the NAVSS were being debated, 'You are talking about this as if it were them and us, it is not. We are part of them, our representatives go up there. They should be our servants.'

This discussion has been introduced as a note of caution against generalizations being drawn from our research. As we illustrated in Chapter 6, while it is possible to draw a picture of the 'average' scheme, in terms of organization, the reality is that there are enormous differences both within and between regions. However, in developing our research we have aimed to provide a framework whereby, even where our findings are specific to certain types of schemes, the questions are more universally pertinent.

Having described, albeit briefly, some of the distinct characteristics of schemes in the South West, we wish now to move on to describe in more detail the workings of individual schemes.

## The research

The local research developed as part of a much larger project on which one of us (M.L. Gill) was employed as a full-time researcher for three years (1983–6). The research as a whole sought to provide a comparative analysis of the use of volunteers within different areas of the criminal justice system, most especially focusing on the police (special constables), the probation service (voluntary associates) and victims support schemes. Essentially, we were concerned with two aspects. First, we were interested in the *organization* of voluntary work, most especially in the context of volunteers used by different statutory agencies and a voluntary agency. Second, we were drawn to consider the pool of potential volunteers and assess how far those volunteering for these rather different aspects of the criminal justice system were similar to, or different from, one another, in terms of their social characteristics, motives, and wider ideological perspectives, for example. Within this context, then, while it would be rash to argue that the average volunteer in victims support schemes in *Britain* has typical characteristics, it is useful to be able to compare volunteers within the region and point out that specific types of people have been drawn to work in victims support, differing in significant ways from those attracted to voluntary work with the police or with probation.

In the context of victims support, then, the research focused in particular on two aspects of services: the organization of victims support schemes and the volunteers themselves. It thus complements and is complemented by the research of Maguire and Corbett (1986), which emphasizes the services provided to specific victims.

Five research approaches were utilized in fulfilling these objectives. First, informal discussions and observations were adopted to gain familiarity with the schemes and general impressions of the issues involved in the everyday running of the schemes. One of us (M.L. Gill) thus visited each co-ordinator and sat in on management and volunteer meetings for each of the schemes, including some of the initial meetings of schemes founded during the research period. Regional meetings were also attended, in order to obtain comprehensive insight into the workings of victims services in the South West.

Second, we gained permission from twelve schemes to code data on all volunteers registered with each scheme, in all 107 individuals, using this to compare the basic characteristics of volunteers working in victims support with those in probation (n=219) and a sample of police special constables (n=250). Third, using the records as a sampling frame, a random sample of volunteers was drawn, ensuring that representatives of each scheme were included. All but four agreed to be interviewed, and extensive interviews were conducted with fifty-five volunteers, providing details of the volunteers and their role in and perceptions of victims services, and allowing comparisons with similarly sized samples of probation and police volunteers.

Fourth, we selected a random sample of police officers in the police authority and conducted a postal questionnaire aimed at discovering their attitudes and perceptions of victims' needs and victims services, as well as their views on volunteers in their own organization. Replies were received from 179 officers, a response rate of 65 per cent. Finally, we constructed a similar questionnaire, which was sent to all probation officers working for the probation service in Devon and Cornwall, receiving replies from seventy-one (49 per cent).

Clearly, the themes covered in the different research exercises overlap considerably. Thus, in the following sections we shall set the scene by discussing the organization, management, and operation of victims services, principally using data from informal discussions, observations, and interviews with volunteers. Then, in Chapter 9 we shall concentrate on the police and victims services, using observational material, interview data, and the results of the postal questionnaire to the police. Similarly, in Chapter 10 we concentrate on the relationship between the probation service and victims support schemes, using observational methods, interviews, and the probation postal questionnaire. In Chapter 11 we shall focus in more detail on the volunteers themselves, based on findings from the scheme records, interviews, and observational material.

Before that, however, we shall concentrate on the internal organization of the schemes in terms of their management and volunteer committees, where similarities with schemes elsewhere are perhaps most evident.

## Management and volunteer meetings

We have already noted the importance placed within victims support on the management committee as a panel of experts; in this, schemes in the South West were no exceptions. Some schemes had two or more police representatives, and every scheme had one probation officer (with social-services departments less frequently represented). In many instances a secretary from a local agency was recruited for administrative duties, a solicitor for legal advice, and a bank manager or accountant as treasurer. A variety of voluntary bodies were represented, reflecting local interests and arrangements, but for the most part the people involved and organizations represented remained constant.

The frequency of meetings varied, both between schemes and over time. In the early stages meetings were held monthly, on average, allowing the opportunity to solve teething troubles and consolidate the organization. The more established schemes met less frequently, often quarterly, although in at least two cases an annual meeting was deemed sufficient. If any problems should arise during the year, they were dealt with by the co-ordinator or chairperson.

Meetings were often held in the police station or, if not, in the probation offices, reflecting the local influence of these two groups. Discussion at these meetings focused on the general administration of the scheme, but issues such as referral policy and fund-raising initiatives featured prominently. The management committee always contained the co-ordinator, who usually acted as the volunteers' representative, although sometimes volunteers were seconded in addition to the co-ordinator. It was usual practice for the co-ordinator to advise the committee of the number and types of referrals received, but these were only rarely discussed in any depth. In the main this was left to volunteer meetings, which in all but one small scheme were held separately.

It should be emphasized that where volunteer meetings were held, they were popular, and in the minority of schemes where no meetings took place, this caused dissatisfaction. Meetings were always chaired by the co-ordinator and were almost exclusively concerned with a discussion of individual cases and any related problems. Attendance was high; indeed, 87 per cent of volunteers who were interviewed said they always or usually attended. The popularity appeared to be related not only to the opportunity to discuss their work but also to the advantages of being able to socialize with a peer group, raising morale.[3] Of course, where meetings were not held, volunteers lacked these two components, and the discontent at this was reflected in answers to a question asking them to state how their scheme could be improved; for example:

'More contact between volunteers, like a talk to discuss cases.'

(I 42)

> 'I would like to meet my fellow volunteers socially. They are not my type but I would like to get to know them better.' (I 36)

Others indicated they would like to meet the management committee as well:

> 'Possibly if we come together with the management committee a little more.' (I 06)

The contact between management committee and volunteers varied considerably. In one scheme they were indistinguishable. The vice-chairman was a volunteer, but the co-ordinator did not visit victims, and all meetings were attended by 'volunteers' and 'management' where discussion ranged across a variety of issues. The role of the co-ordinators varied perhaps more than any other. Sometimes they were ostensibly volunteers who acted as committee members. Alternatively, they could be management committee representatives only, and therefore not visit volunteers. In either case there was little doubt, as Maguire and Corbett (1986) have observed, that they were the most important members of the schemes, tending in practice to be involved in all the decisions.

Finally, it is important to note that volunteer meetings were also used, on occasions, as a forum for outside speakers, part of a training exercise. Nevertheless, in line with NAVSS policy, separate induction training was provided for all new volunteer recruits.

## Training

Since Aves (1969) it has been widely accepted that all volunteers would benefit from a training programme to enable them, amongst other things, to pursue their voluntary work more confidently and proficiently and thus create a favourable impression amongst professionals. Given the position of victims services *vis-à-vis* other agencies, the role of training gains further prominence, and the new training manual (NAVSS 1986b) emphasizes the need for sessions on the needs of victims, counselling skills, financial rights, the role of the police, and the role of other agencies. It is a condition of affiliation to the NAVSS that all member schemes run a programme to prepare volunteers adequately, and similar importance was placed on training locally when the regional chairman withheld her signature from the affiliation form of a new scheme on the basis that its volunteers had received insufficient preparation.

In our interviews we included questions on the training programme, although it should be emphasized that this preceded the publication of the new training manual. As Maguire and Corbett (1986) found, there were considerable variations in programmes; in our sample they tended to last between four and ten weeks, although normally six weeks. However, volunteers here were more enthusiastic than Maguire's and Corbett's sample about the training they received (Maguire and Corbett 1986). For example:

> 'It gave me a good instruction and background.' (I 18)

> 'It was fairly comprehensive. It was fairly good actually.' (I 28)

> 'It was very comprehensive even down to role play.' (I 30)

Indeed, few were able to cite instances where the training they had received was unnecessary, and even those who could, isolated individual lectures or lecturers rather than courses.

The principal advantage of training, it was claimed, was that it provided the necessary knowledge and skills to undertake their voluntary duties, but in addition it increased self-confidence. Some argued that the dangers of not receiving training were severe. For example:

> 'There are quite a few occasions when it would be possible to do more damage than has already been done.' (I 20)

> 'Because it is quite easy to give someone incorrect information. Also, depending on the type of crime, you could do more damage than good.' (I 48)

There is, finally, one other principal advantage in training – the opportunity for socializing. As one volunteer noted in casual conversation with the researchers, 'It established camaraderie between all the members'. It will be recalled that this was also a benefit derived from volunteer meetings, helping to build up a sense of mission and purpose among the volunteers, a topic which will be discussed further in Chapter 11.

However, recently the NAVSS has recognized the need to build upon initial training through follow-up courses. Within the research area, additional training was undertaken in a number of ways. First, via volunteer meetings, where instead of, or in addition to, discussing cases, volunteers also received a lecture on some topic of relevance. Second, experienced volunteers were invited and sometimes encouraged to attend courses for new recruits as refreshers. Of course, this would mainly be going over ground already covered, but many volunteers noted that they found this useful. Third, there were attempts to organize regional training days, the most recent of which, on rape, was universally acclaimed a success. Via these methods volunteers were able to acquire more knowledge and skills but also to improve on those they already had, aiding their abilities to help victims, a subject to which we now turn.

## Helping victims

The object of this section is to discuss the service offered by victims support schemes. The data were derived from our volunteer sample. Since many schemes were relatively new, coupled with the low number of referrals received, it is perhaps not surprising to find that 15 per cent of volunteers had not yet visited a victim. Nevertheless, at the other extreme 15 per cent of the sample had attended over forty, and some of these considerably more.

We have already noted that victims support schemes originated from the idea of providing immediate or short-term crisis service to victims of crime. However, until recently there has been remarkably little research on the type of work they do. In our research we were concerned with testing how 'immediate' was the service offered and, second, what type of crisis help was offered.

Volunteers were asked how soon they left home after receiving a call to visit a victim. The results revealed a tendency to respond as soon as possible: 40 per cent stated they would leave within an hour and 87 per cent said they would leave the visit no longer than two hours. Indeed, co-ordinators commented that in an emergency they would ensure that they would select a volunteer who could attend immediately. Nevertheless, there was little other attempt to match qualities of volunteers with the perceived needs of victims, except that in some cases, particularly involving female victims, clients were sent a volunteer of the same sex. However, for the most part the service was immediate, and always was where a case was known to be urgent.

Although the initial visit was speedy, it was frequently only the first of a number of visits. It has been stressed that victims support schemes offer short-term assistance, and there is no assumption that revisits would normally be necessary. Nevertheless, over three-quarters of all volunteers had made second visits, and a few more than this. Some volunteers left a support card with the name and telephone number of the scheme so that they could be contacted if necessary. Moreover, some volunteers, against the recommendation of most schemes, left their personal telephone number so that a worried victim could make contact more easily.

For the most part, though, it was left to the volunteer to take the initiative in calling back, either to ensure that other agencies had fulfilled their obligations, or to report back on enquiries made on behalf of the victim, for example over insurance, the housing department, or the electricity board. In other cases, a call back seemed to be primarily for the volunteer's own 'peace of mind', particularly the case with victims considered vulnerable. For example:

> 'Further needs, like when someone had glasses smashed after a mugging and I went and found out details for him to get more, but I never visit more than twice.' (I 27)

> 'I wanted to make sure a girl had got her cheque.' (I 34)

> 'I had an old lady in her eighties who was upset and I wanted to make sure she was coping. I live alone myself and know that things get much harder when living alone.' (I 06)

> 'With somebody who has been shaken up you like to check back a little later. I had one on the go for several months for my own peace of mind. You do this occasionally.' (I 05)

There were also instances where victims were supported over long time periods. In one instance a volunteer met a rape victim soon after the incident and continued with the case until the court proceedings were completed. However, there were very few examples of referring victims on to other agencies for long-term and professional guidance; indeed, it was argued by one volunteer that the victim with whom he was working was keen to distance himself from statutory authority, preferring voluntary assistance.

Overall, then, it appears that volunteers tended to respond more speedily, and revisit more frequently than in other schemes outside the South West (Maguire and Corbett 1986). However, it is also true that unlike busy schemes, most schemes in the South West visited all victims referred. Letters or telephone calls were not very common. The fact of the matter is that there were many willing and underworked volunteers. Schemes did not face financial problems and so were able to pay expenses (where these were claimed), and so most victims received a personal visit from a volunteer.

It was largely because of this that schemes were enthusiastic about accepting non-crime referrals. As we have already noted, nationally this issue has received considerable debate. However, in the South West the opinion of volunteers was quite conclusive, with 91 per cent believing that it was simply another method of supporting people in a crisis. For example:

> 'If there is nobody else, why not? Suffering is suffering whatever the cause.' (I 14)

> 'They are victims of something which is not their own fault, with no agency to help them. Also there are not many victims of crime in this area. We can afford to help them.' (I 19)

> 'It is just support in a crisis.' (I 49)

Nevertheless, a small minority were concerned that the movement was in danger of losing its purpose. For example:

> 'If it went, well, into that it could snowball into other things. We need another little scheme to cope with that.' (I 40)

> 'My own personal view is that I volunteered to help victims of crime, and hardship and distress covers everybody.' (I 36)

Such was the enthusiasm of two schemes to provide this type of help that they offered a similar service to the fire service. Each day the co-ordinator would contact the fire station as well as the police and referrals would be followed up.

However, in some schemes the victims support service went beyond work with victims to work with the offender. For example, at one management meeting a police inspector was being questioned about the low number of referrals and proposed the idea of extending their work: 'I had four or five women in a row, all poor old dears hauled in for shoplifting, all were alone, all had no pets or relatives. In my book they were all victims who wanted support. Do you regard these as within your ambit?' The scheme did consider this to be within their scope and by the end of the year had received three such cases. Similarly, another volunteer in a different scheme explained in the course of conversation how they had been included in helping the offender: 'We did try to help the elderly people in their eighties who stole things. They needed help, victims of society I think. I did about three cases and it was most rewarding. But the probation service did something and we had to drop it.'

In many respects schemes attempted to define their role as it most helped the police. Thus, when one police station was being troubled by a lack of observers while juveniles were being interviewed, the local victims support scheme, in the absence of anyone else, agreed to fulfil this function.

Nevertheless, there was a limit to the range of services they felt happy to offer. For example, while volunteers were in favour of the introduction of reparation as a sentence, when asked whether victims support schemes could play any part in this, 63 per cent answered in the negative. Whereas those in favour of scheme participation outlined a role as assistant to the victim, one of the principal objections was becoming too involved in the criminal justice system.

Given the variety of 'victims' that victims support schemes did offer succour to, it seemed relevant to ascertain which categories of victims volunteers considered most in need of their help. The majority mentioned the elderly and those living alone, and nearly half the sample were also able to cite those who would not require victims services; for example, those with kinship support, the young, or corporate rather than individual victims. Notably, though, while 69 per cent of those who had done four or less visits were able to identify such groups, only 36 per cent of those who had visited more than four victims were able to do the same ($x^2 = 20.7$, $p<0.01$). So, just as Reeves (1984) has contended that the needs of victims cannot be realized by knowledge of either the crime or the victims' characteristics, so too did the more experienced volunteers. For example:

'You never know until you get there. It depends on the person.'
(I 07)

'Whatever the crime there could be people who value some support.'
(I 21)

'It is a matter of personal make-up. It is difficult to say in the sense of groups.'
(I 44)

Nevertheless, in line with national data, the most common crime covered was burglary, and the most common service was 'counselling'. When volunteers were asked what type of work they did with the victim, the majority stated 'listening' or 'talking'. For example:

> 'Listening ear, most of the time, just let them tell you what has happened.' (I 05)
>
> 'Listen. Sometimes when in shock you have to talk. Usually you just listen once they get rid of their frustration.' (I 43)
>
> 'Firstly, I get them to tell me if they are very distressed. I try to get them to make me a cup of tea to get them doing something, and make a point of not knowing anything. Let them talk, tell them it's confidential, and it works.' (I 39)
>
> 'Usually let them talk. Oh God it is tiring. I am a chatterbox as you gather, but listening to someone else is tiring. Really I like to know someone cares, which is corny, but it is true. Oh how cliché!' (I 11)

Nevertheless, in recognizing that victims were in need of company, of having someone to talk to about 'their' crime, volunteers also noted that on occasions they were called on to offer advice or practical help. As some recalled:

> 'It depends; if a meter break-in, you advise DHSS. Normally advice as much as anything.' (I 41)
>
> 'Normally, try to console them and understand their problems. You can help them tidy up, block windows, mend locks. Once I have had to rehouse a lady, but then the cantankerous old bitch wouldn't let go. This was the vicar's words, not mine!' (I 54)

These findings were confirmed when volunteers were asked what they considered to be the purpose of victims support. They stressed assistance to victims via counselling, advice, and practical help. So in addition to taking a wide range of 'types' of victims, volunteers were involved in offering many different types of assistance. Mostly, this was short-term aid, but occasionally it extended beyond this to long-term help, with a tendency *not* to refer to other agencies. What also needs to be stressed here is that the volunteers perceived victims to be very favourably disposed towards their offer of help. Even those victims who required no assistance were apparently happy to know that someone had cared and that such an organization existed, a point which supports British Crime Survey data from victims in general.

## Summary

In this chapter we have set the scene for further discussion of our research, by describing the development of victims services in the South West and our research strategies. We then went on to describe the management and organization of schemes, including training, and the work actually done by volunteers. While in this latter respect crime referrals are below the national average, leading to the extension of help to 'victims of circumstance' (including some offenders where defined as 'deserving'), in most respects this picture is not dissimilar to that found in schemes across the country, and indeed our findings parallel those of Maguire and Corbett (1986), particularly with respect to the services provided for victims.

In other respects, despite the NAVSS blueprint (Reeves 1984) and the opportunity which is often taken to portray the 'average' scheme, the 'typical' scheme is elusive. We would not wish to argue that the schemes in this research are anything more than individual case examples of victims services. However, the issues which we shall raise in subsequent chapters *are* of wider relevance, and we shall use the opportunity to compare our findings with others where this is possible and appropriate.

# 9 Victims support schemes and the police

As has already been noted, the probation service and NACRO provided initial encouragement to the development of the Bristol scheme. However, as the scheme developed, the role of the police became more prominent (Gay, Holton, and Thomas 1975). The appointment of a police liaison officer, at chief superintendent level, not only enhanced working relationships between police and volunteers but also allowed the police to be involved in the vetting of all volunteers and 'to make policy decisions in cases of doubt about the types of victims referred' (Rankin 1977: 4). One notable benefit of such close co-operation was that initial police scepticism was replaced by commitment, to both the principles of the scheme and the use of volunteers.

Police scepticism is not surprising. Even writers identified with police perspectives on policy issues have noted the reluctance of the police to co-operate with outside agencies, and especially those outsiders identified as 'do-gooders' (Moore and Brown 1981). However, while such scepticism may remain among many front-line officers (as we shall illustrate), equally clearly senior police officers built up mutually supportive relationships with the emerging victims movement. For example, the second annual report of the NAVSS noted the dependence of schemes upon police co-operation *and* (based on a survey of the first seventy schemes) the commitment of the police to both victims and schemes:

> First at the scene of the crime, the Police have always been deeply concerned with the well-being of victims and in an increasing number of areas they have welcomed the opportunity to share this vital work with other members of the community. The Schemes depend upon good communication with local police representatives for experienced advice and of course for referrals. It is encouraging therefore that in the 1981 Survey, relationships with the police were consistently described as 'good' or 'excellent', reflecting close local co-operation throughout the country.
> (NAVSS 1982: 9)

The police perspective was further developed in an address by Sir

Kenneth Newman, published in the following annual report. Newman noted the coherence between the goals of victims support and his plans for policing London, with the onus for crime prevention being community based and the spin-offs from inter-agency co-operation. Moreover, while recognizing that crime victims expected sympathy, understanding, and support, he argued that heavy workloads prevented the police from spending sufficient time with victims. Victims support thus enabled the police to improve their image: 'Community support for victims can therefore help to dispel the notion that authority is indifferent and indirectly improve the public's perception of the quality of Police response' (NAVSS 1983: 24).

The role of the schemes in providing reassurance is developed in the evidence of the Metropolitan Police to the House of Commons Home Affairs Committee (1984), and the Metropolitan Police also supported the NAVSS in arguing for full-time, permanent co-ordinator posts. The evidence of the Association of Chief Police Officers was equally supportive of the expansion of the victims support movement.

Formally, the close involvement of the police is recognized on management committees. The NAVSS requires affiliated schemes to include at least one police representative on their committees, and our national review of scheme records indicates that most schemes included at least two police representatives. Moreover, locally it is clear that some schemes had more police representatives than this and that non-affiliated schemes also involved police representatives on their committees.

Police commitment to victims support schemes in the South West of England might have been anticipated, given the official doctrine of community policing, with its emphasis on the involvement of the police in the community (Alderson 1979; Gill and Thrasher 1985; Moore and Brown 1981). Although the first schemes in the South West were not police inspired, police commitment became a central organizational feature of schemes as they emerged. Many schemes held meetings in police stations; the police were regular and active participants on management committees; and, as senior police officers were transferred from one area to another, they often initiated the development of new schemes or were able to add their experience to embryonic schemes. There is a double irony in this. First, it is clear that the involvement of senior police officers at management level developed to such an extent that it has since been subject to restraint. Second, it was frequently out of step with police co-operation at ground level, reflected in referral practices.

At management level, the former chief constable of Devon and Cornwall, John Alderson, encouraged the police to adopt positions of responsibility in the schemes. Some schemes in fact decided within themselves that having police in management positions would be counter-productive, since it would blur the distinction between the scheme and the police and undermine independence. Nevertheless, other schemes involved the police as chairpersons, or former police as co-ordinators, and this drift towards police influence in the schemes was accentuated by the fact that in most cases the more senior local police served on committees – usually a subdivisional commander, chief inspector or superintendent. Moreover, these members were regular attenders at meetings, and on the rare occasions when unable to attend, would ensure a police presence by delegating responsibility to an inspector or sergeant. Overall the police appeared to play a more central role on the committee than is the case in other areas (Maguire and Corbett 1986). Finally, it is evident from participation in management committee meetings that the police were accredited status as the 'crime experts'. They acted as advisers and encouragers, and the importance of police advice was one of the prime reasons why volunteers were so keen to involve them on committees.

Such direct involvement was not without its costs, particularly in time. As one chief superintendent noted at a regional meeting, 'The squeeze is on in the police force and many of us will not have the time to spend with volunteers and the VSS.' The warning was translated into policy under a new chief constable following the creation, in 1984, of a new Department of Community Development, responsible for force liaison with, amongst other things, victims support schemes. A policy directive from the chief constable stressed, according to the superintendent responsible for the department, that it was 'important that the police do not get too involved in the running of the scheme' and reflected the feeling that 'we don't want police officers tied up in helping victims, they have not got the time'.

The directive specified that while the police should assist in the running of schemes, they should not become overinvolved through accepting offices of responsibility. This led one scheme to write to the chief constable to complain that their choice of chairperson was based on the person's suitability for the post, the fact that the person was a police officer being incidental.

The second irony in the enthusiastic involvement of senior police officers in the management of victims support schemes derives from the contrast between this and the referral practices of reporting officers. The issue of referrals is a crucial one, nationally in Britain (Maguire and Corbett 1986) and perhaps especially in the South West, and it is one which will feature centrally in this chapter. At this stage, however, it is worth reminding ourselves that referrals of cases by the police to victims support schemes in the South West have been relatively low, and in the case of some schemes this has fed a sense of pessimism and cynicism about the viability of victims support without total police commitment. As a result, one of the key functions performed by senior police representatives in management committees was to reassure other members of the commitment of the police to the work of victims support. They were needed to reassure the committees, where necessary, that disappointing levels of referral were not indicative of police hostility or lack of confidence in the schemes, but a more practical problem of convincing individual officers of the schemes' existence and value. Just what the views of individual officers were is the focus of much of this chapter. Before concentrating on the police perspective, however, we shall consider VSS–police relationships from the other camp, that is in terms of the views held about the police by co-ordinators and volunteers.

## Volunteers' perceptions of the police

Details of the fifty-five volunteers interviewed as part of the research are contained elsewhere. Here it is appropriate to consider those sections of the questionnaire which pertain to the police.

The questions of relevance fall under three headings. First, we can consider a series of questions aimed at ascertaining volunteers' general perceptions of the police. Second, we can review volunteers' views of the role of the police on management committees. Finally we can focus on co-ordinators' and volunteers' attitudes towards the ongoing involvement of the police in referring cases to the schemes.

Taking first the general perceptions held by volunteers, we included at the end of the interview a series of statements on police, offenders, and the crime problem, and asked our sample to state whether or not they agreed with each, and to what extent. The statements were a modification of those included in an earlier household survey (Bottoms, Mawby, and Xanthos 1981) and have been used – among other things – to illustrate variations in attitudes

158   *Crime Victims*

Table 9.1 *VSS volunteers' responses, as percentages, to individual items on police scale (n=55)*

|  | agree strongly | a little | mixed neither | don't know | disagree a little | strongly |
|---|---|---|---|---|---|---|
| The majority of police in Devon and Cornwall do a good job. | 78 | 13 | 2 | 7 | 0 | 0 |
| The police are not interested in serving the interests of our community. | 2 | 0 | 4 | 2 | 9 | 84 |
| There are quite a lot of dishonest policemen in Devon and Cornwall. | 2 | 9 | 16 | 27 | 4 | 42 |
| There are not enough policemen in Devon and Cornwall at present. | 38 | 26 | 6 | 20 | 9 | 2 |
| People criticize the police too often. | 44 | 36 | 2 | 4 | 7 | 7 |

according to age and gender (Mawby 1983). We used them here to discover the attitudes, and indeed the wider and politically based ideological stances of volunteers, comparing volunteers in victims support schemes with probation voluntary associates and police special constables.

On each of the five statements related to the police, victims support scheme volunteers demonstrated considerable support for and approval of the police. As can be seen from *Table 9.1*, the majority strongly agreed that the local force did a good job and firmly rejected the idea that the police were not interested in serving the interests of the community. A majority also felt that more police were required and that the police were too often criticized. Scaling the five items, we find volunteers to be extremely supportive of the police (*Table 9.2*).

Table 9.2 *Mean scores on scales of victims support schemes (VSS) volunteers, police special constables (PSC), and probation voluntary associates (PVA)*

|  |  | VSS | PSC | PVA |
| --- | --- | --- | --- | --- |
| *police scale* (min. 5, max. 25) high score indicates support for police | mean: sample size: | 21.055 55 | 22.176 51 | 18.741 58 |
| *offender scale* (min. 6, max. 30) high score indicates distancing from offenders | mean: sample size: | 20.321 53 | 20.647 51 | 16.246 57 |
| *crime problem scale* (min. 5, max. 25) high score indicates concern over crime problem | mean: sample size: | 18.549 51 | 19.098 51 | 16.842 57 |

Although VSS volunteers were significantly less positive in their views on the police than were police special constables ($z=2.34$; $p<0.05$), they were far more favourably disposed than were probation voluntary associates ($z=3.80$; $p<0.01$). On the other two scales, their mean scores were similar to those of special constables and significantly different from those of probation voluntary associates in terms of both their attitudes towards offenders ($z=5.06$; $p<0.01$) and their perspectives of the crime problem ($z=2.32$; $p<0.05$). Moreover, on all three scales the mean scores of VSS volunteers were considerably closer to those of police specials than to those of probation voluntary associates. The implications of this for relations with the probation service will be developed in Chapter 10. Here, though, it is clear that, in our survey at least, VSS volunteers' perspectives of their moral universe were closely allied to a police perspective, providing the basis for mutual understanding and co-operation.

Volunteers were then asked about the involvement of the police on the committee of their own individual scheme; in particular whether they considered there to be a justification for police involvement. All but five answered in the affirmative. There were principally two reasons offered: first, that victims services are dependent upon police co-operation for referrals, and thus close liaison was deemed essential; second, that the police have the training, experience and influence to assist the volunteers in their function. Comments typical of the first view were:

> 'Without them the scheme would not work at all. You need their co-operation, their sympathy, their interest, without that it can't succeed.'
>
> (I 05)

> 'They are the ones who refer people to us.'
>
> (I 15)

> 'Without them we really wouldn't be in existence. You need to know their side of the story. How they work.'
>
> (I 16)

> 'All the referrals are from them so they need to be represented, also they need to know our views and who we are.'
>
> (I 18)

> 'Because they ought to know our function and sell us to the police, and that takes a policeman.'
>
> (I 19)

> 'Yes, then we understand each other better. Anyway they take us out for drinks.'
>
> (I 45)

Views typical of the second include:

'Most definitely, they have a unique turn of phrase and I suppose training and a lawful attitude to it.'
(I 10)

'It is useful apart from anything else to hear an official view on things and hearing a qualified view and professional.'
(I 11)

'We have found their advice and assistance of help. Also as volunteers we need to have groups about for advice, and they are here. Besides, they all have more money than anybody else.'
(I 54)

'They are the professionals who are dealing with the situation. In any event who will have to bring the offender to court?'
(I 55)

What, then, of attitudes towards the ongoing involvement of the police? The scheme member most in contact with the police is the co-ordinator. It is the co-ordinator's responsibility to liaise with the police, to accept referrals and pass them on to volunteers to visit. In some schemes the co-ordinator contacts the police daily (normally by phone but sometimes by visiting the station personally); in other schemes the arrangement is for the police to ring the co-ordinator when needed; in others the police ring the co-ordinator daily as routine. What is worthy of attention here is the co-ordinator's own impression of police co-operation.

Because victims support schemes are autonomous locally organized bodies, they tend to vary their organizational arrangements to meet their own needs. Thus in some schemes the co-ordinator was seen principally as a volunteer undertaking visits to victims in addition to co-ordinating. In other schemes the co-ordinator was viewed primarily as a committee member detached from visiting the actual victims, acting as a reference point for volunteers and police alike. Since in this study interviews were conducted with a sample of *volunteers*, it meant that only some of the co-ordinators would be interviewed. In fact, four co-ordinators (or former co-ordinators) were. All of them noted that they were known by the officer in charge of referrals at the police station. For example:

'I am now, it is very nice we have it very well taped, but I have always made the point of going to meet them. Also, if a superintendent changes, I go and see him.'

(I 07)

'We used to be on Christian name terms, but it was a telephone acquaintance, actually I never met them.'

(I 50)

'Yes, I know the officers. Certainly they know my face.'

(I 05)

Additionally, informal interviews were conducted with all other co-ordinators and also some committee members, as well as observation at many management and volunteer meetings as already discussed. From these it was clear that in many schemes the lack of police referrals was often a topic on the agenda causing considerable frustration. However, far from manifesting itself in any adverse attitude towards the police, frustration tended to strengthen the resolve of the schemes to prove to the police that they had a valuable function, and indeed, that victims merited help. As one co-ordinator noted:

> 'It is like getting blood from a stone. I keep saying do you know this or that, but they say this is all they know. When a motor-bike was stolen, a sergeant said to me, "that will be doing him a favour and save him getting killed, he doesn't need any support. Anyway it is a luxury, he does not need it!" '

This same attitude was apparent among volunteers. While in almost all other respects being pro-police, volunteers were extremely critical of the referral process. Asked an open-ended question about how they thought their own scheme could be improved, 19 per cent mentioned police reluctance to refer cases. For example:

> 'By having one or two victims! We have to get the volunteers involved. Something I am thinking of is an agent provocateur to do a burglary. Hey, how are you equipped for a rape case?'

(I 35)

> 'Better communication from the police. More willingness to refer, not the present lax attitude. We need someone at Headquarters saying, if they don't they are on a disciplinary charge. Some could not be bothered.'

(I 30)

'I don't think we can improve it until we get more work.'
(I 53)

Moreover, when asked directly whether or not the scheme was used enough, 55 per cent said not, and 29 per cent said they were unsure. Criticisms included:

'We are not used enough here, because from the local paper so much crime goes past us. Perhaps it is too petty to give to us.'
(I 54)

'Purely from our point of view we have not been used as much as we would have liked.'
(I 29)

'You quite often see something in the paper you could have helped with. Because the police force is always changing its manpower, there is no continuity.'
(I 13)

'I am sure that things are happening to which we could have been called.'
(I 02)

*Lack* of referrals was, unfortunately, only one of the referral problems identified. We asked respondents whether any of the information they received from the police was ever wrong. As many as half those who had undertaken some work said that they had received incorrect information. Most of the time volunteers complained at addresses being incorrect. For example:

'Seventy-five per cent of the time, at least one of address, age, telephone number, is wrong. Even what the police tell us is not always true. You need to be quite a detective.'
(I 45)

'Almost always how to get to the house. I have never found one house, I am sure it does not exist.'
(I 43)

'The address was wrong and I went round for three-quarters of an hour in the rain.'
(I 19)

Frequently, the circumstances of the case were false; on other occasions the time the incident occurred was incorrect. During one interview with a volunteer the phone rang. The co-ordinator had just heard from the police inspector who had returned from a week's leave to find that some important cases had not been referred to the scheme. The volunteer said:

> 'This is bloody poor, an old woman got mugged in her home. The chief inspector is ape-shit apparently. It is an administrative error and he is going to jump on them for this. A whole bloody week.'
> (I 30)

Another said:

> 'Often it is not so much wrong as incomplete, but some is wrong. I got to a suicide they said happened 48 hours previously, when I arrived it only happened 2 hours previously.' (I 48)

Sometimes other details of the case are inaccurate or incomplete:

> 'They said the offender was in custody when I was visiting the wife when he walked into the room.' (I 14)

> 'You also get called to Mrs so and so and find that Mr so and so is there to look after her.' (I 19)

Like Maguire and Corbett (1986) we found that many volunteers did not fully understand the referral process. Nevertheless, it was problematic as far as many volunteers were concerned. It is evident that the very positive attitudes held towards the police by volunteers, their approval of police involvement on committees and the explicit enthusiasm of the police active at management level does not tell the whole story. The role of officers in charge, their apparent reluctance to refer cases to schemes and the inaccuracy of information provided in some cases, cast a shadow on the efficiency and effectiveness of many schemes. In moving on to consider police perspectives, it is therefore important to consider these in the context of the referral issue.

## Relations with police at the operational level

The role of the police in early initiatives to develop victims support schemes has already been noted. Moreover, as the number of new schemes accelerated in the early 1980s, the NAVSS recognized a greater willingness among police forces to take the lead. Thus, in the 1983/4 annual report, the NAVSS attributed a large proportion of the new schemes to initiatives from just eight police authorities (NAVSS 1984: 14).

More crucial, though, as we have seen, is the role of the police once a scheme is in operation, in terms of *referral policy*. From the outset, victims support schemes limited demand by placing restrictions on the types of crimes with which they felt able to deal, or in some cases excluding self-referrals. Nevertheless, as schemes expanded, the funding and political requirements to demonstrate a level of unmet need, and the practical importance of providing enough work for volunteers, encouraged schemes to stress the number of victims who were not being referred to victims support schemes. The problem of police discretion in limiting referrals was noted in the second annual report of the NAVSS:

> 'Referral statistics from some local schemes still suggest a tendency for officers to refer only those people assumed to be most vulnerable, invariably people over retirement age and women. Evidence from outside research suggests that as many young people as old may be distressed following an offence and that anyone of us may need special information to deal with the particular and unexpected problems arising from a crime.'
> (NAVSS 1982: 9–10)

Although in following annual reports the NAVSS noted a general increase in police referrals (NAVSS 1983, 1984), the problem of depending on the police to identify need and refer victims continued to receive attention. Evidence from the second British Crime Survey (Hough and Mayhew 1985: 30–31), which demonstrated both that only a minute proportion of those who reported crime to the police were given an offer of help from a victims support scheme and that a large minority of victims felt that *all* 'victims of crime' should be contacted by schemes, was cited as evidence of the need for automatic referral – at least of victims of particular types of offence. Based on a comparison of police and victims support schemes' statistics, the NAVSS estimated that only some 19 per cent of reported burglary victims were referred, with proportions lower for other offences (NAVSS 1985: 11). Yet many of those not referred may well require help: 'Experience has shown by selecting people who are apparently vulnerable: older people, those living alone and so on, only half the people with serious needs will come to light' (NAVSS 1985: 12).

Despite these concerns, echoed in literature from the United States, and those of the volunteers interviewed in our survey, there was no evidence from other research of police decision-making *vis-à-vis* referrals. We therefore decided to attack the issue through a postal questionnaire sent to a random sample of 10 per cent of police officers in Devon and Cornwall. With regard to victims support schemes, we focused on four specific issues:

1. *Knowledge*   Did the police know about the schemes operating in their areas? Had their training included material on victims services?
2. *Attitudes towards schemes*   Did the police feel that the local scheme, and schemes in general, provided a valuable service and why?
3. *Use of schemes*   Had police officers ever referred victims to their local schemes? Who had been referred, and why some and not others? With what sorts of problems might VSS help?
4. *Perceptions of need*   Do certain sections of the community require support more than others? What needs do crime victims have?

We received replies from 179 police officers, a response rate of 65 per cent, which is relatively high for a postal questionnaire (Moser and Kalton 1979). Only 7 per cent of respondents were female, slightly less than the police authority figure of 9 per cent. Three-quarters of those who replied were working as uniformed officers in one of the six police divisions; 10 per cent were currently in traffic, 8 per cent in CID, and 3 per cent working at police headquarters. In terms of age, respondents could be divided into three roughly equal groups, with 31 per cent aged 30 or less, 37 per cent aged 31–40 and 32 per cent aged 41 or more. The majority (82 per cent) were married.

Although over two-thirds of the police were constables, and only 9 per cent above the rank of sergeant, they had amassed between them considerable police experience. Only 15 per cent had under six years' experience in the force and 48 per cent had been in the police for at least sixteen years. We therefore anticipated that our respondents would give a good indication of police relations with victims support schemes at grass-roots level.

## Police views on victims services

Most of our respondents were aware of the existence of victims support schemes. Nearly four-fifths said that a scheme was currently operating in their area, which, given the distribution of schemes in the South West at the time, was fairly accurate. Rather less, however, were able to give a precise name to their local scheme.[1]

This degree of uncertainty increased when we asked whether their local scheme provided a valuable service. A number who knew about the existence of a scheme did not feel able to give an opinion, in some cases due to their lack of direct experience, in others – understandably – where the scheme was relatively new. Nevertheless, of the 106 officers who felt able to give an opinion, a large majority (86 per cent) were favourable. For example:

> 'They can provide sympathy which sometimes is unconsciously lacking when a police officer has dealt with quite a number of crimes.'
> (POL 001)

> 'Yes, because a member of the VSS can give the sympathy/support and guidance that is required because they have the time, whereas the PC who attends has got a lot to do and not much time to do it in.'
> (POL 004)

> 'Yes, it brings the public and the police closer together. Assisting in emotional problems and financial difficulties for the victim.'
> (POL 084)

However, even here some qualified their answers. For example, some saw schemes as relevant for particular types of victim, while others felt that police reluctance to refer victims limited schemes' usefulness:

> 'Yes. For old, weak, or similar people.'
> (POL 212)

> 'Yes, but due to referral method, not many cases are provided by the police to the scheme.'
> (POL 029)

'It could, but not many referrals made to it.'

(POL 097)

These responses have, nevertheless, been coded as positive. A further *seven* were clearly negative, while *eight* replies were intermediate, including one respondent who clearly felt that volunteers needed victims more than victims needed volunteers: 'On occasions they provide valuable support, but are only rarely required much to their chagrin' (POL 088).

We subsequently asked respondents whether they felt that schemes *in general* provided a valuable service. In fact, even in this context 32 per cent were unable to say. Of the remainder, though, positive responses predominated, with 95 per cent feeling that a valuable service was provided. Again, the needs of victims, particularly for comfort and support, were cited. Additionally, a number of officers pointed to services for victims as a necessary but previously missing dimension of penal and welfare services:

'To fill the vacancy between social services and duty police officers.'

(POL 005)

'Social services cannot give the time to victims. Volunteers have the dedication and time.'

(POL 007)

'Provide a service that no other statutory or voluntary body can provide.'

(POL 008)

'Victims for years have been ignored and they should be helped in times of stress and need.'

(POL 069)

'It fills a vacuum left in the welfare state.'

(POL 213)

By way of comparison, we also asked for views on Women's Refuges. In fact, perhaps surprisingly in view of earlier critiques of police response to domestic violence and refuges (Borkowski, Murch, and Walker 1983: 5; Dobash and Dobash 1979; Pahl 1978), responses were equally favourable. Thus 120 officers felt that refuges provided a valuable service, and only seven disagreed. However, views of why refuges were useful contrasted with those on victims support schemes. First, there was a greater emphasis on the *practical usefulness* of refuges, in terms of both safety and emergency accommodation:

> 'Protection from potential violent husbands/boyfriends. Women are very often in a position when having left home with a couple of kids, having nowhere to go, whereas a man, who doesn't normally take the kids can find somewhere to stay easier if the family unit breaks down.'
> (POL 020)

> 'To provide a "place of safety" for the generally weaker sex who are subject to abuse and violence from uncaring men.'
> (POL 026)

> 'To provide shelter and protection albeit on short term, from violent spouse, and so on.'
> (POL 062)

Additionally, though, there was a shift in emphasis regarding the problems which victims support schemes and refuges sought to solve. Whereas victims support was often seen as necessary to provide help which the police were unable to give, but which was both necessary and deserved, the advantage of refuges was sometimes that it solved problems *for the police*, in allowing them to 'refer on' cases which they themselves were reluctant to deal with:

> 'Women the subject of domestic violence are Jekyll and Hyde characters. Ten minutes after the assault they want to complain, press charges; 24 hours later they don't. The refuge provides a useful stop gap.'
> (POL 009)

> 'Solves a problem for police officers. Prevents or could prevent further problems in the short and long term.'
> (POL 027)

> 'It solves a problem for the police. At domestic disputes police officers are tied up for hours calming the situation in order that in many cases the female may be re-accommodated in the marital

home to be the subject of possibly more violence for the want of somewhere to go.'

(POL 213)

These quotes perhaps *overemphasize* the more cynical aspects of police perspectives. Indeed, not only was there a considerable amount of appreciation of the very real needs of battered women and the important roles played by refuges, but more, and fuller, comments appear here than almost anywhere else on the questionnaire! In the wider context of services for the victims of crime in general and domestic violence in particular, though, the police clearly identified with the problems faced by victims and saw victims support schemes and refuges as providing valuable and necessary services.

## Police contact with victims support schemes

Although a number of the police quite clearly had little or no contact with a victims support scheme in their locality, most had considerable lengths of service in the force and might have been expected to have worked at some stage in divisions – such as Exeter, Torbay, and Plymouth – where schemes had been well established. Moreover, the overwhelmingly favourable views held about victims support schemes, allied to the positive light in which the police were seen by volunteers, and management level co-operation, suggest that the conditions for inter-agency co-operation at ground level would be favourable. This was clearly not always the case, as our interviews with volunteers have indicated.

The responses we received when we asked whether our police sample had ever referred any victim to a victims support scheme were, in this context, somewhat mixed, with 40 per cent of respondents replying that they had made at least one referral.

The level of this response raised mixed feelings between us.[2] On the one hand, the fact that a significant minority of police had made referrals may be seen as an encouraging sign. On the other hand, the fact that nearly six in ten had not may give fuel to the arguments about unmet need that we have previously noted. It is therefore perhaps most important to consider the various reasons why referrals were no higher, relating to issues raised in response to different sections of the questionnaire. In essence, these relate to perceptions of *victims' needs* and perceptions of *schemes*.

*Victims support schemes and the police* 171

As some of the quotes cited already illustrate, many of those who held favourable views of victims support schemes identified the frail and elderly as particularly in need (as indeed did some volunteers). This became more apparent when we asked whether our respondents considered certain sections of the community to be in particular need of support following a crime. A large majority, 93 per cent, answered in the affirmative. Moreover, of those identified as in special need, the elderly were cited (in response to an open-ended question) by no less than ninety-nine officers. The image of easily identifiable vulnerable groups, especially the elderly living alone, was presented over and over again:

> 'Elderly and disabled victims of crime often find it harder to recover from the trauma of the incident.'
>
> (POL 042)

> 'Old-age pensioners who invariably live alone and need suitable advice, comfort, and money.'
>
> (POL 101)

> 'The elderly and vulnerable people in the area could benefit from a visit from a non-police-officer.'
>
> (POL 207)

> 'It can provide great comfort to old or lonely people.'
>
> (POL 221)

Now, there is no reason to doubt that the elderly, particularly those living alone, *are* in particular need of assistance following a crime, and indeed much of the research evidence supports this. The problem arises where the stereotyping of easily identifiable groups as a 'referral category' allows the needs of others to be ignored. Thus, when we asked for the circumstances in which officers had referred victims to schemes, the elderly were again cited more frequently than others:

> 'An elderly lady's house had been burgled and she was distressed and frightened.'
>
> (POL 097)

> 'Elderly person victim of robbery.'
>
> (POL 112)

172  *Crime Victims*

'Elderly woman living alone – following a burglary of her premises.'

(POL 255)

In contrast, among those who had not referred anyone to a scheme there was a feeling that very few 'ordinary' victims required help:

'I haven't dealt with anything suitable.'

(POL 015)

'I have not dealt with a case which in my opinion was necessary to refer to the victims support unit.'

(POL 016)

'In my opinion the residents I have attended do not warrant attention by the VSS.'

(POL 111)

Clearly, if the elderly are less likely to be the victims of crime than are other age groups, and if the elderly are singled out as one of the few categories where victims support groups are required, then police perceptions of demand for victims services are drastically at variance with those of the NAVSS. To illustrate this further, we can refer to the final question on our questionnaire.

Here we provided a checklist of the types of problem which, according to earlier research (see Ch. 2), victims frequently experience: emotional needs, help with repairs, advice on financial matters, information on the progress of the case, and support in appearing as a witness. We first asked the police whether 'victims *sometimes need* the help described'. Responses are contained in *Table 9.3*.

Even on this minimal estimate of needs, none of the five problems was identified by more than two-thirds of respondents. Significantly, the two problems most commonly recognized by the police fell in areas where police expertise and police interests were most evident. Thus appreciation that some victims need help with repairs, getting new locks fitted, and so on, arises from crime prevention work with which the police can claim specialist competence, while police awareness of the advantages of victims being 'good' witnesses is self-evident. At the other extreme, and in complete contrast to Shapland's (1984) conclusion that victims wish to be informed of police progress (or even lack of progress) on their case, barely

Table 9.3 *Number and percentage of police officers who felt that victims sometimes needed help, in five areas of support*

| area of support | no. | % |
| --- | --- | --- |
| Victims are upset and need emotional support. | 87 | 48.6 |
| Victims often need help with house repairs, getting new locks fitted, and so on. | 115 | 64.2 |
| Victims often need advice about their financial rights for compensation and insurance claims. | 80 | 44.7 |
| Victims frequently appreciate being kept in touch with police progress regarding the crime. | 65 | 36.3 |
| Victims sometimes need help and support if they are required as witnesses in court. | 92 | 51.4 |
| total | 179 | 100 |

one-third of police officers saw this as even sometimes necessary.

Perceptions of need and awareness of the role of victims support schemes are to some extent engendered by the police training programme. We therefore asked officers whether they had ever received any training on the function and purpose of victims support schemes, and if so, when and how much training had been provided.

Given the almost universal image of the Devon and Cornwall Constabulary as community/service-orientated, and the commitment of senior officers to victims services, one might have expected at least some training input. Instead, only 19 per cent said they had had any such training.[3] The extent of input, even for these, varied, from a 'ten minute talk by police liaison officer' (POL 022) to 'Half a day' (POL 096).

The timing of this input varied, but the most common answer was at constables' refresher courses, held at police headquarters.[4] However, the importance of some input is illustrated by a comparison of respondents' referral practices according to training. Of those who had received some training input on victims services, 81 per cent had made referrals; of those with no training input, only 32 per cent had ($x^2=25.52$, $p<0.001$). There was, moreover, some indication that those who had received some relevant training were senior officers, and thus less likely currently to be in direct contact with victims, although perhaps more able to affect policy.

174  *Crime Victims*

Finally, with regard to the checklist of typical problems experienced by crime victims, we asked whether, in each case, victims ought to receive help from victims support schemes. In each case, police were even less likely to see schemes as important providers of services than they were to appreciate the existence of needs. The overall responses are contained in *Table 9.4*.

Table 9.4 *Number and percentage of police officers who felt that victims ought to receive help from victims support schemes, in five areas of support*

| area of support | no. | % |
| --- | --- | --- |
| Victims are upset and need emotional support. | 60 | 33.5 |
| Victims often need help with house repairs, getting new locks fitted, and so on. | 41 | 22.9 |
| Victims often need advice about their financial rights for compensation and insurance claims. | 72 | 40.2 |
| Victims frequently appreciate being kept in touch with police progress regarding the crime. | 60 | 33.5 |
| Victims sometimes need help and support if they are required as witnesses in court. | 54 | 30.2 |
| total | 179 | 100 |

Three points stand out in *Table 9.4*. First, the problems which the police most readily recognized – regarding support as a witness and repairs – were least likely to be seen as the responsibility of victims support schemes. Second, in contrast, although a minority of police felt that victims required information on police progress, this was often seen as a 'job for victims support schemes', again opposing Shapland's (1984) view of this as a responsibility of the police. Third, only about one-third of the police felt that victims should receive emotional support from victims support schemes.

The reasons for low rates of referrals to victims support schemes seem, therefore, to stem from two interrelated sets of perceptions. On the one hand, the police appear to have a low estimation of the needs of crime victims; they frequently see only certain types of victim as requiring help and underestimate the types of needs which victims experience. On the other hand, they are often vague about the services provided by victims support schemes and are reluctant to acknowledge the part schemes might play *vis-à-vis* a variety of needs. That this occurs against a backcloth of wide police support for the notion of victims support schemes, and an extremely pro-police perspective within the schemes in our research, is striking.

## Police, victims support schemes, and gatekeeping

Although we have focused in this chapter on the relationship between police and victims services, our findings parallel earlier evidence on victims' perspectives of the police. Thus Shapland, Willmore, and Duff (1985), for example, argue that police prioritizing of technical efficiency results in victim *serving* (through concern, help, sympathy, and overall, the appreciation of victims as mattering) receiving low priority. In this context two questions arise which are at the heart of police work with victims: can the police provide a better service for victims, and can the police be entrusted with responsibility for gatekeeping victim access to other services? Here we have considered them through a review of police relations with victims support schemes on various levels and, ultimately, through an analysis of police perceptions of victims' needs.

As we have noted in this chapter, the relationship between victims' services and the police is a strong one. On a national level, the NAVSS has developed with strong police support, and schemes throughout the country have benefited from a positive attitude within police management. On a local level, the role of senior police officers has been significant, although it clearly varies with changes in personnel. Moreover, on different levels of interaction we have indicated very powerful influences towards good relations between police and victims support schemes. First, at management committee level, senior police officers have accepted their responsibilities seriously and shown commitment to the schemes. Second, at volunteer level, our survey of local volunteers reveals that victims support scheme volunteers show a considerable affinity towards police perspectives on issues related to the police, offenders, and the crime problem. There is thus no evidence of a clash of ideologies, which, as we noted in Chapter 5, has been the hallmark of conflict between police and some other agencies like Rape Crisis Centres. Moreover, police at all levels hold very positive views of victims services.

Despite this, lack of referrals – a key issue nationally – is a serious problem in many schemes in the South West, and continues despite initiatives to improve the situation. The extent of the problem varies between schemes, and as we noted in Chapter 7, not all areas have a low ratio of cases to volunteers. However, given the fact that the South West is a traditionally good recruiting ground for volunteers, the fact that relatively few cases are passed on to volunteers is a worrying one, liable to affect morale.

This is an issue to which we shall return in Chapter 11. At this point it is more pertinent to note the basis for this low rate of referrals. Our survey of local police officers has suggested that the root of the problem lies in the vagueness of many police officers' knowledge of victims support and, especially, in restricted police definitions of victims' needs.

This is not, as an issue, specific to the context of police relationships with victims services. A whole variety of studies of gatekeeping, the operation of 'street-level bureaucrats' (Lipsky 1980), has noted the problems which arise when one agency is responsible for referring clients to another organization. The problems seem to stem from inter-agency conflict, lack of awareness by gatekeepers of the appropriate referral agency, and low gatekeeper acknowledgement of need. In this case inter-organizational relationships do not appear problematic. However, the police do not always effectively fulfil a gatekeeping function *vis-à-vis* crime victims, due to lack of knowledge of victims support schemes and lack of awareness of the needs of victims.

We have already stressed that many victims may be inconvenienced rather than harmed by crime (Ch. 2). Despite this, the evidence here demonstrates that the police do seriously underestimate the needs of victims. The police officers we questioned felt that only a minority of victims required help, and only a few areas of need were evidenced. In contrast, many victims of crime who do not receive help from victims support schemes could benefit if they were so referred. The question thus becomes, how can needs be best matched with services? The answer could fall in two directions – improve the role of the police as gatekeepers, or alternatively, minimize the gatekeeping function of the police.

Given that there was a close relationship between training on victims services and referrals, it is tempting to assume that the police will prove more effective gatekeepers to victims services if they receive more appropriate training on needs and services. Thus initial training might include more information and the extension of services to victims as an important feature of good policework, and the training period could incorporate sessions with victims support group volunteers. This could then be reinforced by sessions in refresher courses and courses for newly promoted officers.

However, while we have some sympathy with this approach, we are somewhat sceptical of its ultimate success. The translation of this increased awareness into action through referral is, perhaps, vulnerable, given the strength of the police occupational culture. As a number of researchers have noted, police organizations, particularly in the lower ranks, develop strong subcultural allegiances, based around commitments to certain key principles of the job – often the key reasons for joining the police – and the need to avoid trouble (Cain 1973; Holdaway 1983; Manning 1982; Van Maan 1974). Such principles may be introduced during training, but if not, appear extremely resistant to 'counter-training' (Fielding 1984). While we would not advocate the acceptance of the priorities given in the occupational culture to 'action' (as opposed to 'service'), we remain sceptical of the viability of attempts to encourage the police to enhance their gatekeeping strategies *vis-à-vis* victims. The alternative is a pattern of direct referrals which pre-empts the police role at the referral stage while stressing the need to strengthen the service role of the police and to improve police response to victims.

The NAVSS has moved towards a policy of encouraging automatic referrals, and this has received some police and political support (House of Commons 1984). On a local level, force policy – as yet unimplemented – recommends a move to automatic referral. What this would mean is that the local victims support scheme and the police would agree a policy whereby all victims of incidents of particular kinds would be referred to the scheme. Depending on local arrangements, certain non-crime incidents might be included, and many minor crimes (like car thefts) might be excluded. However, all other crimes would be automatically referred to victims support schemes, *irrespective of the social characteristics of the victim*.

Many police forces and victims support schemes now operate policies of automatic referral, which partly account for the number of schemes with very high victim–volunteer ratios, which we noted in Chapter 6. This problem of excessive demand is likely to be considerable, particularly in many urban areas where volunteer recruitment is most difficult. There are, clearly, implications for the funding and organization of schemes, as we have stressed. At this juncture, we conclude our analysis of the relationship between the police and victims support schemes with two policy recommendations. First, as we have emphasized, it is important that the police are made more aware of the needs of crime victims, and that they redefine their role so as to incorporate serving victims as a more central feature. Second, and despite this, we feel that the needs of victims can be most effectively met through a direct-referral system.

# 10 Victims support schemes and the probation service

Since the inception of the first victims support scheme in Bristol, probation officers have played a key role in the development of victims services. In the South West, as we have already noted, the probation service was a driving force in the creation of both the Exeter and the Torbay schemes, and John Harding, the then Assistant Chief Probation Officer, later wrote the first British text on victim restitution (Harding 1982).

To a certain extent the probation focus on crime victims has been geared to stressing the benefit – to offender, victim, and society – of shifting the emphasis in the criminal justice system from punishment to restitution and reparation. Thus probation officers, including Harding (1978), were strongly in favour of the introduction of community service orders, and the *Probation Journal* recently included a series of articles on reparation.[1] A comparison of one of the major texts on the probation service in the 1970s (Haxby 1978) with a more recent one (Raynor 1985), moreover, illustrates the shifting emphasis towards a concern with crime victims.

The role of probation within victims support has been equally significant. Some officers of the NAVSS are, or have been, in the probation service, including the director, Helen Reeves. It is perhaps not surprising then that whereas the House of Commons Home Affairs Committee recognized that the 'organisation with which a victims support scheme maintains the closest relationship is the police' (House of Commons 1984: vii), it was also 'aware that a close working relationship often exists between victims support scheme co-ordinators and the probation service' (p. x) and recommended closer organizational ties.

The provision of offices is one part of the 'organizational infrastructure' which is provided by probation to sixteen of the seventy-six schemes with office accommodation (NAVSS 1985: 23). However, the importance of a close link with probation is clearly more than this, as is illustrated in a NAVSS document on 'the role of the probation service in victims support schemes'.[2]

The document identifies three major advantages of involving the probation service. First, the probation service is considered to have particular expertise in the use of volunteers.³ Second, a probation presence is seen as helpful in improving police confidence in schemes. Finally, it allows a better understanding of the dynamics of interpersonal offences, where victims services are likely to be involved with only one of the parties concerned.

Similarly, the document identifies three advantages for the probation service: namely, involvement in victims support helps create closer ties with the community, police, and the voluntary sector; it may benefit the probation service's public image; and it may feed back to improved services for offenders.

Perhaps most significantly, the document stresses the *political* advantage to both the NAVSS and the probation service:

> 'It is useful to consider what Victims' Support Schemes could become if the Probation Service were *not* involved. Many people expect a "victims" organisation to be involved in political campaigning, e.g. for stiffer penalties or criticisms of police questioning, etc. This already occurs in other countries and in this country outside the NAVSS. The issues can easily become polarised, leading to competition for resources, press campaigns and a far less constructive service to the public.'

The involvement of probation, then, is at least partly symbolic, providing a balance to the police presence and enabling a focus on victims' needs rather than an intrusion into the 'law and order' debate. Thus, as we stressed in Chapter 6, a probation presence is crucial to victims support in its present form.

Clearly, not all representatives of the probation service are as supportive of victims services as those noted here. For example, the National Association of Probation Officers (NAPO) has been somewhat ambivalent, fearing that resources will be redirected from probation to victims support, and we have already cited some advocates of the victims movement who encourage such 'worst fears' scenarios. Nevertheless, on an official level, and in the development of victims support schemes, the link between agencies appears strong. This chapter considers the relationships in more detail, starting with the volunteers' perspectives and then going on to review the attitudes of a sample of probation officers.

## Victims support schemes and the probation service

While it is only a requirement of the NAVSS that each affiliated scheme should contain a representative of *either* the probation or social services, in Devon and Cornwall probation participation on management committees was usual. Conversely, social workers were less frequently represented. This high profile for probation officers is allied to their role in initiating some of the earlier schemes and fuelled by the commitment of senior officers to involvement in the local community.

Probation officers, like police officers, were discouraged from assuming the chair of schemes, and for similar reasons. However, at management level, the officers in question were no less committed to the aims of victims support. Indeed, at committee level police–probation alliances were evident. Never, at the numerous meetings observed, were the probation and police officers ever in dispute over matters which could be traced to the specific orientation of their agencies. Indeed, the reverse was true. Frequently, police and probation officers operated as a team.

The role that probation officers played in the running of schemes was again much the same as that of police officers, not least in offering advice in areas for which they retained a particular expertise. For example, they were particularly likely to be involved in the running of the training programme.

As in the case of the police outlined in the previous chapter, victims support volunteers were asked whether they considered it 'necessary' for the probation service to be represented on the committee of victims support schemes. Here the results were glaringly at variance. Whereas 91 per cent of volunteers considered a police presence on the management committee necessary, only 52 per cent felt the same way about the probation service. Those arguing in favour of probation presence stressed advantages in terms of the probation services' range of knowledge with regards to their experience of crime, some adding that they were able to offer an understanding of the 'other side of the coin'. For example:

> 'I think it is a good thing I suppose, it is the other side of the coin. It gives more completeness and roundness. Round here the probation service have a tremendous lot to offer.'
>
> (I 05)

> 'The vast experience they have in dealing with people who are the subject of crime. Also they are in touch with so many voluntary organizations.'
>
> (I 46)

> 'It won't do any harm. The more you have who are involved the better. They can certainly give some guidance.'
>
> (I 16)

The notion that the management committee should involve as wide a variety of groups as possible also gained wide support: 'The management committee should be as broadly based as it can possibly be' (I 03) and 'The more we know about each other's work the better' (I 13). Thus the presence of probation officers was justified not only on the basis of their specialist knowledge of crime and the offender but also because volunteers appreciated the advantages of having as broad a base in the community as possible.

In contrast, for those who answered negatively to probation involvement the most common reason was that the probation focus on the offender has little to do with the victim. For example:

> 'I can't see how, their knowledge is with the criminal.'
>
> (I 43)

> 'One can always call them in if we need them. This involves the perpetrator and we are concerned with the victim.'
>
> (I 18)

Nearly as many argued that while probation involvement may not be 'necessary' as the question suggested, they were nevertheless a valued addition. Some typical comments included:

> 'I think that if you need to know anything about that side of it, you can invite them in; it is not necessary to have them there all the time.'
>
> (I 40)

> 'It was nice to meet them at the training session, but I don't see why they need to be there all the time.'
>
> (I 38)

> 'But I do think it is advisable, I have a high opinion of them, they have a lot of experience to share.'
>
> (I 25)

At the extreme, three volunteers demonstrated hostility to the service. One volunteer was in favour of corporal punishment and opposed probation on the grounds of principle. Two others were less precise in their reasoning:

'Me personally, I haven't a lot of time for the probation service.'
(I 17)

'I can't see the point. Anyway, I don't like probation officers or social workers, no teacher ever does.'
(I 31)

Thus only three volunteers could be viewed as being against the probation service. This particular point was enforced when we asked volunteers to state whether they were in favour of probation as a sentence. Again, three volunteers (different from those quoted above) were not in favour, all because they felt that sentences should be harsher.

Generally speaking, therefore, victims support scheme volunteers displayed a mixed attitude towards probation officers and the probation service. While only a small majority considered them a necessary part of victims support schemes, many others felt that they could contribute valuable experience. There was, however, a significant minority who felt that any work with the victim would not, or should not, be the concern of an agency geared towards the offender. It was an observation which held true for other questions. For example, as we noted in Chapter 8, the majority were against direct involvement in reparation initiatives. Nevertheless, within the South West, two direct comparisons can be made. First, clearly volunteers accredited the police with considerably more legitimacy than they did the probation service. Second, victims support scheme volunteers were, as we indicated in the previous chapter, similar in their outlook to police special constables and distinct from probation voluntary associates in some respects. The pool of volunteers drawn into work with crime victims is thus different from that attracted to probation work.

The different moral universes of these groups of volunteers is best illustrated by the offender scale, where victims support scheme volunteers were significantly more likely to hold anti-offender views than were probation volunteers. Linked to the views expressed here vis-à-vis reparation, this raises an element of doubt about the feasibility of merging offender-orientated and victim-focused services, a point we shall return to in the next chapter. Nevertheless, it is only an undercurrent. The majority view, from the volunteers at least, is that the involvement of the probation services holds more advantages.

184 *Crime Victims*

**Survey of probation officers in the South West**

As with the police, we attempted to investigate further the relationship between the probation service, victims, and victims support schemes through a postal questionnaire. In order to gain maximum comparability we included a number of identical questions. Again, we asked a series of questions about volunteers within the respondents' own agency – probation voluntary associates. However, given the different nature of probation contacts with victims and schemes, some of the questions asked were original. Overall, we included questions on victims and schemes regarding:

1. *Knowledge* Did probation officers know about the schemes operating in their areas?
2. *Attitudes towards VSS* Did they feel that the local scheme, and schemes in general, provided a valuable service, and why?
3. *Contact with schemes* Had probation officers ever been involved in running a scheme? Had they had cases referred to them by schemes?
4. *Perceptions of need* Do certain sections of the community require support more than others? What needs do crime victims have?
5. *Victims and the criminal justice system* What role should probation and victims support schemes play in helping victims? Should the criminal justice system be modified to meet the needs or rights of victims more directly?

The questionnaire was sent to all probation officers in Devon and Cornwall. The response rate, at 49 per cent, was considerably lower than for the police, but was satisfactory for a postal questionnaire. Replies were received from seventy-one probation officers, of whom 69 per cent were 'maingrade', and 19 per cent were 'senior' probation officers.[4] As might have been anticipated, respondents were relatively older than police respondents, with only 16 per cent aged no more than 30, 32 per cent aged 31–40, and 48 per cent aged 41–65. In contrast, they had somewhat less experience as probation officers: 50 per cent had served for no more than ten years and 27 per cent for sixteen or more years. Predictably, their educational qualifications were more extensive than were those of the police.

In all, 63 per cent of respondents were male, showing the probation service to fall somewhere between the police and social work (Walton 1975) in the recruitment of females. The majority (81 per cent) were married.

Thus, compared with our police sample, probation officers were somewhat older and better qualified, but had less 'on the ground' experience. Given the lower response rate, we were concerned to guard against the possibility that respondents were markedly different from those who did not respond. To some extent we were reassured by feedback that much non-response was a reaction against additional form-filling, although we were still wary of the possibility that respondents might be more victim- or volunteer-orientated than other probation officers.

A further cause for concern arose from the specialist nature of much probation work. As many as forty of our sample described themselves as specialists, and even though many of these would have been generalists previously, this might impinge on contacts with agencies such as victims support schemes. However, a review of the specialist posts described reveals a range of activities, from juvenile work to divorce court welfare, from community specialisms to institutional work. Thus, while the probation officers whose views we received covered a wide variety of tasks, some were in specialist fields which might have influenced their current contacts with crime victims and support services. Such possible constraints must be borne in mind in reviewing the replies we received.

## Probation officers and crime victims

As already noted despite the caution of NAPO, many probation officers have maintained a high profile as advocates of victims' rights and needs. From an initial interest in compensation, and involvement in early victims service initiatives, the debate within probation over mediation, compensation, and reparation is a lively one. We therefore sought out the level of grass-roots commitment by asking whether officers agreed that 'our criminal justice system is far too much *offender*-orientated, and that little is done for the victim'. The extent of support for additional victims initiatives is indicated by the fact that four times as many agreed with this statement as disagreed. For example:

> 'It is the offender who tends to get all the support, the casework, the legal advice, and so on.'
>
> (PR 004)

> 'Totally, utterly and without any scrap of reservation. Why?

Because after ten years as a P.O. I'm *still* bemused at the "all stops out to help the offender" approach.'

(PR 007)

'For every pound spent on offenders, less than one penny on victims. Victims are *central* to issues involved, not peripheral.'

(PR 056)

On the other hand, 16 per cent of respondents disagreed and 24 per cent were uncommitted, indicating some ambivalence and a certain amount of mixed feelings. Indeed, this was illustrated in the responses of some who agreed:

'But in many ways offenders are the victims of society. I would rather see a system that cares for all victims.'

(PR 041)

'The system should be more evenly balanced. The probation service could be expanded to cover both areas, without reduction of the service to offenders.'

(PR 053)

'It would help to prevent attitudes towards offenders and perhaps victims being polarized.'

(PR 055)

The fear that the issue might be interpreted in 'zero sum' terms, especially when resources were at stake, was explicit in the replies of many of those who disagreed, leading some to accept voluntarism as a compromise:

'There is need for greater victims support but that does not mean less offender help.'

(PR 001)

'The CJS is too state-orientated to the exclusion of the victim. It isn't that too much is done for the offender, it's just that *nothing* is done for the victim (historically the state has acquired much kudos and revenue from dispensing of justice so that the system we have is now firmly entrenched).'

(PR 022)

'I think it is better to keep the roles separate and I believe the voluntary schemes fill the gap well.'

(PR 047)

Clearly, most probable officers felt that the system *was* too offender-orientated. Others, however, considered statutory responses to victims to be inappropriate. Yet members of both camps viewed the concept of balance with some suspicion. Improved services for victims, and greater involvement of victims in the system, were considered important. But for most there was a concern that this should not disadvantage the offenders. Some looked towards expansion of victims services at nil-cost to offenders; others optimistically saw the victims' movement as advantageous to offenders as well. Nevertheless, almost all our respondents agreed that tipping the scales in favour of the victim should not be at the expense of services for offenders. A similar picture emerged when we then asked if any new initiatives should be introduced to enable the offender to repay the victim for any harm, damage, or distress caused. Again, a majority (59 per cent) agreed, and a minority (20 per cent) disagreed. Once more, there was considerable ambivalence.

As anticipated, those who agreed stressed the advantages this held from the point of view of the offender as well as the victim. For example:

'Offenders would perhaps become more aware of the distress to their victims caused by their criminal behaviour.'

(PR 047)

'It would be a sentence which would bring the victims' needs back into the court setting. It would be a sentence which might have more meaning for the offender.'

(PR 050)

'In appropriate cases this would provide a medium for a psychological benefit of both. It may (a) make the offender more aware of the unexpected damage he does, and (b) help the victim through the trauma, despair he/she might feel. It is a more human and personal approach, debureaucratizes the system.'

(PR 071)

On the other hand, those who disagreed varied from some who felt sufficient opportunities already existed in sentencing options, through some who saw the victims' interests as often at variance with such a concept, to others who were dismissive of any re-emphasis:

> 'No need for new laws. Can be part of existing law, e.g. Community Service, Deferred Sentence, and so on.'
>
> (PR 025)

> 'Danger of victim suffering further.'
>
> (PR 019)

> 'Tried before – waste of time.'
>
> (PR 034)

What, then, of the role of the probation service? We asked officers whether they felt that the service should play a more direct role in helping the victims of crime. Again, there was no unanimity – 48 per cent felt it should, while 39 per cent disagreed. Interestingly, the former stressed the advantages of more direct involvement for the service itself (echoing the NAVSS), and for the offender, as well as for the victim:

> 'Probation officers tend to overlook this side of the equation – maybe their relationships with other offenders/clients would be more realistic if they also dealt with victims, and maybe thereby more helpful to the offender himself.'
>
> (PR 004)

> 'I believe that the probation service should focus on "crime" rather than criminals; that is, crime as a social phenomenon, not "criminals" as "patients". Therefore anything which widens our approach is in my view, to be encouraged.'
>
> (PR 101)

> 'Probation is often seen by public as only being interested in criminals rather than crime and its effects.'
>
> (PR 017)

However, while most of these saw a role for the probation service *vis-à-vis* mediation, views on probation involvement with victims' wider needs were rather more mixed. The following two quotes from probation officers answering in the affirmative illustrate the variations:

'Our role is to moderate offending behaviour, hopefully by inducing understanding and responsibility and by lessening the perceived wide gap between the two groups. Often the gap is not that wide. It could be help to *both* parties if they met. It is this hope for conciliation which I feel makes victim/offender work relevant for this agency. Work specifically with victims and only for their sake should perhaps be handled chiefly by an alternative agency at this time.'

(PR 028)

'It is unfortunate perhaps that for years the police have seen their role as that of pursuing and prosecuting the criminal to the exclusion of concern for the victim. It must therefore be even more galling for the victim to learn that welfare services exist to assist offenders with their problems. Present victim support schemes appear to rely too much on the goodwill of volunteers who are prepared to give up their own time to work for the victims. I believe that the time is long overdue when such schemes should form an official part of the duties of all social workers and probation officers; especially the latter.'

(PR 043)

This perhaps represents the extreme probation advocacy for a role in victims services. Those who disagreed with greater probation service involvement were not, however, dismissive of victims' needs and/or rights. Rather, they either saw dangers in a greater widening of the role of their agency (following NAPO) or felt that victims support schemes were a more appropriate response:

'Unless we receive extra funding and staff, resources are currently stretched enough. Victims should be supported, but by an agency specifically funded, not as an afterthought, tacked on to existing agency and run "for free".'

(PR 009)

'Role confusion would result.'

(PR 033)

'There is plenty of scope for an independent body to deal with victims. I feel a more direct role by the probation service will create a dilution of our own response to the offender – which after all is the reason for our being.'

(PR 041)

The views of probation officers in our sample clearly illustrate the complexity of issues surrounding the needs and rights of crime victims. A majority felt that greater involvement of the victim in the criminal justice system was advantageous, but a large minority saw problems in a shift of emphasis. A majority considered that the probation service could play a more direct role in helping victims. However, whether this should be confined to mediation and reparation was unclear. Moreover, while victims' wider needs were appreciated by many, the extent to which these should be incorporated into the terms of reference of the service, or left to other agencies, varied between different respondents.

We should not, however, fall into the trap of assuming that a general concern for victims incorporates any more specific appreciation of their needs. In questioning police officers, where the referral issue is dependent upon perceptions of need, we identified problems of under-recognition. We therefore included, for probation officers, similar questions on victims' needs. As for the police, we first asked whether they considered that certain sections of the community were in particular need of support following a crime. A majority (77 per cent) answered in the affirmative, although this was notably lower than among police officers. In contrast to the police, though, while the elderly were again cited more commonly than other categories, the focus on the elderly was less evident and a number of probation officers appreciated the dangers of predicting response to crime and the wide impact of crime on a variety of victims. For example:

> 'Often people who have lived alone, or with little family or community support, but because people's response to crime is individual it is important that everyone has the opportunity of support, even if they refuse it.'
>
> (PR 013)

> 'The effect of certain crimes can be devastating. As well as the immediate effect upon the victim there can be a general increase of fear within a community and in some instances, particularly criminal damage, the environment could be worsened.'
>
> (PR 050)

Moreover, as one respondent who answered in the negative observed:

> 'I think support should be accorded to the individual's needs

rather than whether they fit into a certain section of the community; for example, it would be easy to say the elderly, children, women, and so on, need help but research has shown that young men in their 20s (who are most vulnerable to physical attack) need emotional support.'

(PR 022)

As we might anticipate from a better-educated group with an emphasis in training on individualizing clients' needs, these responses are somewhat more sophisticated than those we received from the police, and many probation officers appeared aware of the dangers of associating needs with particular client groups. Consequently, when respondents were faced with the same set of problems which the victim of crime might experience, we anticipated a considerably greater awareness of need from probation officers compared with the police. Surprisingly, probation officers were overall no more likely than were the police to feel that victims sometimes needed help. More predictably, the needs they identified differed in degree from those of the police.

In fact, each of four types of problem were identified by about half our sample – help with house repairs (55 per cent), financial advice (55 per cent), upset/emotional support needed and greater knowledge of police progress (49 per cent). Rather less (42 per cent) thought that victims sometimes need help and support as witnesses. The two police-related concerns (repairs, witness) were less likely to be cited by probation officers than by the police, but probation officers were more aware of the financial needs of crime victims and of victims' desire to be kept informed of police progress. Notably, the proportion of probation officers who felt that victims were sometimes upset and needed emotional support was not significantly greater than among the police.

The impact of police understatements of the needs of crime victims may be greater than that of probation officers, given the police role as referral agents. However, both police and probation officers had similar views of the level of victims' needs. Arguably, perhaps, this degree of equivalence is the result of the police having direct experience of victims but little training on victims' needs, and probation officers having considerable training emphasis on clients' (but not specifically victims') needs but little direct experience of crime victims.

## Probation officers and victims support schemes

Turning to probation officers' perceptions of victims support schemes, we first asked whether there was a scheme operating in the respondents' own area. Most answered in the affirmative (88 per cent). However, as with the police, there was a general vagueness about detail – only twenty-eight probation officers actually named a local scheme.[5]

Probation contacts with victims services might, we anticipated, be pronounced in two contexts. First, probation officers might have been involved in setting up the schemes, or in the day-to-day running of the schemes (through the management committee). Second, probation officers might have had clients referred to them by schemes, where long-term counselling of victims was needed or where mediation was required.

We first asked whether respondents had ever played a role in the running of *any* victims support scheme. Fifteen probation officers (21 per cent) answered in the affirmative, citing eight local schemes and one from elsewhere. Apparently, despite the part played by the probation service at a policy level, and the high profile maintained by particular individuals, victims support schemes do not feature in the working lives of more than a minority of probation officers.[6] Among this minority, though, nine were involved on management committees, of whom two held office and three more had major responsibility for the selection and training of volunteers. In addition, two had been instrumental in starting schemes in different parts of the region.

We then asked respondents if they had ever had a case referred to them from a victims support scheme. Only three in fact said they had, and these were in special circumstances; for example, one respondent was a volunteer in a scheme, another had had an offender who was victimized. Thus, while national policy may focus on the role of the probation service as treatment/casework specialists, it seems that the direct use of probation officers' skills is minimal and is more evident where officers are involved in the training of volunteers.

In general, probation officers held somewhat mixed feelings about the involvement of the service with victims of crime. In practice, it emerges that actual involvement with victims services is by a minority. What then do probation officers feel about victims support schemes? As with the police, we first asked about attitudes towards local schemes.

In common with the police, few respondents (in fact three) categorically said that the scheme did not provide a valuable service. At the other extreme, eighteen officers felt that it did. Others, however, raised difficulties, with referrals again the main item, showing recognition that police referral practices were less than satisfactory. For example:

> 'Yes. It has run for over a year. Referrals dropped off after six months, but even so it is still important that it is available for the few people who can benefit from it.'
> 
> (PR 013)

> 'Yes. But limited. Needs a better organizational structure and links with police and probation service.'
> 
> (PR 046)

> 'Yes, though it would be more effective with some co-operation from the police – principally the delay in referring victims.'
> 
> (PR 269)

In common with the questionnaire for police officers, we later included a question on attitudes towards victims support schemes in general. Again, answers were largely positive. Only two respondents felt that victims support schemes did not provide a valuable service, while the majority (74 per cent) felt that they did. Overwhelmingly, these respondents focused on victims' needs and the void in service provision which victims support schemes filled:

> 'Support for victims for whom crime can bring pressing short and longer term distress.'
> 
> (PR 001)

> 'Helps to overcome the terrible shock/harm and other feelings expressed.'
> 
> (PR 025)

> 'It involves the community in caring for its members and thereby improves the quality of life in that community.'
> 
> (PR 048)

> 'There is no other official assistance for victims and they have to

rely on relatives and friends – if they have any. Need advice on insurance, Criminal Injuries Compensation, and so on.'

(PR 053)

One aspect of schemes of which we anticipated probation officers would have some knowledge was the involvement of the police, particularly given the importance of co-operation between agencies. We therefore asked directly for attitudes towards police involvement.

The replies fell into five categories. At one extreme, four respondents were critical of any police involvement, arguing against a wider definition of the police role. A further three specifically criticized the police for inadequate referrals, while twelve noted that police involvement was essential because of the referral process. Another twelve respondents accepted a police involvement, but were cautious that the police should not assume control:

– 'It is right that they should be involved, but their role in a scheme should not be a controlling one.'

(PR 057)

– 'Very necessary, but important that they play an equal part with other officials of the organization and don't try to take it over. It is essentially a community response to victims.'

(PR 269)

A large minority (45 per cent), though, had no such doubts, being extremely positive in their approval of police involvement. Stressing the welfare role of the police, many probation officers saw the police as a suitable agency to be involved; others, perhaps ironically,[7] saw this as advantageous in helping to *redefine* the police role:

– 'A direct referral from police who are on the spot seems effective. They are welfare minded and give good service to victims, therefore should be able to refer for extra help where needed.'

(PR 009)

– 'I believe that any scheme which helps the police to be able to see people as individuals is helpful.'

(PR 045)

– 'Very much in favour. The police are invariably first on the scene and can assess needs. It is often the case that the victim will see the policeman as his one and only friend at this time.'

(PR 262)

Thus, despite some notes of caution, most probation officers saw the police as a necessary part of victims support schemes and saw this as beneficial, so long as the police did not attempt to monopolize schemes. Their major criticisms centred on referral problems. Indeed, it seemed that most officers approved of a model based on community involvement, with a balance of statutory agencies, reaffirming the NAVSS ideal type (Reeves 1984).

We have, however, already noted that probation officers, like the police, had rather more restricted ideas of victims' needs than the NAVSS. Finally, then, we asked our sample which of the five specified problems faced by some victims they felt ought to be the responsibility of victims support schemes.

Their replies were in marked contrast to those of the police, and indeed to their own perceptions of victims' needs. For four of the five problem areas, more probation officers felt victims ought to receive appropriate help from victims support schemes than felt that such problems arose in the first place! As is clear from *Table 10.1*, some seven out of ten probation officers felt that where victims needed help and support to act as a witness in court, this should be provided by victims support schemes. Six out of ten agreed that schemes were appropriate *vis-à-vis* financial advice and emotional support. At the other extreme, nearly half felt that victims support schemes should play a role in keeping victims informed of police progress on the case. Indeed, for each of the five, probation officers were significantly more likely to identify a role for victims support schemes than were the police. In marked contrast, few probation officers felt that schemes in their area were providing these services, illustrating

Table 10.1 *Percentage of probation officers and police officers who felt that victims ought to receive help from victims support schemes, in five support areas*

| area of support | probation | police |
|---|---|---|
| Victims are upset and need emotional support. | 60.6 | 33.5 |
| Victims often need help with house repairs, getting new locks fitted, and so on. | 56.3 | 22.9 |
| Victims often need advice about their financial rights for compensation and insurance claims. | 60.6 | 40.2 |
| Victims frequently appreciate being kept in touch with police progress regarding the crime. | 47.9 | 33.5 |
| Victims sometimes need help and support if they are required as witnesses in court. | 70.4 | 30.2 |

partly the lack of fully operating schemes, partly a lack of awareness, and perhaps partly reflecting concerns at the operation of local schemes, for example with regard to referral practices and services available.

## Attitudes towards volunteers

In the last two chapters the views of police and probation officers towards victims support schemes have been documented and appear to have degrees of congruence. Both agencies reflect, at management and operational level, a general support for victims services; both see their own role as facilitating rather than directive. For the police, official policy stresses the lack of police time to devote to victims' needs, and this was at least partly reflected in the views of our sample. For probation officers, official enthusiasm for victims services has been counterbalanced, nationally, by some ambivalence about these becoming a feature of the probation service, and within our sample even mediation and restitution initiatives were greeted with some scepticism.

However, in neither case is there a clear image of the appropriateness, or otherwise, of *voluntary*-based victims support schemes. As noted in this chapter, probation views are mixed. Some felt that such schemes provided the best medium for meeting victims' needs, and indeed saw advantages in the greater involvement of the 'community', albeit *via* the voluntary sector. Others, however, felt that schemes were not always as efficient as they might be, identifying referral issues as a particular problem, while a very small minority voiced some unease at the influence of the police in some schemes.

Clearly, the efficiency of voluntary bodies is an important issue, and it is one which, as Brenton (1985) has recently observed, receives somewhat lukewarm attention. Unfortunately, our questionnaire was not designed to provide direct evidence of the extent of commitment to the current structure for providing services for victims. However, there are additional political reasons why a voluntary body should be preferred.

We have already noted the importance accredited by the NAVSS to the concept of victims support as a service based on both the community and a balance of relevant agencies. For both probation and police, a lack of commitment to taking responsibility for the service itself leaves a 'neutral third party' as the most suitable alternative. The voluntary organization may thus be seen as a compromise solution between two statutory agencies neither of whom wishes full responsibility nor would wish the other to have sole responsibility. The importance of victims support as an impartial body is thus confirmed, not just in its own eyes but also from the perspective of the relevant statutory agencies.

Nevertheless, it is possible to argue that police and probation officers may hold positive attitudes towards voluntary involvement in victims services. This can be tested by comparing their views on victims support scheme volunteers with their views on volunteers in their own agencies, police special constables and probation voluntary associates. A high proportion of respondents said that they had worked with such volunteers (75 per cent of police, 99 per cent of probation officers). We therefore asked respondents to indicate their own views of volunteers in their own agency, *and* the views of their colleagues in general. Although both police and probation were less willing to be critical themselves than they were to see their colleagues as holding unfavourable views, the police were considerably, and significantly, more critical on both counts. Thus 91 per cent of probation officers, but only 60 per cent of the police, said that they personally were in favour of volunteers, whilst 49 per cent of probation officers but only 12 per cent of the police said that they thought their colleagues held favourable views. Moreover, while police criticisms tended to focus rather more on volunteers as untrained amateurs, and there was concern over the threat to overtime work, probation officers were rather more likely to see volunteers as of benefit in bridging the gap between the organization and the community. For example, voluntary associates were of benefit because:

> 'Less formal contact, to befriend and give more time to clients – support and advice from basically "ordinary" people. Facilitates client contact with community, removes feeling of "us and them".'
> (PR 009)

> 'To involve the community in the care and so on of offenders.'
> (PR 031)

> '1. Represent the community – paid professional.
> 2. Offer time.
> 3. Personal talents.
> 4. Offer something significantly different and sometimes more appropriate than professional input.' (PR 269)

Although these questions were directed at volunteers within police and probation officers' own agencies, they do suggest a markedly different basic attitude to the volunteer. The police were somewhat sceptical about the usefulness of special constables, and certainly saw their use as limited. Probation officers, in contrast, were keen to stress the positive advantages of involving non-professionals.

It is something of a leap to relate these responses to attitudes towards victims support schemes. However, bearing this in mind, we might anticipate that behind police approval of victims support schemes lie some doubts on the effectiveness of volunteers, and suggest this as an additional factor influencing referral patterns. In contrast, the positive view of voluntarism held by probation officers, perhaps reflecting the official 'party line' of social administration teaching, may provide some further understanding of the willingness of many probation officers to limit their involvement in victims services and to see the victims support scheme model as appropriate.[8]

**Summary**

The dilemma for probation is well illustrated in the words of NOVA, in its review of the role of probation in victims services in the United States:

> 'If the administrator perceives the role or mission of probation to be limited to recommending dispositions and to supervising probationers, then the concept of victims services is an absent one. However, if the mission of probation is perceived to include delinquency and crime prevention, community education, dealing with the impact of crime and building good community support for quality correctional services, then the administrator will place a high priority on providing services to victims, particularly victims of violent crime.'
>
> (Rowland *et al.* 1984: 10)

In the United States, several probation departments have chosen this second route, providing crisis counselling for victims, advice on compensation and the legal process, and escort services, presenting victim impact statements in court and playing a major role in co-ordinating victims services. In Britain, some writers have advocated a move to a similar, but not identical, community role for probation (Raynor 1985). This chapter has well illustrated the difficulties in making such a shift, from the perspective of both probation and victims support schemes.

Along with the police, the probation service has played a crucial role in the development of victims services and, as we have noted, provided an important counterbalance to the police. However, whereas the last chapter suggested that the key issue in police–victims service relationships was operational, and that ideologically there was a large degree of affinity, probation–victims service relationships appeared rather more questionable on an ideological level. Most especially, we found a minority of volunteers to be sceptical of the role of probation officers, and our sample of volunteers espoused markedly different views on law and order and offenders than did probation volunteers and, we would assume, probation officers. This was ironic because, while many probation officers were wary of increased involvement with victims services without additional resources, they were positive about the role of victims support schemes and showed considerably greater enthusiasm for the volunteer ideal than did the police.

Perhaps the most significant finding to emerge from the last two chapters, however, is that which relates to the ideological perspectives of our victims support scheme volunteers. This point will be followed through in the following chapters. In Chapter 11 we shall focus on the volunteers in more detail and consider their motivation to become involved in voluntary work in general and victims services in particular, and relate this to their tasks. Then, in the concluding chapter, we shall consider this in the wider context of the politics of the victims movement.

# 11 Volunteers and victims support schemes

In line with other volunteer initiatives, the use of volunteers by victims support schemes is extolled in terms of community participation. Caring by the community, for the community, is considered preferable to reliance on paid employees of the state. Thus, even such a stalwart of the welfare state as Titmuss (1971) could, in the context of blood donorship, agree to the merits of a system where members of a society freely gave for the benefit of their fellows.

At the same time, somewhat ironically, it is widely accepted that those who voluntarily give their time, services, or money are scarcely typical members of society. From Aves (1969) to Humble (1982), the typical volunteer has been identified as distinctive in various respects – age, sex, or social class, for example – in the latter case leading one commentator to define voluntary effort as the new 'middle class imperialism' (Webb 1981).

Nevertheless, while reviews have for the most part accepted such generalizations (for a recent review see Brenton 1985), the methodological basis for them is both narrow and suspect. For example, samples of volunteers are generally drawn from two alternative sources. First, samples of those volunteering to work with a particular agency may be taken. Studies of this kind in fact seem to either consciously limit themselves to one agency and restrict their conclusions, or focus on one or two agencies, particularly in fields such as personal social services, health, or (more recently) employment, and assume similar patterns would be discovered in other areas. Second, data may be drawn from national surveys, where members of the public are questioned about any voluntary work they might have done. Here the major problem relates to difficulties in defining 'voluntary work' – relatively large minorities of the population are invariably discovered to have volunteered for something, yet the variety of tasks and the vagueness of definition limit the conclusions.

Having identified the characteristics of volunteers, some studies go on to consider one further feature, motivation, in terms of why people volunteer. In this context generalizations are again easy to make but equally dangerous. Thus the public may be drawn into voluntary work for altruistic reasons – a vague desire to help others (or less vaguely a religious commitment to do so) – or from self-interest (to relieve boredom, or an entry route to a career).

We do not claim to have succeeded in solving the methodological difficulties associated with identifying altruism and self-interest through an interview. Nevertheless, in other respects our approach has, we would argue, made a significant break from earlier research in at least four respects.

First, in our wider research design, we deliberately incorporated different, but related, avenues of voluntary work, such that our analysis was comparative. Thus we considered three groups of volunteers within the criminal justice field, where the aims of the organization were rather different: probation voluntary associates, police special constables, and victims support scheme volunteers. Essentially, we were concerned to see whether different subgroups of the population were drawn to these rather different forms of voluntary activity, and if so, how and with what consequences.

To do this we compared the social characteristics of volunteers, but then went on to consider in more detail attitudinal features. However, we would argue that our approach was distinct in a second respect, because we were only partly interested in why individuals became involved in voluntary work and primarily concerned with motivation *vis-à-vis* a *particular form* of voluntary work. For example, the goals of victims support schemes are *care-orientated* towards a specific target group, *crime victims*, the probation service is care-orientated towards a distinctly different target group, *offenders*, while the police are *control- or help-orientated* towards a more amorphous target group, the public.[1] We were therefore interested to see whether different volunteers were attracted to different areas of voluntary work within the criminal justice system, *and* whether their motives reflected distinctive patterns as to what form of help was required, or merited, by whom.

Third, in this context we saw it as necessary to move beyond a concern with 'motives' as such. Rather, we saw ideology as the key issue, where ideology subsumes a moral universe incorporating perceptions, attitudes, and values. Specifically, this involved comparing different groups of volunteers according to their perceptions of the crime problem, its solutions, and their part in these solutions. More generally, it involved considering the political orientations of our sample.

Fourth and finally, though, it is important that we do not see ideology as a static concept. Equally, we should not view motives to participate in voluntary work as constants. True, those who volunteer because they identify with the goals of a particular organization may remain in that voluntary work because they find their expectations met, or they may leave, disillusioned. But they may also come to modify their ideology through a series of interchanges between self and organization; or rather between self, other volunteers, paid employees of the organization, representatives of other agencies, and members of the public – processes which may incorporate official or unofficial reward structures. In the context of victims support, for example, we were interested in volunteers and how they interact with their schemes. This is a two-way process. On the one hand, it requires a consideration of volunteers; on the other, an understanding of schemes' policies. These are not mutually exclusive.

The remainder of this chapter, then, is devoted to a discussion of our findings for victims support scheme volunteers, contrasted, where appropriate, with police and probation volunteers. (For a fuller comparative analysis, see Gill 1986b.) In the next section we consider the ways in which volunteers were recruited by the various schemes. Then we review data on the social characteristics of volunteers. Having done this, we concentrate on the motives, ideologies, and subcultures of volunteers working in the victims support schemes in our survey.

**Recruitment**

Recruitment strategies are, of course, important since they determine to a considerable extent the composition of the pool of interested potential volunteers. Media appeals, welcomed by Wolfenden (1978), elicit a big response but suffer from a high drop-out rate (Hodgkinson 1980). If a specific type of volunteer is required, volunteer bureaux can be attractive because, in screening applicants, they can sift out those most likely to meet the requirements of a particular agency. However, the most recognized method of recruitment is via 'word of mouth' (Aves 1969; Humble 1982), although few agencies rely solely on this (Jackson 1985). Nevertheless, where it is found that people are persuaded into volunteering by friends (Hadley and Scott 1980; Morris 1969), self-perpetuation of particular types of volunteer may occur.

Yet 'word of mouth' was the most common source of recruitment among victims support schemes. When volunteers were asked where or from whom they initially heard of victims support schemes, the majority cited someone they knew as their source. A few noticed articles in the local or national press. Some schemes recruited their volunteers by writing to other recognized voluntary organizations enquiring as to the availability of volunteers for work with crime victims; others advertised in the local volunteer bureau or press. But in the main, schemes relied on word of mouth.

Indeed, it was not unusual for a request for possible new recruits to be made at either a volunteer or a management meeting. In such cases someone – often a police representative – was willing to suggest a name, and arrangements were made to approach the person concerned.

In one area the management committee was formed by the police representative (a chief inspector) writing to local voluntary and statutory agencies seeking interest. Once a working group had been formed, an advertisement for volunteers was placed in the local press. In contrast, one other scheme recruited the initial group of volunteers exclusively from the WRVS. Here, as elsewhere though, police involvement in recruitment was evident in the vetting of volunteers for criminal records.

With the exceptions of Plymouth and Exeter, schemes rarely suffered any permanent shortage of volunteers. In one other instance there was concern at the lack of male volunteers. In general, though, in an area not troubled by high crime rates and with some referral blockages, the workload was well within the capabilities of a small group of volunteers. As a result, schemes could be selective in their choice of volunteers, perhaps reinforcing tendencies in the recruitment process towards a certain amount of homogeneity.

## The social characteristics of volunteers

Data on the social characteristics of volunteers were available from files and from interviews with a random sample of volunteers. In the case of victims support schemes, records on 107 volunteers were filed for information on gender, age, marital status, and social class. The interviews, conducted with fifty-five of these, allowed these details to be further considered, plus other information on education qualifications and voluntary-work experience. Comparisons were then made with probation volunteers (n=219, n=58 respectively) and police special constables (n=250, n=51, respectively).[2]

Scheme records revealed that a slight majority of victims support scheme volunteers were female (59 per cent), similar to probation voluntary associates, but not surprisingly in contrast to police specials, where only 21 per cent were female. These findings were not unexpected, but it is perhaps worth mentioning that in both probation *and* the police, women were better represented among volunteers than among full-time employees.

Rather more surprisingly, victims support scheme volunteers tended to be considerably older than volunteers working in most welfare agencies, other than those specializing in services for the elderly (Hadley and Scott 1980). Only two from our survey were in their 20s, and five in their 30s, and half were aged over 55, with nearly one-third aged over 60. This contrasted, not surprisingly, with police specials, where there is a maximum age, but victims support scheme volunteers were also significantly older than probation voluntary associates.

The combined influence of age and gender resulted in only 47 per cent of victims support scheme volunteers being employed, with 21 per cent housewives and 31 per cent retired. Notably, in an area of high unemployment, the unemployed were significant by their absence.

Those who were employed were grouped according to social class; 62 per cent fell in social class I (professional) or II (managerial), and only 2 per cent were in semi-skilled or unskilled manual work. While, as already noted, volunteers do tend to be disproportionately drawn from high social classes, as *Table 11.1* illustrates, those volunteering to work with crime victims were significantly different in this respect from probation volunteers and especially police specials, and these differences were maintained when we used interview data ($x^2 = 15.93$, $p<0.01$). A similar pattern emerges from interview data on education, with a higher percentage of victims support scheme volunteers having proceeded to higher education ($x^2 = 22.51$, $p<0.01$).

How, then, can we best summarize our findings on victims support scheme volunteers? Overall they reflect earlier findings in that volunteers were slightly more likely to be female than male, and that higher social classes were heavily overrepresented, although in terms of age they were considerable older than might have been anticipated. Making comparisons with volunteers working for probation and police, however, allows us to identify somewhat

Table 11.1 *Social class of volunteers (percentages)*

|  | VSS (n = 58)* | Probation (n = 156) | Police (n = 229) |
| --- | --- | --- | --- |
| I/II | 62 | 57 | 28 |
| III non-manual | 19 | 16 | 20 |
| III manual, IV, V | 19 | 27 | 52 |
| total | 100 | 100 | 100 |

$x^2 = 48.29$, $p<0.01$
Note:
*Lower numbers here caused by the larger number of female and retired volunteers; an analysis of previous employment for the latter revealed the same pattern.

different populations being attracted to these different agencies. Quite distinct, police specials tended to be younger males employed in routine non-manual or skilled manual work, with poorer educational qualifications. In contrast, probation and victims support scheme volunteers were more similar in gender, social class, and education, although the latter were particularly concentrated in the higher social classes. The most notable difference between these two groups, however, was in terms of age, with victims support scheme volunteers being significantly older.

Were we to halt our analysis here, it would be tempting to conclude that those volunteers for *care-orientated* work with victims and offenders share many characteristics in common, and are distinct from those joining the special constabulary. Fortunately, we are able to provide further analysis which undermines such a straightforward conclusion.

## From motives to ideologies

Assessing motivation to volunteer is a complex task. People may undervalue their motives, be embarrassed about stating purely altruistic intentions (or indeed self-interest) or may simply not recollect their original states of mind. Some may confuse their original motives with their current ones, which for some may be distinctly different.

In order to minimize these various problems, respondents were, during the interview, asked a number of questions about their motives, those questioned being asked why they had originally been attracted to voluntary work, and then how they decided on this particular agency. Following these two open-ended questions, they were asked whether it was more true to say they had originally been interested in voluntary work *per se* or specifically work with this agency. Later in the questionnaire, we asked why they *continued* in this voluntary work. Finally, towards the end of the questionnaire, respondents were offered a list of statements 'typical' of why some people volunteer and were invited to rank them in order of importance.

Considering first why volunteers became involved in voluntary work, victims support scheme volunteers fell into five main groups. The largest of these, accounting for 40 per cent of responses, encompassed the volunteers' own particular needs, interests, or availability. For example:

- 'I just felt I needed something to do after being made redundant.'
(I 05)

- 'I hate to sound pi but when I came down here I had no job and needed to be part of the community.'
(I 19)

A further 18 per cent replied in ways which could be identified broadly as altruistic motives – a desire to help other people. However, less predictably, almost as many (16 per cent) could best be described as having 'drifted' into voluntary work; that is, the volunteer could think of no conscious decision having been made. Notable here, in the context of recruitment strategies, were those who became involved because a current volunteer asked them.

A further 13 per cent said they did voluntary work out of religious commitment:

- 'Just a natural follow-on from my beliefs. If you have a Christian outlook, this is automatic.'
(I 41)

- 'Because of the fact that I am a Christian.' (I 01)

Finally, 9 per cent spontaneously gave answers which were specific to victims support schemes. For example:

'I didn't think of it as voluntary work. It was this particular scheme, and I was keen to do it.' (I 05)

'I suppose because of experience as a policeman having visited loads of homes, and the growing realization that we were doing so much for the offender rather than for victims, and recognized the need as a policeman but like social services had no time. This was an area of much development.'

(I 33)

Not surprisingly, when we asked specifically about motivation for joining victims support schemes, this view was reflected in considerably more replies. Thus 38 per cent mentioned an interest in victims or the victims' movement, although interestingly only one referred to personal experience as a crime victim. Of the rest, the following examples well illustrate the extent to which previous experience in the criminal justice system provided openings:

— 'I worked with the offender and wanted to find out about the other side.'

(I 14)

— 'I was speaking to a probation officer about how much the system was offender-orientated and the victim was missed out. So this led to him getting me a place on victims support schemes.'

(I 29)

— 'Having been a magistrate, I saw the opposite side of the coin and trauma of the victim.'

(I 35)

Nevertheless, those who appeared to have joined victims support as a conscious, perhaps well-planned decision, were in a minority. Just over half the sample (54 per cent), in contrast, were classified as having 'drifted' into work with victims. Many said they had joined because they were asked, again signifying the importance of recruitment methods. Others responded to an advertisement, where any other advertisement at the time might have received the same response; others were directed to victims support by a volunteer bureau. For example:

— 'I was asked if I would be interested when it started up.'

(I 15)

— 'One of the people I know said I had been recommended – would I like to try it? Well I thought this sounded a good thing, so I thought I'd try it.'  (I 38)

'A local policeman came to see me and said, "Do you think it would be a good idea?" and so I said, "Yes", and that was it.'  (I 43)

'It wasn't particularly victims support; it came along when I needed it.'  (I 04)

Thus, while a small proportion of our sample 'drifted' into voluntary work, about half drifted into work with victims support schemes. In contrast, a large minority appear to have been attracted to work with victims specifically, a proportion similar to that for probation (37 per cent)[3] but well below that for the police (59 per cent).

This hint that victims support scheme volunteers were less specific than some others in their choice of agency is supported by replies to a question asking which of two statements best described their original motivation; 62 per cent chose the statement indicative of an interest in voluntary work in general. In contrast, 50 per cent of voluntary associates and 59 per cent of police specials identified an agency-specific motive, a difference which was not quite statistically significant ($x^2 = 4.57$, $0.05 < p < 0.1$).

The key features leading to the decision to volunteer for work with victims support were, excluding the 'drift' factor, reflected in responses to the 'cafeteria'-style question asked towards the end of the interview (Moser and Kalton 1979). Here nine alternative motives were 'offered', and respondents were asked to rank each which applied. A mean rank score was then calculated for each alternative. Probation and police respondents were offered a similar list.[4] In *Table 11.2* we have itemized the rank scores for the victims support scheme sample, and included where appropriate the rank score for police and probation volunteers.

Considering first the responses from the victims support scheme sample, it is not surprising that respondents ranked first the choice with most esteem attached to it, namely a concern to help others. In other respects, though, choices reflected the issues raised already. Thus volunteers identified victims' needs as important, felt the work was interesting, had time on their hands and saw this as an

Table 11.2 *Ranking of reasons for becoming volunteers for victims support schemes, the probation service, and the police*

| reasons | VSS | probation | police |
|---|---|---|---|
| Genuine desire to help other people. | 1 | 1 | 1 |
| Victims of crime were a group who particularly needed assistance. | 2 | NA | NA |
| This type of voluntary work would be interesting and exacting. | 3 | 2 | 2 |
| Committed to the need to uphold law and order. | 4 | 7 | 4 |
| Had time on hands and wished to use it constructively. | 5 | 3 | 5 |
| Saw this as an opportunity to meet new people. | 6 | 6 | 6 |
| Had previously been a victim and thus wished to help other victims. | 7 | NA | NA |
| Considered that at some point might like to work in criminal justice field.[5] | 8 | 4 | 8 |
| Would enhance occupational promotion opportunities. | 9 | 8 | 9 |

opportunity to meet new people. In contrast, they rarely saw it as a career route (either directly or indirectly), not surprising given their age, and were not particularly led into this work after personal experience as a crime victim.

Comparison with the other two samples has to be made with care, given that in each case two scale items were different. Nevertheless, two general points are evident. First, probation volunteers were distinctive in that a number of respondents saw their voluntary work as a route into a course involving a Certificate of Qualification for Social Worker (CQSW) and ultimately work as a probation officer or social worker. Second, and in direct contrast to our comparisons on the social characteristics of volunteers, victims support scheme volunteers and special constables responded similarly. Indeed, their rankings of the seven items they shared in common were identical, most notably with each seeing the need to uphold law and order as an important motivation, in contrast to voluntary associates.

We shall take this point on board later. Here, though, we can summarize our findings on motivation to join, and compare victims support scheme volunteers with our other samples.

In terms of the process of becoming involved in voluntary work, a similarly sized minority in all three samples gave answers which indicated that they drifted into voluntary work, and similar numbers from victims support and probation (but less for the police) gave altruistic motives. However, while probation volunteers were to a certain extent drawn into voluntary work as a route into a welfare career, and police specials were more inclined than others to cite agency-specific reasons, victims support schemes volunteers were best typified by the numbers indicating an eagerness to get involved, use their spare time, or meet people, with rather less focus on any particular type of voluntary work. This is supported by the additional finding that they were more likely than the others to be involved in other forms of voluntary activity. For example 62 per cent of victims support scheme volunteers were, at the time of interview, also engaged on other voluntary work, compared with 50 per cent of probation volunteers, and 41 per cent of special constables ($x^2 = 4.57$, $0.1 < p < 0.05$).

However, when we turn to consider motivations to join a specific agency, the picture changes somewhat. Each agency included a number of volunteers who cited a particular interest in this area of work and, in contrast, those who appeared to have drifted into this type of voluntary work. Among probation volunteers the goal of a career in probation remained distinctive. But in victims support, the numbers who seemed to have drifted into this work were both considerable and larger than in either of the other agencies. To a certain extent, then, there is some indication that many victims support scheme volunteers could well have been found, in different circumstances, immersed in other forms of voluntary activity.

In the discussion so far, only one finding jars with this view, namely the relative popularity of the 'law and order' item on our prompt card. This does, however, become more understandable if we consider other issues.

First, we can refer to the question of why volunteers *continued* to do voluntary work, which, as Blau and Scott (1977) have suggested in the context of paid workers, is distinct from the reasons for joining originally. A large minority (27 per cent) said that they continued in the work for altruistic or other-directed reasons, and a further 6 per cent because of their religious beliefs. However, most significantly, 26 per cent gave replies which we categorized as 'agency committed', and an additional 14 per cent were coded as 'stickability'. These two categories were closely related. In the former were those who stated quite explicitly that they were committed to victims support schemes. For example:

'I felt what I have done has been worthwhile. Our particular group is a good one. We are all interested in each other's work. And also all the victims have been so appreciative.'

(I 13)

'Because I believe there is still a worthwhile role to be fulfilled and if we can help them I am happy to do so. It can fulfil a worthwhile function.'

(I 32)

'Because I think it is a good thing. It seems to me an admirable thing.'

(I 37)

In the 'stickability' category we included those who said that they did not give up something to which they had committed themselves. For example:

'I feel committed at this stage because it hasn't got off the ground.'

(I 15)

'If you commit yourself, you are committed. You always need people in case you get a rush of happenings.'

(I 28)

The fact that the agency was new and the victims movement as a whole was struggling to establish itself was influential in building up a sense of commitment among volunteers. The cause was seen as worthwhile, and volunteers wanted to be a part of its development. In contrast, both probation volunteers and especially police special constables cited 'enjoyment' of the work as their main reason for continuing in voluntary work. But victims support schemes were new organizations, where work was in many respects lacking and by its nature less structured and predictable. Volunteers were thus less in a position to say that they enjoyed the work but rather stressed their commitment to it.

This suggests two avenues for further consideration. First, we should ask whether victims support schemes draw into them volunteers who are particularly sympathetic to their goals in ways we have not yet tapped. Second, we should consider how the organization itself impacts on the volunteers who are recruited. To address these issues, we need to shift the emphasis from motives to ideologies and subcultures.

**Victims support schemes and the volunteer subculture**

In their attempts to make sense of the world in which they live, and reassure themselves that the world is a meaningful and just place, individuals are drawn towards others who share their views and will reciprocate their attempts to create stability and order out of unpredictability and injustice. In considering involvement with agencies from the criminal justice system, volunteers are not alone in seeking organizations which share with them a particular view of order in society, subsuming explanations for disorder or lawlessness and social and political solutions. Incorporated within this are, at the very least, perceptions of the current crime problem, views of offenders and their reasons for offending, and evaluations of personnel and policies applicable to law enforcement.

As we have already noted, victims support scheme volunteers rated very close to the police on our crime problem scale. With a mean score of 18.6, well above the scale mean of 15, they scored 0.5 less than police specials but 1.8 more than voluntary associates. Their view of contemporary Britain was of a society in which crime featured as a major social problem, where moral chaos reigned, where criminal gangs ran amok in many cities, and where it was unsafe for women to go out alone after dark.

Similarly, on our offender scale, victims support scheme volunteers had a mean score of 20.3, above the scale mean of 18, only 0.3 below the scores for police specials, and well above probation volunteers whose score of 16.2 was considerably below the scale mean. Unlike the latter, they were willing to see offenders as a distinctive subgroup of the population, sometimes 'more like animals than human beings', and were less likely to accept that offenders were themselves society's 'victims'.

What then of current law-enforcement personnel and policies? As we demonstrated in Chapters 9 and 10, victims support scheme volunteers had very positive views of the police, both on our police scale and as reflected elsewhere in the interviews and informal discussions. Equally, they were rather more ambivalent about probation officers and probation.

This was not, however, extensively reflected in attitudes towards sentencing in general. Thus, although we asked only one, very general and unsophisticated question on sentencing to all three samples, it is evident from *Table 11.3* that responses from victims support scheme volunteers were similar to those from voluntary associates and in marked contrast to those from police specials. There were significant differences between samples in terms of attitudes towards capital punishment ($x^2 = 31.79$, $p<0.01$), corporal punishment ($x^2 = 13.31$, $p<0.01$), and community-service orders ($x^2 = 12.21$, $p<0.01$). However, while in the latter case this was due to differences between all three samples, in each of the former it reflected the distinctive views of police specials compared with the other two samples. Moreover, in terms of attitudes towards probation orders and cautioning, differences were not significant, although victims support scheme volunteers were significantly less likely than police specials ($x^2 = 5.11$, $p<0.05$) to reject probation as an alternative for adults.

Table 11.3 *Percentage of each volunteer sample\* who felt that certain 'sentences' might sometimes be appropriate for adult offenders*

| 'sentence' | VSS | probation | police |
| --- | --- | --- | --- |
| capital punishment | 47.1 (n = 51) | 43.6 (n = 55) | 92.2 (n = 51) |
| corporal punishment | 47.2 (n = 53) | 40.7 (n = 54) | 75.0 (n = 48) |
| probation order | 94.5 (n = 55) | 96.6 (n = 58) | 80.0 (n = 50) |
| community-service order | 86.8 (n = 53) | 98.2 (n = 56) | 75.5 (n = 49) |
| caution | 80.0 (n = 55) | 91.1 (n = 56) | 82.0 (n = 50) |

Note:
\* In each case excluding those who said they did not know.

On this item at least, then, victims support scheme volunteers did not demonstrate distinctly punitive views on sentencing and were certainly not aligned with the perspectives of special constables. Combined with other responses discussed already, they felt that the criminal justice system was too offender-orientated, and approved of reparation, even though two-thirds did not feel that victims support schemes should be involved in this.[6]

What seems to be indicated is a mixture of care-orientation and conservatism; a concern with the crime problem, an acceptance of the responsibility for this falling on an identified group of offenders (rather than being the fault of society, or of offending being widespread in society), support for the police, yet no dramatic or distinctive wish for harsher sentences. To a large extent it indicates a balance between care and control, which may be allied to the conservative penal philosophies of the pre-1970s period (Ryan 1983). Although we have no direct evidence of shades of conservatism within our sample, the voting patterns were certainly clear. Thus, when asked about current voting intentions and past voting behaviour, the volunteer samples differed significantly in their responses (*Table 11.4*), with police specials to the right, voluntary associates to the left, and victims support scheme volunteers somewhere in between, on a political spectrum which was not that far right of current voting intentions in the South West. If we link voting with social class, we have, in our three samples, three broadly distinctive groups: upper-middle-class liberals (voluntary associates), lower-middle/upper-working-class conservatives (special constables), and upper-middle-class conservatives (victims support scheme volunteers). Ideologically, the latter two, we would argue, while sharing common definitions of the crime problem, differ somewhat in their views of the solution, with special constables more

Table 11.4 *Voting behaviour and intentions of volunteers*

|  | voting, 1983 gen. election | | | current* voting intentions | | |
| --- | --- | --- | --- | --- | --- | --- |
|  | VSS (n=55) | probation (n=58) | police (n=51) | VSS (n=55) | probation (n=58) | police (n=51) |
| (i) Conservative | 49 | 38 | 65 | 38 | 28 | 53 |
| (ii) Alliance | 35 | 33 | 22 | 46 | 41 | 26 |
| (iii) Labour | 4 | 21 | 6 | 6 | 16 | 2 |
| (iv) Other | 2 | 0 | 0 | 2 | 0 | 0 |
| (v) NA/DK/ no vote | 11 | 8 | 8 | 9 | 16 | 20 |
| total | 101 | 100 | 101 | 101 | 101 | 101 |

*At time of interview, i.e. before the 1987 election
Comparing (i), (ii) and (iii), $x^2 = 14.82$, $p<0.01$
Comparing (i) with (ii)/(iii) combined, $x^2 = 10.21$, $p<0.01$

punitive than their perhaps paternalistic conservative equivalents in victims support.

To understand this further, however, it is necessary to look at the relationships between volunteers and the organization, where the latter finds slightly different expression at local and national levels.

Compared with our other two samples, victims support scheme volunteers were more likely to drift into this area of voluntary work, and consequently had less clearly formed expectations of the organization. They were therefore somewhat dependent upon the victims' movement for defining for them the goals and priorities of the agency. In this respect, while the focus on victims as the forgotten people of the criminal justice system, or indeed the welfare state, touched a chord amongst our respondents, the policy of the NAVSS explicitly discourages volunteers from associating this with wider sentencing philosophies. It is also possible that the incorporation of both police and probation representatives on management committees helps fulfil NAVSS objectives of maintaining balance.

The structure of schemes at local level provided both the raw materials and the constraints upon which a volunteer subculture might develop. Being autonomous agencies, schemes were dependent upon the police for referrals and needed to convince an agency, which was already somewhat sceptical about volunteers, that they were useful.

This raises the question of volunteers' commitment. Police specials, immersed in both voluntary work and the police subculture (see Gill 1986b), were committed on two levels: to the nature of the work and to the police as an organization. Probation volunteers, though grossly underdeployed, to a lesser extent enjoyed their work but were also committed to helping others, and despite the somewhat ambivalent attitudes of probation officers, were highly committed to the agency. What, then, of the commitment of victims support scheme volunteers to the work and the organization?

In terms of the nature of the work, there was potential for greater volunteer involvement. In contrast to police and probation volunteers, victims support scheme volunteers had considerably more autonomy. Once a case had been referred to the scheme, only the co-ordinator came between volunteer and victim; clients 'belonged' to volunteers to a far greater extent than in the other agencies. This does of course bring its dangers, for example where volunteers are reluctant to refer victims to professionals for long-term help. However, in the present context we merely wish to observe that the nature of the organization might impose a greater degree of commitment upon volunteers, because 'its' clients become 'their' clients.

However, in the South West the potential for this level of commitment was restricted by the lack of referrals. Volunteers had a commitment to giving 'their' time freely, but there was insufficient work. They therefore committed themselves to the agency itself.

This was undoubtedly reflected in our schemes, where victims support scheme volunteers showed a greater involvement in the organization and felt themselves to be an important part of it. They were, for example, notable in their attendance at volunteer meetings and were positive about training sessions. Commitment was, moreover, encouraged by the fact that schemes were new. Because the victims movement was still young, volunteers could identify with the new movement – if not there at conception, they could at least share in the joys of birth. A sense of mission and purpose could therefore be built up, and management and volunteer meetings and training provided the forum for such commitment to be reaffirmed.

The problem here is that by definition such a basis for commitment is only temporary – schemes cannot remain 'new' for long. Thus there is the potential for volunteer disinterest or disenchantment under present conditions in the South West. Volunteers work on their own and have few clients to help. It is thus easy to see them drifting off into other areas of voluntary work where they feel more appreciated.

The solutions would appear to be at least twofold. First, it is crucial that volunteers are not under-used and thus seemingly undervalued. This implies that changes need to be made to the referral process, that volunteers need to be used in rotation where possible (rather than some receiving more of the referrals), that schemes should not over-recruit, and that volunteers should be given a realistic estimate of the extent of commitment required. Clearly, the problem of under-use varies regionally. However, in areas where volunteers are plentiful and initial commitment high, it is important that such commitment should not be lost, as indeed most management committees appreciated.

Second, and rather differently, we wish to stress the role of the organization in maintaining commitment. As we have noted, the autonomy of schemes gives them an advantage over voluntary structures which are incorporated into statutory agencies. However, volunteers who provide services for victims do so in relative isolation from other volunteers. It is thus important that volunteers are provided with opportunities to build up a corporate identity through interchange with other scheme members. As we have noted, training sessions and meetings provide this opportunity. However, despite the recommendations of the NAVSS (1986b), ongoing training is not fully developed. We would therefore see it as important, not only as a means of improving volunteer efficiency but as a mechanism for maintaining morale and identity, preventing the trough in commitment which appears to hit schemes after a few years (Maguire and Corbett 1986).

## Summary

We began the review of our findings on volunteers in victims support schemes on familiar ground. Apart from their age, volunteers were fairly typical of volunteers generally, and scarcely representative of the communities from which they came. However, in age they were somewhat more typical of the victims who were most likely to be defined as in need of help.

Nevertheless, there was little evidence that volunteers were motivated to work with victims support schemes because of previous victimization. Rather, the high profile of elderly volunteers could be explained in terms of two advantages: their life experience and their availability to respond to calls at most hours of the day (and particularly during the daytime). Notably though, the life experience of lower-class potential volunteers, with more direct experience as crime victims, and the ready availability of the unemployed, did not result in these groups being overrepresented. Indeed, their near total exclusion was striking.

The comparative nature of our study did, moreover, allow us to take the notion of an '*identifiable volunteer*' further by considering the ideologies of volunteers working in three different agencies. Here we found that victims support scheme volunteers fell somewhat between the more punitive philosophy of special constables and the offender-orientation of probation volunteers, reflecting a mixture of concern over the crime problem and anti-offender perspectives and a care-orientated philosophy. This is perhaps understandable given the non-political role of the NAVSS, the balance of police and probation in scheme management, and the caring aspects of work with victims. In practical terms, volunteers did not express more punitive views on sentencing than did probation volunteers, but they were notably reluctant to become involved in reparation and mediation initiatives; where there was 'spare capacity', work with non-crime victims provided a more acceptable alternative.

The precise mix of volunteer motivation and initial ideological perspectives, on the one hand, and organizational influences, on the other, will vary between schemes. In our study, it is not precisely clear as to what the relative influences of each are. Volunteers in victims support schemes differed in their social characteristics from the other volunteer samples but were typical in other respects. Equally, while many more appeared to drift into victim services than was the case for the other samples (probably because such services are so recent), in other respects motivations were broadly similar. Nevertheless, informal recruitment methods allowed all three agencies to avoid volunteers they considered unsuitable.

However, volunteers, whether they rationally choose or drift into an agency, whether they are carefully selected or not, are only likely to remain with that agency where their wider ideologies incorporate the role of the agency as meaningful and just. Those involved with victims support schemes in the South West tended to be politically to the right (if not to the extent of special constables); they perceived the crime problem as a serious one and had little sympathy with offenders, and they supported the police. At the same time, they demonstrated a caring philosophy towards both crime and non-crime victims. In victims support schemes they found a medium which, while discouraging any 'anti-offender' backlash, allowed these attitudes to be maintained, and indeed provided them with support.

However, while the voluntary nature and autonomy of schemes encouraged commitment, lack of work and the isolation of volunteers from one another limited the influence of the agency to maintain commitment. In the short term, volunteers were able to reaffirm their commitment because the victims movement was in its infancy and many schemes were struggling to get off the ground. In the long term, we have suggested that unless the relationship between organization and volunteer is strengthened, through better referral policies and more opportunities for volunteers to meet one another, the influence of the agency on its volunteers will be undermined.

# PART V
## *Discussion*

# 12 Discussion

**Summary**

In Part I we focused on crime and its victims. We argued that while, in terms of actual risk, serious crime is not particularly common and that other contemporary problems may be more prevalent, this is not necessarily the case for all groups of the population. Some, notably those most vulnerable and disadvantaged in other respects, may be particularly at risk of crime. Moreover, reflected in the political salience of crime, fear of crime is itself an issue paramount in the minds of many, whether or not such fears are based on actual risk.

In Chapter 2 we assessed the impact of crime in terms of the effects of crime on victims. Although only a small minority of victims appear to experience long-term problems, crime does affect a large number of victims at least in the short term, and many victims experience financial or emotional difficulties. Moreover, while offender characteristics are only vaguely related to crime impact, victims who suffer at the hands of offenders whom they knew prior to the offence register the most concern. Further, those victims who appear most affected – women, the divorced or separated, one-parent families, those living alone, the elderly, and the poor – are among the most vulnerable and powerless groups in our society. For some such groups, risk may be great, impact considerable, and fear correspondingly disabling. For others, risk may be no more than average, but fear of crime is none the less a significant intrusion on their lives.

As in most areas of social policy, however, it is difficult to translate victims' perceptions of their problems into a menu of 'needs' which can be referred to appropriate 'services'. Nevertheless, we have argued that while crime is for most victims a nuisance rather than a disaster, this is no reason for governments to avoid responsibility. Moreover, for some victims, and for some offence situations (notably personal crimes where the offender is well known to the victim), many victims do experience considerable distress. Alternative responses to such grievances and greater concerns were the subjects of subsequent chapters.

In Part II we provided a critical analysis of the development of state services for the victims of crime. In Britain, as elsewhere, these have been minimal and based within the criminal justice system rather than welfare agencies. There are, of course, exceptions; medical provisions for those injured by crime are, for example, provided free by the National Health Service and thus victims are not faced with medical costs as in some other countries. Nevertheless, the 'giant evils' identified by Beveridge did not encompass crime, and state services for victims in Britain have in the postwar period emerged gradually and with apparent reluctance.

The most notable developments are in terms of criminal injuries compensation and compensation orders. However, as we noted in Chapters 3 and 4, despite the humanitarian concern of Margery Fry these innovations drew much of their *political* appeal from the right, balancing and partially reinforcing punitive sentencing philosophies. Additionally, in each case it was explicit that victims had won no *rights*. Indeed, there is no obligation on any state agency to inform victims of the possibility of either form of compensation!

Mediation and reparation are rather different initiatives, which raise somewhat different issues regarding victims' rights. Largely originating (in present-day form) in North America, they are very much in the experimental stage in Britain. Indeed, as we have indicated, even in North America their use is largely restricted to non-violent crimes and juvenile offenders. It may thus be too early to pass judgement, although we see much of positive value in reparation and mediation for both offender and victim. Furthermore, as we have noted, *public* response to such initiatives is encouraging, even if – in Britain at least – victims support schemes have more mixed views.

Despite these developments, it remains true that most services for crime victims in Britain are provided by the voluntary sector. Part III was therefore devoted to a critical analysis of voluntary organizations. In Chapter 5 we introduced our own classification of voluntary-sector provision, suggesting that agencies may be compared on four criteria: their relationship to conventional statutory services, sources of funding, goals, and the relationship between helper and helped. To illustrate the model, we described the emergence of, and shifting emphasis within, Women's Refuges and Rape Crisis Centres in Britain and North America.

Then, in Chapter 6, we focused on the growth of victims support schemes in Britain between 1971 and 1987 – perhaps the most notable voluntary-sector expansion of the last twenty years. These schemes, originating in Bristol, emerged as independent local organizations aimed at addressing the difficulties posed for victims by crime and particularly non-vehicle property crimes. However, rapid growth in the number of schemes led to both the foundation of a national association, the NAVSS, and a degree of variation between schemes. Additionally, as earlier lessons from the voluntary sector have suggested, regional variations in the emergence of schemes and their ability to attract sufficient volunteers have created disparities. Nevertheless, it is possible to construct an ideal type to illustrate that victims support schemes differ markedly from the feminist-inspired services described in Chapter 5.

The contrast with innovations in the United States is, however, equally vivid, as we note in Chapter 7. In the United States the victims movement owes rather more of its impetus to a concern with system-efficiency, the law-and-order lobby, and victims' rights campaigns. Partly as a result, it is better funded, more closely identified with statutory agencies (particularly the police), and more political in its operational presence than is the NAVSS. It thus provides a contrast, not only with mainstream British developments but most especially with victims services in the South West of England, where the voluntary ideal is more closely maintained than is the case nationally.

In Part IV we consequently detailed the current structure and operation of schemes in the South West, which not only depict voluntary services in relatively 'pure' form but also allow us to consider the expansion of such services in a largely rural area.

As one might have hypothesized from previous work on the voluntary sector, victims support schemes in the South West originated relatively early on, and have now multiplied to cover almost all of the two counties. Recruitment of sufficient volunteers is not a problem for the majority of schemes, which has itself helped schemes maintain their early commitment to the pure voluntarism principles. Interestingly, the district with the most pronounced difficulties has been Plymouth, the most urbanized area.

Nevertheless, in many respects the structure and organization of schemes is similar to that in other parts of the country. Volunteers provided a direct contact for victims, including some victims of non-crime incidents, for the majority of whom the expression of concern, 'counselling', and basic information and advice were sufficient. Second visits were, however, possibly more common than elsewhere, understandable given the workload of different schemes.

In Chapters 9 to 11 we focused on three key features of victims support schemes: (1) their relationships with police, (2) with probation, and (3) the characteristics and role of volunteers. In so doing we identified a number of problems. Most especially, police discretion over referrals was a source of difficulty, even where police–scheme relationships were found to be strong in most other respects. The relationship between probation officers and volunteers and schemes was slightly more ambivalent, and many volunteers were unhappy about extending their role to include mediation and reparation. Interestingly, such concerns were shared by many probation officers, who saw their priorities as lying with offenders as clients, and consequently while many officers aimed criticisms at the operation of victims support schemes (including again the referral issue), support for the basic principles of schemes was considerable. It is thus important to stress that the need for victims services and acceptance of independent voluntary organizations as the providers of services gained widespread support from both police and probation.

Our discussion of those who volunteer to work with victims support schemes in the South West is relevant to a number of themes in this book. For example, where we outlined the political context of the victims movement, the comparative nature of our local research allowed us to elicit the political – or more broadly ideological – perspectives of volunteers. Additionally, this has a number of practical implications, in terms of recruitment, volunteer morale, and the willingness (or otherwise) of schemes to widen their work to include reparation and non-crime victims. Clearly, the local form of victims support will vary in different areas, and in this context the leadership provided by the central body attains significance. Thus we suggested that NAVSS policy described in Chapter 6 may have helped local schemes avoid the intermingling of victims' and law-and-order issues which pervades the North American scene. On the other hand, despite central policy, recruitment appears highly selective in the South West, resulting in a startling degree of homogeneity among volunteers.

We have, overall, attempted to provide a critical analysis of victims' needs and services, using national data and international and local detail for comparison. However, given the recent expansion of the victims' movement, here more than in most areas of policy, one might anticipate rapid changes. In order to confront this situation, the following four sections take us forward from 1987. Thus, we consider recent developments, first in Britain in terms of government initiatives in the 1986–7 period (what we term a needs-based response), then internationally through the victims' rights movement. Following from this, we provide a philosophical foundation for future services, by addressing the politics of victims' rights. Finally, on the basis of the preceding discussions, we provide our own suggestions for possible reform.

## Current initiatives in Britain

In its proposals for the 1986–7 parliamentary session, the government renewed its promise to put the Criminal Injuries Compensation Board on a statutory footing, and to modify the position regarding compensation orders. Despite this, there was no move to give victims any *right* to crime compensation.

The most significant developments, however, occurred with regard to finance. In an effort to cut expenditure, the minimum award from the board is to be raised once more, further restricting the scope of compensation to all but the seriously injured. On the other hand, policy towards victims support schemes has been reversed with proposals to provide £9 million for schemes over a three-year period,[1] the bulk being for the payment of full-time local co-ordinators.

The implications of this U-turn are at least twofold. First, in organizational terms the regional structure of the NAVSS is to be changed, to allow districts to act as local companies to employ co-ordinators. Instead of the regions described in Chapter 6, then, schemes will be organized on a county basis. Within the South West, Devon and Cornwall will thus be separate.

The second and major implication is financial. The government has made it clear that it expects most of the additional finance to be spent on full-time co-ordinators, and thus the number of schemes with such staff would be increased. Precisely how many is difficult to estimate at this stage and the NAVSS are rightly cautious in making predictions. However, as an approximation we would expect funding to be sufficient for between 150 and 200 full-time co-ordinators in 1987–8, possibly rising to over 300 by 1989–90. The total number of full-time co-ordinators in post would, of course, also depend on whether or not current sources of funding are phased out, and if so how quickly. As far as the additional finance is concerned, co-ordinators would be employed for three years in the first instance, but with the intention of making the posts permanent. No scheme would have more than one paid post. Schemes which do not warrant a full-time co-ordinator may be eligible for a part-time appointment or running expenses.

Clearly, the proposals have a number of advantages, building stability into the role of co-ordinator, which we and Maguire and Corbett (1986) have identified as crucial. It is, however, doubtful whether the number of posts funded will be sufficient for all schemes that require a full-time co-ordinator, and the problem of schemes which appear to need more than one full-time post remains unresolved. Moreover, clearly the proposals assume that volunteer potential is adequate (or at least can be solved if there is one paid post). However, while a committed full-time co-ordinator may be able to improve recruitment and minimize wastage, evidence of regional variations in recruitment suggests that the problem is not so easily solved.

As far as rural areas are concerned, the current situation is vague. However, if – as a minimum – it is possible to appoint one permanent full-time co-ordinator at *county* level in both Devon and Cornwall, this would appear to have a number of advantages, facilitating co-operation within counties and nationally. Thus, while we are doubtful about whether the measures are sufficient to address the problems facing schemes in metropolitan areas, they should be applauded as a step in the right direction.

That they are no more than a step is perhaps not surprising, given the philosophical foundation from which they are drawn. For despite the cosmetic modifications to the Criminal Injuries Compensation Board contained in the 1986/7 Criminal Justice Bill, the emphasis remains on needs rather than rights. Moreover, the impression is that only a minority of crime victims, who may suffer serious harm or upset, 'require' victims services or compensation.

Such a focus on needs-based services is, however, compatible with current government philosophy on the provision of welfare, particularly since it minimizes state obligations and directs attention at the voluntary sector as main provider. Although we have some reservations about voluntary-sector provision, national and local evidence of the operation of victims support schemes leaves us in no doubt that, *given adequate funding*, voluntary-sector provision holds considerable advantages. Nevertheless, we are less certain about the adequacy of services based on needs, rather than rights, for a number of reasons.

For example, as we argued in Chapter 2, it is extremely difficult to define needs in the context of crime victims, except in terms of demand. This notwithstanding, we feel that while only a small minority of crime victims experience problems which can be described as evidence of unmet needs, victims *in general* deserve to have their rights addressed.

In Chapter 3 we noted that in rejecting the notion of rights for crime victims, the Advisory Council Working Party (Home Office 1970a) argued that acknowledging rights was paramount to accepting responsibility for allowing any crime to occur. This is clearly nonsense. To translate this argument into other areas of welfare, this is to suggest that we refuse citizens the right to free health services because the state cannot accept responsibility for all illness! On the contrary, rights are an acknowledgement of 'what constitutes the good society' (Titmuss 1974: 49).

As we noted in Chapter 7, victims' *rights* have been more explicitly stated by the North American victims movement, with attendant problems. However, they have also received attention recently on an international level. It is thus appropriate to consider whether or not such initiatives provide a more useful basis than those undertaken in Britain.

## The international victims' rights movement

Within the last few years, much due to the World Society of Victimology and influenced by North American Victimologists (Lamborn 1984; Waller 1984, 1985), the issue of victims' rights has been addressed at the international level, notably through the United Nations. Thus a declaration on the 'Protection and Assistance of Crime Victims' was discussed at an International Workshop on Victim Rights in Dubrovnik in 1984 and the Fifth International Symposium on Victimology in Zagreb in 1985, and accepted by the Seventh UN Congress on the Prevention of Crime and Treatment of Offenders in Milan in 1985.

Nevertheless, such progress towards an international charter of victims' rights is not without its critics. On the one hand, it has been argued that crime prevention is not strictly speaking a victims' issue, and that mediation is not necessarily in the victims' interests. Most potently, Cressey[2] has argued that greater victim involvement in sentencing is dangerous, and the NAVSS has stressed the injustices which may accrue to both offender and victim should such a policy be fully implemented:

'It is anticipated that a victim will express views about bail, sentence and parole – with a chance that they might be ignored, which could possibly make their frustration even worse? Alternatively, should the actual effects of each crime be taken into account in sentencing – in which case a burglar who, by chance, does not cause distress to the people who happen to be living in the house he has chosen would presumably receive a lighter sentence?'[3]

Discussions at the 1985 Zagreb Conference well illustrated the conflicting ideologies within the victims movement and suggest that these will dominate the victimology agenda in coming years. Since we see policies aimed at victims' rights as the most positive response to the problems of crime, it is thus imperative to confront the politics of the victims movement.

## The politics of the victims movement and victims' rights

Clearly, the victims movement is multifaceted. It is supported by those whose concern is directed only at victims' needs, by those who see victims–offender relationships as the key issue, and by those concerned at 'law and order' or 'the crime problem'. In Britain, as we have noted, it has gained major impetus from those on the right. Only in the last few years has the Labour Party seen the need to explicitly direct its attention at law and order in general, much less crime victims (Birley and Bright 1985; Downes 1983).

Our own research in the South West of England equally suggests a right wing, law-and-order focus among victims support scheme volunteers, although *not* in terms of views on sentencing. While we would not wish to generalize nationally from this, scheme volunteers did fall between volunteers working with police and probation, which was not unexpected. In Britain as a whole, the NAVSS – with its NACRO and probation origins – has played a major part in maintaining this balance, most notably in avoiding involvement in wider penal policies. However, to a certain extent it has been aided in this by the focus on victims' needs rather than victims' rights. In contrast, the victims movement in North America has been more directly concerned with rights. Partly because of this, it has openly acknowledged, indeed encouraged, perceptions of crime as a serious problem, and its policies have implications for the rights of defendants and offenders (see also Fattah 1986).

While we wholeheartedly support NAVSS policy in avoiding

dramatizing the crime problem, this nevertheless leaves one fundamental issue. How can victims' rights be acknowledged without undermining the rights of offenders?

In addressing this issue it is important to justify our stance on offenders' rights. While victimologists often suggest that victims gain far less from the criminal justice system than do offenders, such a point is simplistic. First, many services are provided not for *offenders* but for *defendants*. Second, in any case, moves in Britain in recent years, and those envisaged for the 1986–7 parliamentary session, in fact curtail defendants' rights in certain respects. Third, the bulk of spending on the criminal justice system goes on the police force, scarcely in the offenders' interests, and of the rest much is directed at the prison service, where offenders' interests are scarcely paramount and offenders' rights somewhat restricted. The point is not that the £5,600 million or so spent on the criminal justice system in 1985/6 was lavished upon offenders, but rather that in this context the £4 million per annum due to be spent on victims support schemes, allied to the costs of the Criminal Injuries Compensation Board, hardly suggests that more than a pittance (approximately 1 per cent of the total) is lavished upon victims!

Thus, at the outset we wish to make clear that while victims' rights should be acknowledged, this should be done without caricaturing the state of law and order or the so-called 'privileges' accredited to defendants or offenders. With these points in mind, we shall briefly review future possibilities for increasing the rights of victims.

## Rights for crime victims

There are at least four areas in which victims' rights require strengthening: the right to play an active part in the process of the criminal justice system; the right to knowledge; the right to financial help; and the right to advice and support. Here we shall focus on each area in turn, but given the emphasis of this book on victims support schemes, we shall pay particular attention to the latter.

First, however, there is the contentious issue of the right of the victim to play an active role in the process. We accept the arguments that the development of the criminal justice system over the past century or more has excluded the victim. Nevertheless, to reorientate the system towards a mandatory focus on victims' perspectives and the impact of the crime is misconceived, both because it invites injustice (where the impact of the crime is unrelated to criminal intent) and because it ignores the fact that many crimes are the concern of the state as well as the victim. We therefore reject the North American model for mandatory victim impact statements with a sentencing recommendation and for increased victims' power over sentencing, parole, and so on. Instead, we would suggest two possible ways of increasing victims' power. First, we recommend further experiments with mediation and reparation, where, subject to victim and offender acceptance of this, the scope for victims to express their views is greater. Second, we suggest that victim impact statements (including a clear statement of acceptable compensation *but not* sentence)[4] might be introduced on a trial basis in the criminal courts, *after sentence has been passed*. The sentence of the court might then be adjusted down and (partly or wholly) replaced by compensation, but would not be increased as a result of the victim impact statement.

This is, we recognize, a new proposal which is directly opposed to moves since 1982 to make the compensation order a sentence in its own right. However, if compensation is to be implemented more fully by the court, it is essential for victims to present considerable detail of the impact of the offence, much of which might be subjective. But, for the reasons we noted earlier, this might be unjust to offenders and thus influence sentencing practices. This alternative solution would thus allow victim impact statements to be introduced as a 'sentence bargaining stage', and allow the offender, where desirable, to quite literally work off the sentence.

Second, in terms of victims' rights to knowledge we see more potential for change. Here there are at least four areas of knowledge which need to be addressed, at two stages. At the *criminal investigation stage* (i.e. commonly prior to an arrest or summons), the victim has the right to be kept informed of police action on the case, and on what facilities or services are available to help the victim. The police should therefore have an obligation to (1) keep the victim informed of police progress (or otherwise) by sending a 'closure' letter when the case is either passed on to the Crown prosecution service or closed for lack of further evidence and (2) immediately inform the victim of the possibility of criminal injuries compensation (if appropriate) and the availability of victims support and/or a Rape Crisis Centre or Women's Refuge. All victims reporting crimes covered by any of these services would then be provided with written details of the services.

At the *offender processing stage*, victims should have the right to information on the decision to caution or prosecute; in the latter case they should be kept informed of the court processes, along the lines of the North American model, and should be informed of their right to claim compensation. At this stage it would seem most appropriate that these obligations should become a feature of the Crown prosecution service, appropriately funded.

Third, we feel that the rights of victims to financial help need to be strengthened. As implicit in the above points, this would entail the victim's right to claim compensation through the courts. This would be facilitated by the extension of mediation and reparation alternatives, and by requiring the prosecution service to inform victims of their rights. However, in making the claim for compensation a right while avoiding any implication for sentencing severity, we have suggested that sentencing should precede the discussion of compensation, which should itself be informed by a limited victim impact statement as described earlier.

However, compensation orders and reparation are only applicable where offenders are caught. In consequence we feel that more concrete steps are required to ensure that where physical harm is caused, or financial loss sustained, victims have the right to compensation. We therefore recommend a comprehensive system of crime insurance, financed by either national insurance or taxation, but allowing those who wish for private insurance to opt out of the system, under certain safeguards. This would establish criminal injuries compensation as a *right* but also incorporate rights for property losses exceeding, say, £50. In order to avoid anomalies, such an insurance scheme, as in New Zealand, would incorporate accident victims.

Fourth, we have argued that all victims have the right to specialist advice and support. In this context, although we have concentrated here on victims support schemes, it is crucial not to ignore the role of Women's Refuges and Rape Crisis Centres, which provide necessary services for some victims and should not be 'freezed out' because of their less acceptable political profile.

It is, however, here more appropriate to focus on victims support schemes. Our principal recommendations cover six aspects of their development. First, our research on the referral process provides unequivocal evidence that discretionary referral is an inadequate solution, and we therefore stress the need for mandatory automatic referral with (as noted above) the onus on victims to refuse.

Second, our evaluation of the operation of schemes and the views of police and probation leave us in no doubt that, despite operational deficiencies, the voluntary-body model is the most acceptable basis for providing a comprehensive service. Third, however, we feel that it is vital that such a service should be adequately funded, and that therefore all schemes or, where appropriate, county schemes, should have paid co-ordinators. Given regional variations, it may also be necessary for some schemes to have more than one paid co-ordinator, and some inner-city schemes may need paid counsellors if the recruitment of volunteers is shown to be a persistent and intractable problem. Moreover, a structure within which paid co-ordinators are the norm would appear to hold at least four advantages. It would improve liaison with the national organization, consolidate contacts with local agencies, improve the status of schemes *vis-à-vis* such agencies, and provide the basis for the development and retention of expertise within the scheme.

Fourth, and related to this last point, we would encourage the provision of additional training. This is clearly crucial for co-ordinators, where management and administrative as well as counselling skills are important, and it may be that a one day per week secondment training programme is appropriate. However, as has been stressed elsewhere (Gill 1986b), training is important for volunteers also, both as a means of imparting relevant knowledge and skills and as a way of maintaining morale. We therefore fully support the emphasis placed by the NAVSS on training, for both new volunteers and as a continuous part of the operation of schemes. For volunteers, training should thus be provided within each scheme or at county level.

Fifth, it is important to recognize the varying needs of crime victims and the similar needs expressed by some non-crime victims. Recent initiatives, which include long-term support, for example for rape victims, thus seem appropriate, and indeed necessary where victims support widens its role to include support in court. It would, however, be regrettable if such initiatives were taken at the expense of alternative services, like Rape Crisis Centres. Furthermore, it is important that where long-term services are required, co-ordinators should be fully aware of the circumstances and feel able to refer victims to other specialist agencies where appropriate. As well as providing services for crime victims, as we have noted many schemes accept non-crime referrals. While this will necessarily be only a small part of schemes' functions, there seem to be advantages in continuing services to non-crime victims where there is a demand and where schemes have sufficient volunteers to provide this service.

Sixth, and finally, this raises the question of whether the work of victims support might be widened in any other way. Essentially, if reparation, mediation, and compensation are to become more central features of the criminal justice system, we feel it is important that victims support schemes should play an active part as advocate, representative, or adviser of the victim. Despite the equivocal view of mediation held by many in victims support, we feel that schemes have a part to play in maintaining the balance of interests in these initiatives. Schemes should therefore be represented on the management committees of mediation programmes, be willing to recommend cases where – in discussion with the victim – mediation is considered appropriate, and provide support for the victim in the mediation process. Further, should the limited form of victim impact statement we have suggested be introduced, victims support schemes could be given responsibility for helping victims to complete the forms.

Clearly, some of our recommendations with regard to victims support are more contentious than others. One point is, however, uncontentious: we see a marked shift in the form of victims support, according to the criteria we identified in Chapter 5. Most notably, we see victims support schemes becoming more dependent upon state finance, almost inevitably resulting in some slight loss of autonomy, and possibly widening the gap between helper and helped. Nevertheless, two points require stressing here. First, we feel that victims support can become more dependent upon the government for finance without losing its independence and without becoming seen as no more than another service provided by 'experts' for 'clients'. Second, such shifts are easily subsumed within the model we introduced in Chapter 5; they entail a modification in the form of the voluntary organization, not the destruction of the voluntary base, which some scheme members seem to fear.

In summary, then, we feel that all crime victims have the right to services aimed at addressing the difficulties and inconveniences caused by crime. Fundamental to this is the right of victims to advice and support, through readily available victims support schemes, which should remain independent of state agencies.

However, voluntary-sector development is not an *alternative* to state financial commitment, and here we have suggested concrete steps that might be taken to advance the victims' cause beyond political rhetoric.

## Finale

In this last chapter we have therefore suggested that while victims support schemes should not be 'taken over' by the state, it is essential that the government provides adequate finance. We see this as necessitating a shift towards the acceptance of victims' rights, but are concerned that policy developments should avoid the political and ideological controversies which pervade the international victims movement. Consequently, in the preceding section we have made some preliminary recommendations about future policies.

As we noted in our introduction, despite the growth of victimological research and developments in victims services, victim-related policies are only briefly discussed in the literature and even in social-work-related courses. It is, consequently, possible that policies will be formulated reactively, perhaps laced with electoral appeal, rather than stemming from rational debate. We thus offer this text as a minor contribution to ensuing debates. If victims are indeed the forgotten people of the welfare state, it would be a double irony were they to become, in the late 1980s, the victims of political expediency.

# Notes

### Chapter 1: Crime and its victims

1. In fact, the homicide rate is greatest for infants (i.e. aged under 1 year), then those aged between 1 and 4, but falls dramatically for those aged from 5 to 15, who have the lowest homicide rates of all.
2. We have focused on these three variables here, but it must be stressed that other variables are also, to a greater or lesser extent, related. Thus victimization rates vary with marital status, for example, with the single and divorced/separated having high risk and the widowed especially low risk. See Mawby and Firkins (1987).
3. Much of the BCS data is published here for the first time. We are especially grateful to the Home Office Research and Planning Unit for access to the data, and to Mike Hough for providing this analysis of victimization rates. All BCS data used has been reweighted to allow for variable sampling.
4. For excellent critical reviews, see Karmen (1984); Clark and Lewis (1977).

### Chapter 2: The impact of crime

1. Respondents included details of up to four incidents each, but only 50 per cent of crimes of malicious damage were included. We are grateful here for the help of Vicki Firkins in data analysis.
2. We include here all incidents where the offender was the current or previous spouse or cohabitee of the victim.

### Chapter 3: State responses to the needs of victims and the introduction of criminal injuries compensation

1. For example, *vis-à-vis* sentencing, or in the United States current moves to make arrest of males involved in domestic violence mandatory. See papers to Lisbon conference, reported in *Victimology* 10 (1985).

### Chapter 4: State responses to the needs of victims: compensation orders and reparation

1. The percentages here are based on the number of potential victim/

236  *Crime Victims*

offender cases; that is, where two offenders and one victim were involved, this constitutes two cases, as does a situation involving one offender and two victims.
2. Personal communication with Mark Umbreit.
3. A feature of the Third International Institute of Victimology in Lisbon was conflict over the appropriateness or otherwise of reparation and mediation in cases of domestic assault.
4. For convenience we have described the proportion answering in the affirmative to the first question as those in favour of reparation.
5. See, for example, the attack launched by *The Sun* describing Home Office reparation initiatives as 'a load of old codswallop' and arguing, 'Criminals do not harm only their victims. They offend against the rule of law. They are a threat to society. They must be punished because they deserve to be punished' (18 Sept., 1985).
6. For discussions within the NAVSS, see NAVSS, 'Establishing a Local Mediation Centre', 'The Victim and Reparation'.

## Chapter 5: The community and the voluntary sector

1. This is particularly important where governments wish to maintain a caring image while controlling use of resources, yet where the victim is clearly deserving. A useful example to contrast with the crime victims issue is current government policy towards the elderly; see, for example, DHSS (1981).
2. It has been pointed out to us by some voluntary bodies that 'appeasing' sometimes has negative connotations. It is thus important to stress that here and elsewhere the term 'appeasing' and indeed 'opposing' should be taken as objective descriptions; no judgemental comment is intended.
3. Based on a visit by one of us (R.I. Mawby) to the Clearwater Shelter, discussions with Pat Gerard and Joanne Snair (former director of Refuge House of Leon County), and data from the annual report for 1984–85 of the Florida Domestic Violence Program.
4. One example of this was the march through the streets of Leeds in an attempt to claim back the streets during the Women Against Sexual Violence Conference, 22 November, 1980.
5  The purpose of the LEAA is described more fully in Chapter 7.
6. Based on a visit to the Hillsborough County Centre and discussion with the director, Lerea Goldthwaite.

## Chapter 6: Victims support schemes in Britain, 1971–87

1. We are especially grateful for the help we have received from former and current officers of the NAVSS, especially Kay Coventry, Helen Reeves, and John Pointing, and to officials of the sample of schemes we

contacted in 1986, who responded with annual reports and further details of their programmes. We also appreciate the comments made on a draft of this chapter by Martin Wright, John Pointing, and Helen Reeves.
2. It is possible for schemes to be set up and operated without being affiliated to the NAVSS, either through choice or because the NAVSS refuses affiliation.
3. The number of regions has been increased from an original five. We have excluded here Northern Ireland (which currently has one scheme in Belfast) and Scotland, which was Region 14 but is now a separate Scottish Association, with three schemes (figures for June 1985). This structure will change in 1987; see Chapter 12.
4. In some schemes the co-ordinator sits on the committee as the volunteer representative, in others there is a separate volunteer representative.
5. The constitution adopted 23 March 1982 thus includes under 'Objects', section 2A: 'To relieve poverty, sickness and distress among persons who have suffered the same as a result of any criminal offence committed by any person *or through any means whatever* and the families of such persons who are in need' (our italics).
6. See, for example, a NAVSS discussion paper, undated, 'Non-Crime Referrals'.
7. Each victim was only asked these questions for the *first* crime recorded.
8. It only raised some £3,000 and was in fact one of the lowest appeal totals in this television slot.
9. Although, as the NAVSS notes, some areas may have misclassified Urban Aid money as county council or local authority grants (NAVSS 1986a: 26).
10. For example, a grant of £136,000 to be used in 1986 to 'support the work of local Schemes facing particular financial difficulties' (NAVSS 1986a: 10).
11. Victims of Violence recruitment pamphlet.
12. Letter from Age Concern to director-general of BBC, 7 October, 1980.
13. See, for example, the discussion paper 'The National Association of Victims Support Schemes and Penal Policy'.
14. Salford VSS, Annual Report 1986: 10.
15. $a = 36.2 + 0.931 b - 33.8 c$, where 'a' is the referral–volunteer ratio, 'b' the population of the police authority per hectare, and 'c' the proportion of police specials per 1,000 population.
16. Lambeth VSS, Annual Report and Accounts 1985: 2.
17. In speech to Annual Conference of South-West Region, November, 1986.

## Chapter 7: Victims services in the United States

1. We are particularly indebted to John Dussich for much of the material

included here, and especially for his unpublished paper 'The First Six Years: the Early History of NOVA, 1972–1978'.
2. References to the response of NOVA to the report are taken from our discussions with Marlene Young at the Fifth International Symposium on Victimology (1985), Zagreb, and more public controversy involving most especially Marlene Young and Donald Cressey, who, as we note elsewhere, was particularly forceful in his criticisms of the political focus of the victims' movement.
3. For a useful summary, see NOVA, 'Network Information Bulletin', Vol. I, No. 2, November 1984, 'Starting a Victim Service Program'.
4. This is based on a trip to a number of schemes in Florida by one of us (R.I. Mawby). We are particularly grateful for the help afforded by Sara Sopkin, Penny Goatcher, Denise Hassee, and Doris Hundley.
5. We are most grateful to officials from AARP who helpfully provided details of their schemes.
6. We are grateful for the help of Mary Wiley and Pat Oles, of the Orange County Chapter. Other data included here comes from the MADD national newsletter, its student newsletter, and a number of MADD booklets, principally:
   'Helping Children Cope with Death in the Family'
   'Your Grief: You're not going Crazy'
   'Victim's Rights in Alcohol Impaired Crashes'
   'Victim Information Pamphlet'
7. Formerly, Mothers Against Drunk Drivers.
8. See, for example, *NOVA Newsletter* 9/12 (Dec., 1985) and 10/2 (Feb., 1986).

## Chapter 8: Victims services in a rural area

1. *Unemployment Unit Bulletin*, May, 1986.
2. The role of the Council for Christian Care and other local welfare work, notably with alcoholics, is reported in Mills, Mawby, and Levitt (1983).
3. For a fuller description of this in the context of other groups of volunteers, see Chapter 10 and especially Gill (1986b).

## Chapter 9: Victims support schemes and the police

1. This may be slightly misleading, since some could have avoided naming their local scheme to preserve anonymity.
2. This is perhaps a good illustration of where it is possible to draw different conclusions from one statistic! Our discussions among ourselves and with practitioners and academics suggest that for some, 40 per cent is a high figure. However, given that these 40 per cent in many cases had only referred one of a number of victims seen, it is also possible to see it as illustrating levels of untapped needs, especially

given the length of service of many respondents.
3. Indeed, it appears that police in Devon and Cornwall receive little training about other groups of volunteers, even their own special constabulary. For more details see Gill (1986b).
4. Our discussions with victims support scheme co-ordinators suggested that their input to training had increased, and so this situation may be changing. However, it is also clear that police inputs to training, which have more impact than those by outside speakers, contain very little on victims' needs and services.

## Chapter 10: Victims support schemes and the probation service

1. Special Issue of *Probation Journal* 31/4 (1984).
2. NAVSS, 'The Role of the Probation Service in Victims Support Schemes'.
3. For a fuller critique of the use of volunteers in probation, see Gill (1986b).
4. Including Senior Probation Officers and Assistant Chief Probation Officers.
5. Again, as for the police, this is probably an understatement since some probation officers may have been concerned to retain anonymity.
6. This may be accentuated where probation services see involvement with victims support schemes as a specialist role, which was certainly the case in Devon.
7. This is particularly ironic given, as we said in Chapter 9, that some police encouragement for victims support derives from a reluctance among the police to take personal responsibility for victims' needs.
8. In marked contrast, police volunteers were much better integrated than probation volunteers into the agency and its subculture. See Gill (1986b).

## Chapter 11: Volunteers and victims support schemes

1. Although, as various researchers have noted, the police may make distinctions in specifying some subgroups of the public as respectable 'clients' and others as disreputable.
2. Where details were available from each source, we have here included those from the records. However, comparisons with the interview data reveal only one notable difference, with victims support scheme volunteers who were interviewed including a higher proportion of widowed than the records would have suggested.
3. These figures are, however, easily distorted. For example, we could have added to the probation sample here a further 23 per cent who cited career reasons as a factor in becoming a voluntary associate, which could easily be reclassified as an interest in the agency itself. In contrast,

240  *Crime Victims*

only one victims support scheme volunteer gave a career reason. See Gill (1986b) for further details.
4. Each list contained nine alternatives, of which seven were comparable (see note 5).
5. Item on the other two questionnaires referred specifically to either police or probation, on victims support scheme volunteers' questionnaire it referred to both.
6. These questions were unique to the victims support scheme volunteers' questionnaire.

**Chapter 12: Discussion**

1. From April 1987: £2 million for the year ending March 1988, £3 million the year ending March 1989, and £4 million for the year ending March 1990.
2. Discussion at Fifth International Symposium on Victimology, Zagreb, 1985. See particularly Geis, Chappell, and Agopian (1985).
3. Summary of NAVSS communications with World Society; see *World Society of Victimology Newsletter* 4/1 (1985): 48–50.
4. This is quite distinct from the move in the United States to include a sentence recommendation in victim impact statements.

# References

Abarbanel, G. (1976) Helping Victims of Rape. *Social Work*, November: 478–82.
Abrams, P. (1977) Community Care: Some Research Problems and Priorities. *Policy and Politics* 6: 125–52.
Adleman, C.S. (1976) Psychological Intervention into the Crisis of Rape. In E. Viano (ed.) *Victims and Society*. Washington, DC: Visage Press.
Alderson, J.C. (1979) *Policing Freedom*. Plymouth: McDonald & Evans.
Amir, M. (1971) *Patterns of Forcible Rape*. Chicago: University of Chicago Press.
Amir, D. and Amir, M. (1979) Rape Crisis Centres: An Arena for Ideological Conflict. *Victimology* 4: 247–57.
Aurora Associates Inc. (undated) *Law Enforcement and Victim Services*. Washington, DC: NOVA.
Aves, G. (1969) *Voluntary Workers in the Social Services*. London: Allen & Unwin.
Baldwin, J. and Bottoms, A.E. (1976) *The Urban Criminal*. London: Tavistock.
Balkin, S. (1979) Victimization Rates, Safety and Fear of Crime. *Social Problems* 26: 343–58.
Bard, M. and Sangrey, D. (1979) *The Crime Victims' Book*. New York: Basic Books.
Baumes, T.L. (1978) Research on Fear of Crime in the United States. *Victimology* 3: 254–64.
Becker, H.S. (1967) Whose Side Are We On? *Social Problems* 14: 239–47.
Becker, J.V., Abel, G.G., and Skinner, L.J. (1979) The Impact of a Sexual Assault on the Victim's Sex Life. *Victimology* 4: 229–35.
Bentham, C.G. (1985) Which Areas Have the Worst Urban Problems? *Urban Studies* 22: 119–31.
Berg, W.E. and Johnson, R. (1979) Assessing the Impact of Victimization: Acquisition of the Victim Role among Elderly and Female Victims. In W.H. Parsonage (ed.) *Perspectives on Victimology*. Beverly Hills: Sage.
Biderman, A.D., Johnson, L., McIntyre, J., and Weir, A. (1967) Report on a Pilot Study in the District of Columbia on Victimization and Attitudes towards Law Enforcement. *President's Commission on Law Enforcement and Administration of Justice, Field Surveys 1*. Washington, DC: US Government Printing Office.
Binney, V., Harkell, G., and Nixon, J. (1985) Refuges and Housing for Battered Women. In J. Pahl (ed.) *Private Violence and Public Policy*. London: Routledge & Kegan Paul.

Birley, D. and Bright, J. (1985) *Crime in the Community*. London: Labour Campaign for Criminal Justice.
Black, Sir D. (1980) *Inequalities in Health: Report of a Research Working Group*. London: DHSS.
Blagg, H. (1985) Reparation and Justice: The Corby Experience. *British Journal of Criminology* 25: 1–15.
Blair, I. (1985) *Investigating Rape*. Beckenham: Croom Helm.
Blau, P. and Scott, R. (1977) *Formal Organisations*. London: Routledge & Kegan Paul.
Block, R. (1983) A Comparison of National Crime Surveys. Paper to World Congress of Criminology, Vienna.
Blom-Cooper, L. (1985) *A Child in Trust*. Harrow: Kingswood Press.
Bolin, D.C. (1980) The Pima County Victim Witness Program: Analysing its Success. *Evaluating Change*, Special Issue: 120–6.
Borkowski, M., Murch, M., and Walker, V. (1983) *Marital Violence: The Community Response*. London: Tavistock.
Bottomley, A.K. and Coleman, C. (1981) *Understanding Crime Rates*. Aldershot: Gower.
Bottoms, A.E., Mawby, R.I., and Walker, M. (1987) A Localised Crime Survey. *British Journal of Criminology*, forthcoming.
Bottoms, A.E., Mawby, R.I., and Xanthos, P.D. (1981) Sheffield Study on Urban Social Structure and Crime, Part 3. Report to Home Office.
Braungart, R.G. and Hoyes, W.J. (1980) Age, Sex and Social Factors in Fear of Crime. *Sociological Focus* 13: 55–66.
Bready, J.W. (1935) *Dr Barnado: Physician, Pioneer, Prophet: Child Life Yesterday and Today*. London: Allen & Unwin.
Brenton, M. (1985) *The Voluntary Sector in British Social Services*. London: Longman.
Brett, P. (1964) Compensation for the Victims of Crime: New Zealand's Pioneer Statute. *Australian Lawyer* 5: 21–7.
Burgess, A.W. and Holmstrom, L.L. (1974) *Rape: Victims of Crisis*. Bowie, Md.: Brady & Co.
Burnham, D. (1984) In the Name of Reparation. *Probation Journal* 31: 133–5.
Burns, P.T. (1983) A Comparative Overview of the Criminal Injuries Compensation Scheme. *Victimology* 8: 102–8.
Burns, P. and Ross, A.M. (1973) A Comparative Study of Victims of Crime Indemnification in Canada. *University of British Columbia Law Review* 8: 124–8.
Burt, M.R. and Katz, B.L. (1984) Rape, Robbery and Burglary: Responses to Actual and Feared Criminal Victimization, with Special Focus on Women and the Elderly. Paper to Third International Institute on Victimology, Lisbon, reprinted in *Victimology* (1985), 10: 325–58.
Cain, M.E. (1973) *Society and the Policeman's Role*. London: Routledge & Kegan Paul.

Cameron, B.J. (1963) Compensation for Victims of Crime: The New Zealand Experiment. *Journal of Public Law*, 12: 367–75.
Carrington, F.G. (1975) *The Victims*. New Rochelle, NY: Arlington House.
Carrington, F. and Nicholson, G. (1984) The Victims' Movement: An Idea Whose Time Has Come. *Pepperdine Law Review* 11: 1–13.
Carter, R.L. and Hill, K.Q. (1979) *The Criminal's Image of the City*. New York: Pergamon.
Central Statistical Office (1986) *Social Trends, 16*. London: HMSO.
Chambers, G. and Millar, A. (1983) *Investigating Sexual Assault*. Edinburgh: HMSO Scottish Office.
Chappell, D. (1970) The Emergence of Australian Schemes to Compensate Victims of Crime. *Southern California Law Review* 43: 70–7.
Chappell, D. and Wilson, P. (eds) (1977) *The Australian Criminal Justice System*. Sydney: Butterworth.
Chesney, S. and Schneider, C.S. (1981) Crime Victim Crisis Centres: The Minnesota Experience. In B. Galaway and J. Hudson (eds) *Perspectives on Crime Victims*. St Louis: C.V. Molsby.
Christie, N. (1977) Conflicts as Property. *British Journal of Criminology* 17: 1–15.
Clark, L.M.G. and Lewis, D.J. (1977) *Rape: The Price of Coercive Sexuality*. Toronto: Women's Press.
Clarke, R.V.G. and Mayhew, P. (eds) (1980) *Designing Out Crime*. London: HMSO.
Clarke, R.G., Eckblon, P., Hough, M., and Mayhew, P. (1985) Elderly Victims of Crime and Exposure to Risk. *Howard Journal* 24: 1–9.
Conklin, J.E. (1971) Dimensions of Community Response to the Crime Problem. *South Problems* 18: 373–85.
Cook, J.V. and Bowles, R.T. (eds) (1980) *Child Abuse*. Scarborough, Ontario: Butterworth.
Craig, F.W.S. (1975) *British General Election Manifestos 1900–1974*. London: Macmillan.
Curtis, L.A. (1981) Victim Precipitation and Violent Crime. In B. Galaway and J. Hudson (eds) *Perspectives on Crime Victims*. St Louis: C.V. Molsby.
Daniels, R. (1977) Battered Women: The Role of Women and Refuges. *Social Work Today*, 9 (15 November): 12.
Davies, B. (1968) *Social Needs and Resources in Social Services*. London: Michael Joseph.
——(1971) *Variations in Services for the Aged*. London: Bell.
Davies, B., Barton, A., and McMillan, I. (1972) *Variations in Children's Services among British Urban Authorities*. London: Bell.
DHSS (1981) *Growing Older*. London: HMSO.
Dittenhoffer, T. and Ericson, R.V. (1983) The Victim/Offender Reconciliation Program: A Message to Correctional Reformers. *University of Toronto Law Journal* 33: 315–47.

## 244  Crime Victims

Dobash, R.E. and Dobash, R. (1979) *Violence against Women*. London: Free Press, Open Books.
Doerner, W.G., Knudten, R., Meade, A., and Knudten, M. (1976) Correspondence between Crime Victim Needs and Available Public Services. *Social Service Review* 50: 482–90.
Downes, D. (1983) *Law and Order: Theft of an Issue*. London: Fabian Tract 490, Fabian Society.
Downes, D. and Rock, P. (1982) *Understanding Deviance*. Oxford: Clarendon Press.
Du Bow, F.L. and Becker, T.M. (1976) Patterns of Victim Advocacy. In N. McDonald (ed.) *Criminal Justice and the Victim*. Beverly Hills: Sage.
Dussich, J.P. (1976) Victim Service Models and Their Efficacy. In E. Viano (ed.) *Victims and Society*. Washington, DC: Visage.
Edelhertz, H. and Geis, G. (1974) *Public Compensation to Victims of Crime*. New York: Praeger.
Edmunds, C., McLaughlin, K., Young, M., and Stein, J. (1985) *Campaign for Victim Rights: A Practical Guide, 1985*. Washington, DC: NOVA.
Ellis, E.M., Atkinson, B.M., and Calhoun, K.S. (1981) An Assessment of Long-term Reaction to Rape. *Journal of Abnormal Psychology* 90: 263–6.
Ennis, P. (1967) Criminal Victimization in the United States. In *President's Commission on Law Enforcement and Administration of Justice, Field Surveys III*. Washington, DC: US Government Printing Office.
Eve, R.A. and Eve, S.B. (1984) The Effects of Powerlessness, Fear of Social Change, and Social Interaction on Fear of Crime among the Elderly. *Victimology* 9: 290–5.
Fahy, J.L. (1975) The Administration of the Accident Compensation Act, 1972. *Economic Bulletin, Canterbury Chamber of Commerce*, No. 592, section 5.
Fattah, E.A. (1986) Prologue: On Some Visible.and Hidden Dangers of Victim Movements. In E.A. Fattah (ed.) *From Crime Policy to Victim Policy*. Basingstoke: Macmillan.
Feyerherm, H. and Hindelang, M. (1974) On the Victimization of Juveniles: Some Preliminary Results. *Journal of Research in Crime and Delinquency* 11: 40–50.
Fielding, N.G. (1984) Police Socialisation and Police Competence. *British Journal of Sociology* 35: 568–90.
Finch, J. and Groves, D. (1980) Community Care and the Family. *Journal of Social Policy* 9: 487–511.
Foster, P. (1983) *Access to Welfare*. London: Macmillan.
Frazer, D. (1973) *The Evolution of the Welfare State*. London: Macmillan.
Friedman, D.M. (1976) A Program to Service Crime Victims. In E. Viano (ed.) *Victims and Society*. Washington, DC: Visage.
Fry, M. (1951) *Arms of the Law*. London: Gollancz.
——(1959) Justice for Victims. *Journal of Public Law* 8: 191–94.
Galaway, B. (1984) Victim Participation in the Penal-Corrective Process.

Paper to Third International Institute on Victimology, Lisbon, reprinted in *Victimology* 10: 617–30.

—— (1986) Implementing a Penal-Corrective Process with Juvenile Burglary Offenders and Their Victims. Paper to World Congress of Victimology, Orlando.

Galvin, D. (1986a) The Victimology of Terrorism. Paper to Crime Victims Conference, Plymouth, reprinted in R.I. Mawby (ed.) *Crime Victims*. Plymouth: Plymouth Polytechnic.

—— (1986b) American Programmes for Victims. Paper to Crime Victims Conference, Plymouth, reprinted in R.I. Mawby (ed.) *Crime Victims*. Plymouth: Plymouth Polytechnic.

Gaquin, D.A. (1978) Measuring Fear of Crime: The National Crime Survey's Attitude Data. *Victimology* 3: 314–47.

Garofalo, J. (1979) Victimization and Fear of Crime. *Journal of Research in Crime and Delinquency* 16: 80–97.

—— (1986) Lifestyles and Victimization: An Update. In E.A. Fattah (ed.) *From Crime Policy to Victim Policy*. Basingstoke: Macmillan.

Garofalo, J. and Laub, J. (1978) The Fear of Crime: Broadening our Perspectives. *Victimology* 3: 242–52.

Gay, M.J., Holton, C., and Thomas, M.S. (1975) Helping the Victims. *International Journal of Offender Therapy and Comparative Criminology* 19: 263–9.

Gayford, J. (1975) Wife Battering: A Preliminary Survey of 100 Cases. *British Medical Journal* 1: 194–7.

Geis, G. (1976) Crime Victims and Victim Compensation Programs. In W.F. McDonald (ed.) *Criminal Justice and the Victim*. Beverly Hills: Sage.

Geis, G., Chappell, D., and Agopian, M.W. (1985) Rapporteurs' Report: Fifth International Symposium on Victimology, Zagreb, 1985. *World Society of Victimology Newsletter* 4/2: 84–103.

Genn, H. (1984) Criminal Injuries Compensation. In D. Harris, M. Maclean, H. Genn, S. Lloyd-Bostock, P. Fenn, P. Corfield, and Y. Brittan (eds) *Compensation and Support for Illness and Injury*. Oxford: Clarendon Press.

Gill, M. (1986a) Wife Battering: A Case Study of a Women's Refuge. Paper to Crime Victims Conference, Plymouth, reprinted in R.I. Mawby (ed.) *Crime Victims*. Plymouth: Plymouth Polytechnic.

—— (1986b) Voluntarism and the Criminal Justice System: A Comparative Analysis. PhD, Plymouth Polytechnic.

Gill, M. and Thrasher, M. (1985) Problems in Administering Community Policing: Lessons from Implementation Analysis. *Policy and Politics* 13: 37–52.

Gilley, J. (1974) How to Help the Raped. *New Society*, 27 June: 756–58.

Goldstein, A.S. (1982) Defining the Role of the Victim in Criminal Prosecution. *Mississippi Law Journal* 82: 515–61.

Gornick, J., Burt, M.R., and Pittman, K.J. (1985) Structure and Activities of Rape Crisis Centres in the Early 1980s. *Crime and Delinquency* 31: 247–68.

Gottfredson, M. (1984) *Victims of Crime: The Dimensions of Risk*. London: Home Office, Home Office Research Study, No. 81.

Hadley, R. and Scott, M. (1980) *Time to Give? Retired People as Volunteers*. Berkhamsted: Volunteer Centre.

Hafer, B.H. (1976) Rape is a Four-Letter Word. In E. Viano (ed.) *Victims and Society*. Washington, DC: Visage.

Harding, J. (1978) The Development of Community Service. In N. Tutt (ed.) *Alternative Strategies for Coping with Crime*. Oxford: Blackwell, Robertson.

——(1982) *Victims and Offenders: Needs and Responsibilities*. London: NCVO, Bedford Square Press.

Harland, A.T. (1978) Compensating the Victims of Crime. *Criminal Law Bulletin*, 21: 203–24.

Harper, R. and McWhinnie, A. (1983) *The Glasgow Rape Case*. London: Hutchinson.

Harris, Lord J. (1986) Survivor Grief Following a Drunk Driving Crash. Paper to World Congress of Victimology, Orlando.

Hatch, S. (1980) *Outside the State*. London: Bedford Square Press.

Hatch, S. and Mocroft, I. (1977) Factors Affecting the Location of Voluntary Organisation Branches. *Policy and Politics* 6: 163–72.

Haxby, D. (1978) *Probation: A Changing Service*. London: Constable.

Helfer, R.E. and Kempe, C.H. (eds) (1968) *The Battered Child*. Chicago: University of Chicago Press.

Herbert, D.T. (1976) The Study of Delinquency Areas: A Social Geographical Approach. *Transactions of the Institute of British Geographers* 1: 472–92.

Hindelang, M.J. (1976) *Criminal Victimization in Eight American Cities*. Cambridge, Mass.: Ballinger.

Hirschel, D. (1978) Providing Rape Victims with Assistance at Court: The Erie County Volunteer Supportive Advocate Court Assistance Program. *Victimology* 3: 149–53.

Hobhouse, R. (1939) *Benjamin Waugh: Founder of the NSPCC and Framer of the Children's Charter*. London: Daniel & Co.

Hodgkinson, M. (1980) A Review of Television and Radio Volunteer Recruitment Programmes. *Social Action and the Media: A Series of Case Studies* 4, Media Project, November.

Holdaway, S. (1983) *Inside the British Police: A Force at Work*. Oxford: Blackwell.

Home Office (1959) *Penal Practice in a Changing Society*. London: HMSO, Cmnd 645.

——(1961) *Compensation for Victims of Crimes of Violence*. London: HMSO, Cmnd 1406.

——(1964) *Compensation for Victims of Crimes of Violence*. London: HMSO, Cmnd 2323.
——(1970a) *Reparation by the Offender: Report of the Advisory Council of the Penal System*. London: HMSO.
——(1970b) *Non-Custodial and Semi-Custodial Penalties: Report of the Advisory Council of the Penal System*. London: HMSO.
——(1978) *Review of the Criminal Injuries Compensation Scheme: Report of an Interdepartmental Working Party*. London: HMSO.
——(1984) *Criminal Injuries Compensation Board Report and Accounts*. London: HMSO.
——(1985a) *Criminal Statistics for England and Wales, 1984*. London: HMSO.
——(1985b) *Compensation and Support for Victims of Crime*. The Government Reply to the First Report from the Home Affairs Committee, Cmnd 9457. London: HMSO.
——(1985c) The Cautioning of Offenders. HO Circular 14/1985.
Hough, M. and Mayhew, P. (1983) *The British Crime Survey: First Report*. London: HMSO, Home Office Research Study, No. 76.
—— and ——(1985) *Taking Account of Crime: Key Findings from the Second British Crime Survey*. London: Home Office Research Study, No. 85.
House of Commons (1975) *Report from the Select Committee on Violence in Marriage, Together with the Proceedings of the Committee*. London: HMSO.
——(1984) *Compensation and Support for Victims of Crime*. First Report of the Home Affairs Committee, together with Proceedings of the Committee, the Minutes of Evidence and Appendices. London: HMSO.
Hudson, J. and Galaway, B. (eds) (1980) *Victims, Offenders and Alternative Sanctions*. Lexington, Mass.: Heath.
Humble, S. (1982) *Voluntary Action in the 1980s: A Summary of the Findings of a National Survey*. Berkhamsted: Volunteer Centre.
Irving, C. (1977) The State of Victims. *Prison Service Journal* 28: 2–4.
Ishii, A. (1982) Second Tokyo Victim Survey. Paper to Fourth International Symposium on Victimology, Tokyo.
Jackson, H. (1985) *Recruiting Volunteers*. London: HORPU Paper 31, HMSO.
Jacobs, J. (1961) *The Death and Life of Great American Cities*. New York: Random House.
Johnson, N. (1981) *Voluntary Social Services*. Oxford: Blackwell, Robertson.
Jones, E.H. (1966) *Margery Fry: The Essential Amateur*. London: Oxford University Press.
Jones, T., MacLean, B., and Young, J. (1986) *The Islington Crime Survey*. Aldershot: Gower.
Jones, T. and Young, J. (1986) Crime, Police and People. *New Society*, 24 January: 135–36.
Karmen, A. (1984) *Crime Victims: An Introduction to Victimology*. Monterey,

Calif.: Brooks, Cole.

Katz, S. and Mazur, M.A. (1979) *Understanding the Rape Victim: A Synthesis of Research Findings*. New York: Wiley.

Kempe, C.H., Silverman, F.N., Steele, B.F., and Droegemuller, W. (1962) The Battered Child Syndrome. *Journal of the American Medical Association*, 7 July: 17–24.

Kingsley, S. (1981) Voluntary Action: Innovation and Experiment as Criteria for Funding. *Home Office Research Bulletin* 11: 7–10.

Kinsey, R. (1984) *Merseyside Crime Survey: First Report*. Liverpool: Merseyside County Council.

Labour Party (1964) *Crime – A Challenge to Us All: Report of the Labour Party's Study Group*. London: Labour Party.

Lamborn, L.L. (1984) Towards a United Nations Declaration on Crime Abuses of Power, and the Rights of Victims. *World Society of Victimology Newsletter* 3/2: 15–20.

Lawton, M., Mahemow, L., Yaffe, S., and Feldman, S. (1976) Psychological Aspects of Crime and Fear of Crime. In J. Goldsmith and S. Goldsmith (eds) *Crime and the Elderly*. Lexington, Mass.: Lexington.

Le Grand, C.E. (1973) Rape and Rape Laws: Sexism in Society and Law. *California Law Review* 61: 919–41.

Lipsky, M. (1980) *Street-Level Bureaucracy*. New York: Russell Sage Foundation.

London Rape Crisis Centre (1984) *Sexual Violence: The Reality for Women*. London: Women's Press.

Lotz, R. (1979) Public Anxiety about Crime. *Pacific Sociological Review* 22: 241–54.

Lowenberg, D.A. (1981) An Integrated Victim Service Model. In B. Galaway and J. Hudson (eds) *Perspectives on Crime Victims*. St Louis: C.V. Molsby.

Lynch, R.P. (1976) Improving the Treatment of Victims: Some Guides for Action. In W.F. McDonald (ed.) *Criminal Justice and the Victim*. Beverly Hills: Sage.

McCahill, T.W., Meyer, L.C., and Fischman, A.M. (1979) *The Aftermath of Rape*. Lexington, Mass.: Heath, Lexington.

McCann, K. (1985) Battered Women and the Law: The Limits of the Legislation. In J. Brophy and C. Smart (eds) *Women-in-Law*. London: Routledge & Kegan Paul.

McClintock, F.H. (1963) *Crimes of Violence*. London: Macmillan.

McCombie, S. (1976) Characteristics of Rape Victims Seen in Crisis Intervention. *Smith College Studies in Social Work* 46: 137–158.

McDonald, W.F. (1976a) Criminal Justice and the Victim: An Introduction. In W.F. McDonald (ed.) *Criminal Justice and the Victim*. Beverly Hills: Sage.

——(1976b) Towards a Bicentennial Revolution in Criminal Justice: The Return of the Victim. *American Law Review* 13: 649–73.

McGillis, D. and Smith, P. (1983) *Compensating Victims of Crime: An Analysis of American Programs.* Washington, DC: National Institute of Justice.

McPherson, M. (1978) Realities and Perceptions of Crime at the Neighbourhood Level. *Victimology* 3: 319–28.

Maguire, M. (1980) The Impact of Burglary upon Victims. *British Journal of Criminology* 20: 261–75.

—— (1982) *Burglary in a Dwelling.* London: Heinemann.

——(1984) Victims' Needs and Victim Services: Indications for Research. Paper to Third International Institute on Victimology, Lisbon, reprinted in *Victimology* (1985), 10: 539–59.

Maguire, M. and Corbett, C. (1986) *The Effects of Crime and the Work of Victims Support Schemes.* Final Report to Home Office. Aldershot: Gower, forthcoming.

Manning, P.K. (1982) Organisational Work. *British Journal of Sociology* 33: 118–34.

Marshall, T.F. (1984) *Reparation, Conciliation and Mediation.* London: Home Office Research and Planning Unit, Paper No. 27.

Marshall, T.F. and Walpole, M.E. (1985) *Bringing People Together: Mediation and Reparation Projects in Great Britain.* London: Home Office Research and Planning Unit, Paper No. 33.

Martin, D. (1976) *Battered Wives.* San Francisco: Glide.

Mawby, R.I. (1979a) *Policing the City.* Aldershot: Gower.

——(1979b) The Victimization of Juveniles. *Journal of Research in Crime and Delinquency* 16: 98–113.

——(1982a) Contrasting Measurements of Area Crime Rates: The Use of Official Records and Victim Studies in Seven Residential Areas. Paper to Fourth International Symposium on Victimology, Tokyo, reprinted in K. Miyazawak and M. Ohya (1986) *Victimology in Comparative Perspective.* Tokyo: Seibundo.

——(1982b) Crime and the Elderly: A Review of British and American Research. *Current Psychological Reviews* 2: 301–10.

——(1983) Crime and the Elderly: Experience and Perceptions. In D. Jerrome (ed.) *Ageing in Modern Society.* London: Croom-Helm.

——(1984) Bystander Responses to the Victims of Crime: Is the Good Samaritan Alive and Well? Paper to Third International Institute of Victimology, Lisbon. Reprinted in *Victimology* 10: 461–75.

Mawby, R.I. and Firkins, V. (1986) The Victim/Offender Relationship and Its Implications for Policies: Evidence from the British Crime Survey. Paper to World Congress of Victimology, Orlando.

—— and ——(1987) Victims and Their Offenders. Report to Home Office.

Maxfield, M. (1984) *Fear of Crime in England and Wales.* London: Home Office Research Study, No. 78.

Mayhew, P. (1984) The Effects of Crime: Victims, the Public and Fear. Paper to Council of Europe Sixteenth Criminological Research Confer-

ence, Strasbourg.
Meiners, R.E. (1978) *Victim Compensation*. Lexington, Mass.: Lexington.
Miers, D. (1978) *Responses to Victimisation*. Abingdon: Professional Books.
——(1980) Victim Compensation as a Labelling Process. *Victimology* 5: 3–16.
Mills, C., Mawby, R.I., and Levitt, I. (1983) Voluntary Action in a Complex Society: A Case Study of the Plymouth Nightshelter. Paper to Social Administration Association Conference, Canterbury, Kent.
Moore, C. and Brown, J. (1981) *Community versus Crime*. London: Bedford Square Press.
Morris, M. (1969) *Voluntary Work in the Welfare State*. London: Routledge & Kegan Paul.
Moser, K. and Kalton, K. (1979) *Survey Methods in Sociological Investigation*. London: Heinemann.
NAVSS (1981) *First Annual Report*. London: NAVSS.
——(1982) *Second Annual Report, 1981/82*. London: NAVSS.
——(1983) *Third Annual Report, 1982/83*. London: NAVSS.
——(1984) *Fourth Annual Report, 1983/84*. London: NAVSS.
——(1985) *Fifth Annual Report, 1984/85*. London: NAVSS.
——(1986a) *Sixth Annual Report, 1985/86*. London: NAVSS.
——(1986b) *The Training Manual*. London: NAVSS.
Nevitt, D.A. (1977) Demand and Need. In D. Heisler (ed.) *Foundations of Social Administration*. London: Macmillan.
Newman, O. (1972) *Defensible Space*. London: Macmillan.
Nisbet, R.A. (1966) *The Sociological Tradition*. London: Heinemann.
North Tyneside and Blyth Valley VSS (1984) A Report from the Committee of Management to the Chief Constable of Northumbria Police. North Tyneside: NTBV VSS.
Norton, P. (ed.) (1984) *Law and Order and British Politics*. Aldershot: Gower.
NOVA (1983) *Campaign for Victim Rights*. Washington, DC: NOVA.
——(1984) Starting a Victim Service Program. *Network Information Bulletin* 1 (2).
——(1985) *Program Directory*. Washington, DC: NOVA.
Oberg, S. and Pence, E. (1981) Responding to Battered Women. In B. Galaway and J. Hudson (eds) *Perspectives on Crime Victims*. St Louis: C.V. Molsby.
O'Sullivan, E. (1978) What Has Happened to Rape Crisis Centres? A Look at Their Structures, Members and Funding. *Victimology* 3: 45–62.
Pahl, J. (1978) *A Refuge for Battered Women*. London: HMSO, DHSS.
——(1979) Refuges for Battered Women: Social Provision or Social Movement? *Journal of Voluntary Action Research* 8: 25–35.
Parnas, R. (1967) The Police Response to the Domestic Disturbance. *Wisconsin Law Review* 4: 914–60.
Parton, N. (1981) Child Abuse, Social Anxiety and Welfare. *British Journal*

*of Social Work* 11: 391–414.
Pizzey, E. (1974) *Scream Quietly or the Neighbours Will Hear*. Harmondsworth: Penguin.
Pizzey, E. and Shapiro, J. (1981) Choosing a Violent Relationship. *New Society*, 23 April: 133–35.
—— and ——(1982) *Prone to Violence*. Feltham: Hamlyn.
Plant, R., Lessor, H., and Taylor-Gooby, P. (1980) *Political Philosophy and Social Welfare*. London: Routledge & Kegan Paul.
President's Task Force on Victims of Crime (1982) *Final Report*. Washington, DC: US Government Printing Office.
Radzinowicz, L. (1957) *Sex Offences*. London: Macmillan.
Rankin, M. (1977) The Bristol Victim Support Scheme. Paper for Volunteer Centre, Berkhamsted.
Rape Counselling and Research Project (RCRP) (1977) *First Annual Report*. London: RCRP.
——(1979) *Rape – Police and Forensic Practice: Submission to the Royal Commission on Criminal Procedure*. London: Onlywomen Press.
Raynor, P. (1985) *Social Work, Justice and Control*. Oxford: Blackwell.
Reeves, H. (1984) Victim Support Schemes: The United Kingdom Model. Paper to Third International Institute on Victimology, Lisbon, reprinted in *Victimology* 10: 679–86.
——(1985) The Victim and Reparation. *World Society of Victimology Newsletter* 4/1:50–6.
Reiss, A.J. (1971) *Police and Public*. New Haven, Conn.: Yale University Press.
Repetto, T. (1974) *Residential Crime*. Cambridge, Mass.: Ballinger.
Riger, S., Gordon, M.T., and Bailly, R. Le (1978) Women's Fear of Crime: From Blaming to Restricting the Victim. *Victimology* 3: 274–84.
Rose, H. (1978) In Practice Supported, In Theory Decried: An Account of an Invisible Urban Movement. *Urban Regional Research* 2: 521–37.
Rowland, J., Brown, W.E., Donati, D., Helber, N., Hopkins, A.J., Knouff, S.B., O'Ran, S.W., Schuman, A., White, R., and Woody, A. (1984) *Role of Probation in Victim Services*. Washington, DC: NOVA.
Rowntree, S. (1901) *Poverty: A Study of Town Life*. London: Macmillan.
Runciman, W.G. (1972) *Relative Deprivation and Social Justice*. Harmondsworth: Penguin.
Ryan, M. (1978) *The Acceptable Pressure Group: A Case Study of the Howard League and RAP*. Aldershot: Gower.
——(1983) *The Politics of Penal Reform*. Harlow: Longman.
Salasin, S.E. (ed.) (1981) *Evaluating Victim Services*. Beverly Hills: Sage.
Samuels, A. (1973) Criminal Injuries Compensation Board. *Criminal Law Review*, 418–31.
Schafer, S. (1960) *Restitution to Victims of Crime*. London: Stevens & Sons.
Schembri, A.J. (1976) The Victim and the Criminal Justice System. In E. Viano (ed.) *Victims and Society*. Washington, DC: Visage.

Schneider, A.L. and Schneider, P.R. (1981) Victim Assistance Programs. In B. Galaway and J. Hudson (eds) *Perspectives on Crime Victims*. St Louis: C.V. Molsby.

Shapland, J. (1984) The Victim, the Criminal Justice System and Compensation. *British Journal of Criminology* 24: 131–49.

Shapland, J., Willmore, J., and Duff, P. (1981) *The Victim-Complainant in the Criminal Justice System*. London: Home Office, First Report.

——, ——, and —— (1985) *Victims in the Criminal Justice System*. Aldershot: Gower.

Skogan, W.G. (ed.) (1976) *Sample Surveys of the Victims of Crime*. Cambridge, Mass.: Ballinger.

Skogan, W.G. (1986) The Fear of Crime and Its Behavioural Implications. In E.A. Fattah (ed.) *From Crime Policy to Victim Policy*. Basingstoke: Macmillan.

Smith, B.L. (1984) Trends in the Victims Rights Movement and Implications for Future Research. Paper to Third International Institute on Victimology, Lisbon, reprinted in *Victimology* 10: 34–43.

Smith, S.J. (1982) Victimisation in the Inner City. *British Journal of Criminology* 22: 386–402.

——(1986) Social and Spatial Aspects of the Fear of Crime. Paper to Conference on The Geography of Crime, North Staffordshire Polytechnic. Reprinted in D.T. Herbert *et al.* (eds) *The Geography of Crime*. Stoke: North Staffs Polytechnic, Occasional Papers in Geography, 7.

Softley, P. (1978) *Compensation Orders in Magistrates Courts*. London: HMSO, Home Office and Research Study, No. 43.

Sparks, R., Genn, H., and Dodd, D. (1977) *Surveying Victims*. London: Wiley.

Stockdale, E. (1985) *The Probation Volunteer*. Berkhamsted: Volunteer Centre.

Stowers, G. and Snair, J. (1986) Forming Coalitions to Pass Spouse Abuse Legislation in the American States: Why and How. Paper to World Congress of Victimology, Orlando.

Sutherland, S. and Scherl, D. (1970) Patterns of Response among Victims of Rape. *American Journal of Orthopsychiatry* 48: 166–73.

Sykes, G.M. and Matza, D. (1957) Techniques of Neutralization: A Theory of Delinquency. *American Sociological Review* 22: 664–70.

Symonds, M. (1982) Victim Responses to Terror: Understanding and Treatment. In F. Ochberg and D. Soskis (eds) *Victims of Terrorism*. Boulder, Colo.: Westview.

Tarling, R. and Softley, P. (1976) Compensation Orders in the Crown Court. *Criminal Law Review* 422–28.

Taylor, I. (1981) Crime Waves in Post-War Britain. *Contemporary Crises* 5: 43–62.

Taylor, I., Walton, P., and Young, J. (1973) *The New Criminology*. London:

Routledge & Kegan Paul.

Taylor, J. (1979) Hidden Labour and the National Health Service. In P. Atkinson, R. Dingwall, and A. Muscott (eds) *Prospects for the National Health*. London: Croom Helm.

Titmuss, R.M. (1971) *The Gift Relationship*. London: Allen & Unwin.

——(1974) *Social Policy: An Introduction*. London: Allen & Unwin.

Townsend, P. (1979) *Poverty*. Harmondsworth: Penguin.

Umbreit, M.S. (1985) *Victim Offender Mediation*. Report to US Department of Justice.

——(1986a) Victim Offender Mediation with Violent Offences. Paper to World Congress of Victimology, Orlando.

——(1986b) Victim Offender Mediation and Judicial Leadership. *Judicature* 69: 202–204.

United States Department of Justice (1982) *Federal Bureau of Investigation, Uniform Crime Reports, Crime in the United States, 1981*. Washington, DC: US Government Printing Office.

Van Maan, J. (1974) Working the Street: A Developmental View of Police Behaviour. In H. Jacobs (ed.) *The Potential for Reform of Criminal Justice, Vol. 3*. Beverly Hills: Sage.

Vennard, J. (1976) Justice and Recompense for Victims of Crime. *New Society*, 19 February: 379–81.

——(1979) Magistrates' Assessments of Compensation for Injury. *Criminal Law Review*, 510–23.

Volunteer Centre (1978) *Four Victim Support Schemes in Devon*. Berkhamsted: Volunteer Centre.

Von Hentig, H. (1948) *The Criminal and His Victim*. New Haven, Conn.: Yale University Press.

Walklake, S. (1986) Reparation: A Merseyside View. *British Journal of Criminology* 26: 287–97.

Waller, I. (1984) Declaration on the Protection and Assistance of Crime Victims. *World Society of Victimology Newsletter* 3/2: 1–14.

——(1985) Towards a United Nations Declaration on Justice for Victims of Crime and Abuse of Power: Next Steps for Individual States and International Organisations. *World Society of Victimology Newsletter* 4/2: 116–24.

Waller, I. and Okihiro, N. (1978) *Burglary: The Victim and the Public*. Toronto: University of Toronto Press.

Walton, R. (1975) *Women in Social Work*. London: Routledge & Kegan Paul.

Wasik, M. (1978) The Place of Compensation in the Penal System. *Criminal Law Review*, 599–611.

Webb, A. (1981) *Collective Action and Welfare Pluralism*. London: Association of Researchers in Voluntary Action and Community Involvement.

Weir, S. and Simpson, R. (1980) Are the Local Authority Social Services Being Bled Dry? *New Society*, 10 July: 59–62.

Weis, K. and Borges, S.S. (1973) Victimology and Rape: The Case of the Legitimate Victim. *Issues in Criminology* 8/2: 71–115.

Williams, A. (1974) Needs as a Demand Concept. In A. Culyer (ed.) *Economic Policies and Social Goals*. London: Robertson.

Williams, J.E. and Holmes, K.A. (1981) *The Second Assault: Rape and Public Attitudes*. Westport, Conn.: Greenwood Press.

Wilson, J.Q. and Kelling, G. (1982) Broken Windows. *Atlantic Monthly*, March: 29–38.

Wolfenden, J. (1978) *The Future of Voluntary Organisations*. London: Croom Helm.

Wolfgang, M.E. (1958) *Patterns in Criminal Homicide*. Philadelphia: University of Pennsylvania Press.

——(1985) Victim Precipitation. Keynote Address to Fifth International Symposium on Victimology, Zagreb.

Wright, M. (1983) *Victim/Offender Reparation Agreements: A Feasibility Study in Coventry*. Birmingham: West Midlands Probation Survey.

——(1984) The Impact of Victim/Offender Mediation on the Assumptions and Procedures of Criminal Justice. Paper to Third International Institute of Victimology, Lisbon, reprinted in *Victimology* 10: 631–45.

Yin, P.P. (1982) Fear of Crime among the Elderly: Some Issues and Suggestions. *Social Problems* 27: 492–504.

Young, M.A. (1981) *Fundraising and Victim Services*. Washington, DC: NOVA.

Young, M.A. and Stein, J.H. (1983) *The Victim Service System: A Guide to Action*. Washington, DC: NOVA.

Ziegenhagen, E. (1976) Towards a Theory of Victim–Criminal Justice System Interactions. In W.F. McDonald (ed.) *Criminal Justice and the Victim*. Beverly Hills: Sage.

Ziegenhagen, E.A. and Benyi, J. (1981) Victim Interests, Victim Services and Social Control. In B. Galaway and J. Hudson (eds) *Perspectives on Crime Victims*. St Louis: C.V. Molsby.

# Author Index

Abarbanel, G. 81
Abel, G.G. 18
Abrams, P. 67–8
Adleman, C.S. 81
Agopian, M.W. 240
Alderson, J.C. 155
Amir, D. 82
Amir, M. 6, 11, 79, 82
Atkinson, B.M. 18
Aurora Associates Inc. 123, 132
Aves, G. 146, 200, 202

Baldwin, J. 7
Balkin, S. 16–17
Bard, M. 19
Barton, A. 106
Becker, H.S. 3
Becker, J.V. 18
Becker, T.M. 117, 122
Bentham, C.G. 107
Benyi, J. 121
Berg, W.E. 17
Biderman, A.D. 4
Binney, V. 76–7
Birley, D. 228
Black, D. 106
Blagg, H. 56
Blair, I. 84
Blau, P. 210
Block, R. 4–5
Blom-Cooper, L. 39
Bolin, D.C., 118, 126
Borges, S.S. 79
Borkowski, M. 168
Bottomley, A.K. 6
Bottoms, A.E. 5, 7–8, 14, 157
Bowles, R.T. 39
Bready, J.W. 39
Brenton, M. 69–71, 196, 200
Brett, P. 47
Bright, J. 228
Brown, J. 154–5
Burgess, A.W. 18
Burnham, D. 36

Burns, P.T. 47
Burt, M.R. 18, 83

Cain, M.E. 177
Calhoun, K.S. 18
Cameron, B.J. 40
Carrington, F.G., 35, 116, 119
Carter, R.L. 10
Central Statistical Office 15
Chambers, G. 18
Chappell, D. 47, 240
Chesney, S. 124
Christie, N. 54, 56
Clark, L.M.G. 79, 80, 235
Clarke, R.V.G., 3, 9, 12
Coleman, C. 6
Conklin, J.E. 13
Cook, J.V. 39
Corbett, C. 20, 90, 91, 93–7, 102, 109, 111, 139, 141, 143, 146–7, 149, 153, 156–7, 164, 217, 226
Craig, F.W.S. 49, 62

Daniels, R. 78
Davies, B. 106
Dittenhoffer, T. 54, 55, 61
Dobash, R. 77, 168
Dobash, R.E. 77, 168
Dodd, D. 5, 8, 13
Doerner, W.G. 19
Downes, D. 3, 229
Du Bow, 117, 122
Duff, P. 19, 44, 46–7, 53, 68, 175
Dussich, J.P. 92, 123

Edelhertz, H. 39, 40, 47
Edmunds, C. 130, 131
Ellis, E.M. 18
Ennis, P. 4
Ericson, R.V. 54, 55, 61
Eve, R.A. 17
Eve, S.B. 17

Fahy, J.L. 47

Fattah, E.A. 229
Feyerherm, H. 9
Fielding, N.G. 177
Finch, J. 68
Firkins, V. 24, 235
Fischman, A.M. 18
Foster, P. 94
Frazer, D. 27
Friedman, D.M. 124
Fry, M. 36–7, 39, 40–1, 45, 50

Gallaway, B. 54, 55
Galvin, D. 19, 47
Gaquin, D.A. 13
Garofalo, J. 12, 13, 15, 17
Gay, M.J. 21, 88, 154
Gayford, J. 76
Geis, G. 39, 40, 47, 240
Genn, H. 5, 8, 13, 44
Gill, M. 78, 85, 155, 202, 215, 232, 238–40
Gilley, J. 79
Goldstein, A.S. 37
Gornick, J. 83
Gottfredson, M. 7, 9, 10, 12
Groves, D. 177

Hadley, R. 202, 204
Hafer, B.H. 80
Harding, J. 35–6, 49, 56, 58, 137, 179
Harkell, G. 76–7
Harland, A.T. 39
Harris, Lord J. 19, 127–8
Hatch, S. 69, 71, 73–4, 106
Haxby, D. 101, 179
Helfer, R.E. 39
Herbert, D.T. 14
Hill, K.Q. 10
Hinderlang, M.J. 8–9, 17
Hirschel, D. 81
Hobhouse, R. 39
Hodgkinson, M. 202
Holdaway, S. 177
Holmes, K.A. 18
Holstrom, L.L. 18
Holton, C. 21, 88, 154
Home Office 39, 41–4, 46, 51–3, 90, 99, 227

Hough, M. 5–9, 16–17, 88, 119, 131, 165
House of Commons 44, 76, 90, 94, 96, 99, 101–2, 155, 177, 179
Hudson, J. 54
Humble, S. 200, 202

Irving, C. 38–9, 103
Ishii, A. 4

Jackson, H. 202
Jacobs, J. 67
Johnson, N. 69
Johnson, R. 17
Jones, E.H. 40
Jones, T. 5, 8–9, 16, 21

Kalton, K. 166, 208
Karmen, A. 7, 55–6, 117, 235
Katz, S. 18, 33
Kelling, G. 17
Kempe, C.H. 39
Kingsley, S. 70
Kinsey, R. 5, 8, 16

Labour Party 49
Lamborn, J.L. 227
Lawton, M. 16–17
Le Grand, C.E. 79–80
Lessor, H. 28
Levitt, I. 70, 93, 238
Lewis, D.J. 79–80, 235
Lipsky, M. 176
London Rape Crisis Centre, 18, 80–1
Lowenberg, D.A. 118
Lynch, R.P. 118

McCahill, T.W. 18
McCann, K. 77
McCintock, F.H. 6
McCombie, S. 18
McDonald, W.F. 118
McGillis, D. 46–7
MacLean, B. 5, 8–9, 16, 21
McMillan, I. 106
McPherson, M. 14
Maguire, M. 6, 10, 19, 20–1, 90–1, 93–7, 102, 109, 111, 132, 139,

# Author Index

141, 143, 146, 147, 149, 153, 156–7, 217, 226
Manning, P.K. 177
Marshall, T. 56–8
Matza, D. 3
Mawby, R.I. 4–6, 8–10, 14, 24, 67, 70, 93, 157, 159, 235, 238
Maxfield, M. 15, 17
Mayhew, P. 3, 5–9, 16–17, 88, 119, 131, 165
Mazur, M.A. 18
Meiners, R.E. 35–7, 39, 48
Meyer, L.C. 18
Miers, D. 44–5, 47–50
Millar, A. 18
Mills, C. 70, 93, 238
Mocroft, I. 106
Moore, C. 154–5
Morris, M. 202
Moser, K. 166, 208
Murch, M. 168

NAVSS 35, 88–93, 95, 100–3, 105, 146, 154–5, 165–6, 179, 217, 237
Newman, O. 11
Nicholson, G. 119
Nisbet, R.A. 67
Nixon, J. 76–7
North Tyneside and Blyth Valley VSS 139
NOVA 119, 123, 130

Okihiro, N. 168
O'Sullivan, E. 82

Pahl, J. 74, 77, 168
Parnas, R. 75
Parton, N. 39
Pittmann, K.J. 83
Pizzey, E. 76
Plant, R. 28
President's Task Force on Victims of Crime 19, 116, 119–21, 130–1

Radzinowicz, L. 6
Rankin, M. 87, 154
Rape Counselling and Research Project 80

Raynor, P. 178, 198
Reeves, H. 91–4, 99, 104, 151, 153, 195
Reiss, A.J. 6
Repetto, T. 10
Riger, S. 9, 16–17
Rock, P. 3
Rose, H. 76
Ross, A.M. 47
Rowland, J. 198
Rowntree, S. 28
Runciman, W.G. 29
Ryan, M. 214

Salasin, S.E. 19, 29
Samuels, A. 44, 46
Sangrey, D. 19
Schafer, S. 35–7, 51
Schembri, A.J. 16
Scherl, D. 18
Schneider, A.L. 118, 122
Schneider, C.S. 124
Schneider, P.R. 118, 122
Scott, M. 202, 204
Scott, R. 210
Shapiro, J. 76
Shapland, J. 19–20, 27, 44, 46–7, 53, 68, 134, 172, 174–5
Simpson, R. 106
Skinner, L.J. 18
Skogan, W.G. 17
Smith, B.L. 117, 119
Smith, P. 46–7
Smith, S.J. 5, 8, 17
Snair, J. 131
Softley, P. 52–3
Sparks, R. 5, 8, 13
Stein, J.H. 19, 123–4, 132
Stockdale, E. 112
Stowers, G. 131
Sutherland, S. 18
Sykes, G. 3
Symonds, M. 19

Tarling, R. 53
Taylor, I. 3, 38
Taylor, J. 68
Taylor-Gooby, P. 28
Thomas, M.S. 21, 88, 154

Thrasher, M. 155
Titmuss, R.M. 29, 200, 227
Townsend, P. 28

Umbreit, M.S. 54–5
United States Department of Justice 5, 7

Van Maan, J. 177
Vennard, J. 44, 53
Von Hentig, H. 3, 11

Walker, M. 5, 8
Walker, V. 168
Walklake, S. 56
Waller, I. 68, 227
Walpole, M.E. 56–8
Walton, P. 3
Walton, R. 184
Wasik, M. 53

Webb, A. 200
Weir, S. 106
Weiss, K. 79
Williams, A. 28
Williams, J.E. 18
Willmore, J. 19, 44, 46–7, 53, 68, 175
Wilson, J.Q. 17
Wilson, P. 47, 240
Wolfenden, J. 70–1, 106, 137, 202
Wolfgang, M.E. 11
Wright, M. 54, 56–8

Xanthos, P. 5, 14, 157

Yin, P.P. 17
Young, J. 3, 5, 8–9, 16, 21
Young, M.A. 19, 120, 123–4, 132

Ziegenhagen, E. 35, 121

# Subject Index

accidents 15, 19, 25, 42, 95, 97, 124, 126
age and crime: fear 12–13, 15–16; impact 21–2; offenders 23–4, risk 7–12; 60; services, 60, 94, 124–7, 171–2, 190, 217
Arney, Sir G. 37

Bentham, J. 36
Beveridge Report 38
British Crime Survey 5, 6, 9, 12–13, 15–17, 20–5, 26–7, 58–60, 88, 98, 165
bystander intervention 67

community sector 67–8
compensation orders: background 51–2; problems 52–53, 61; purpose 30–1; recommendations 230
Conservative Party 40–3, 49, 62
coordinator: victims support scheme 156; duties 139, 161–2; payment 111–12, 225–6, 232
crime statistics (official) 3–7
Criminal Injuries Compensation Board: background 36–7, 39–42; board membership 43; Criminal Justice Bill 1986/7 226; payments 43–4; politics 48–50, 222; problems 45–8; purpose 30–1
criminological theory and victims 3

domestic disputes: research 9; police 75; victims support in USA 125–6; victims support in Britain 96
drink-driving 19, 124, 127–8, 113

fear of crime 13–17, 25, 104, 221
Fry, M. 37, 39–40, 51, 222

General Household Survey 4–5

Garofalo, R. 37
gender and crime: fear 12–13, 15–16; impact 19, 21–2; offenders 23–4, 60; risk 7–12; services 60, 94, 125
Genovese, Kitty 67

impact of crime 18–25, 26–7, 221

Labour Party 38, 49, 228

Meah case 45–6
mediation 35, 56–9, 61, 222

National Federation of Women's Aid 76–7, 79
NAVSS 35, 85, 88, 90, 93, 99, 104–5, 112, 130, 141–2, 177, 196, 215, 223, 225
Neighbourhood Watch 68
NOVA 119–20, 131

police: officers' attitudes to: volunteers 197–8; victims support schemes 134, 167–8, 174–5; women's refuges 168–70; relationship with VSS 154–7, 175–8; special constables 106, 108, 111, 159, 183, 197–8, 204, 208–9, 212–15; training on VSS 173; VSS volunteers' attitudes to police 159–162 (*see also* referral policy and victims' needs)
private sector 29, 30–1
probation: officers' attitudes to: criminal justice system 185–8; police involvement 194; probation service helping victims 188–91; victims support schemes 192–3, 195; volunteers 197–8; relationship with VSS 179–80; voluntary associates 106, 108, 111, 159. 183, 197–8, 203–4, 208–9, 212–15; VSS

volunteers' attitudes to
probation 181–3, 199 (*see also*
victims' needs)

rape: compensation 45–6; effects
18–19; fear of 16; precipitation
11; treatment by CJS 79; victims
support in USA 124; victims
support in Britain 96, 232
rape crisis centres: America 74,
80–84, 133; Britain 73, 74, 80,
81, 84, 133, 232
Reeves, H. 113, 179
referrals to VSS: number 109–10,
139–40, 148, 162–3, 165, 167–8,
170, 173–6, 193–4; policy 93–4,
139, 157, 161–5, 167, 176–8,
193–5, 198, 216, 231
reparation: definition 56; history
35–7; place in sentencing
process 55–8; victims/offenders
41, 55, 62–3; victims support
schemes 233; VSS volunteers'
views 151, 222; victims' views
59–61; VORP 54–8
research methods 143–4, 157, 164,
184, 201–2, 205–6

south west: description of 137, 139;
victims support schemes in 137–9

Tallack, W. 37

victim impact statements 117, 123,
128, 198, 230
victimization rates 8–13, 15–17
victim precipitation 11–12, 29, 42–3, 79
victim surveys: Britain 5, 8–9, 13,
16; foreign 4–5, 8–9, 13, 15, 17;
methodology 5, 7–8 (*see also*
British Crime Survey and
General Household Survey)
victims' needs: compensation 47–8,
50, 226; definition 28–9; NOVA
131; police officers' perceptions
171–4, 176, 178; probation
officers' perceptions 190–1,
195–6; services 31, 39, 42, 221,
226–7; victims' movement 115;
victims support schemes 87, 130
victims' rights: compensation 41–2,
47–8, 50, 231; crime insurance
231; criminal justice system 229;
internationally 227–8;
knowledge of 230; NOVA 131;
offenders' rights 130, 229;
probation officers 189; services
29, 31, 115, 226–7; victim
impact statements 117, 123,
230; victims support schemes
130, 231–3
victims' support services
(America): background 117–18;
ideological perspectives 116–17,
119–20, 130–3; funding 118,
120–1, 126, 128–9; MADD
127–9, 133; number of services
119; programmes: crisis
intervention 123; victim
advocacy 122–3; victim/witness
121–2; referrals 123–4, 126;
relationship with: clients 132–3;
state services 129; police 123–7,
134; types of crimes dealt with
119, 122, 124–7; types of
services offered 117–9, 121–8; '
volunteers 124–8
victims support schemes: area
variations 107–12; autonomy 98,
141, 215, 233; background 87–9; function 87, 94; funding 100–2, 105, 111–12; goals 103, 105;
relationship with: clients 104–105; state services 99–100, 105,
233; police 100, 154–7, 224;
probation 100, 179–81, 224;
structure 90–2, 99; types of
crimes dealt with 95–7, 150–1,
177; types of services offered
97–8, 148–9, 151–2; victims'
views of 98
victims support scheme volunteers:
attitudes to: crime problem/
offenders 159, 183, 212;
reparation 151; sentencing 213;
characteristics 105, 203–5;

motivations 205–9; numbers per scheme 109, 110, 139–41; recruitment 202–3; reasons for continuing work 210–11; training 146–8, 217, 232; voting behaviour 214
voluntary sector: boundaries 68–70; classification 71–5; disadvantages and advantages 70–1, 106; relation to state 29, 93; victims' services 30–1, 63 (*see also* Rape Crisis Centres, Women's Refuges, and VSS)
volunteer subculture 212–18

welfare state services 29, 30–1, 37–9, 42, 75, 222
women's refuges: America 74, 78–9, 133; Britain 73–8, 133, 168–70
Woolf, Mr Justice 45